PRAISE FOR *ONE IN A BILLION: ONE MAN'S REMARKABLE ODYSSEY THROUGH MODERN-DAY CHINA*

"Like Edgar Snow in *Red Star Over China* in the 1930s, Nancy Pine has discovered a largely unknown Chinese figure in a remote village who encapsulates much of the extraordinary story of modern China. Snow found Mao Zedong. Now Pine gives us An Wei, a bright, ambitious child born to a peasant family in the same region. He and his family suffer through the traditional plagues of old China, drought and locusts among them. Then they must endure the new hardships inflicted by Mao, the grandiose building of communes, starvation during the Great Leap Forward, and the cruelties of the Cultural Revolution. In a modern twist, An Wei finds his own way forward by learning English and becoming a translator for visiting American dignitaries, among them, Snow's widow."

—Fox Butterfield, Pulitzer Prize winner and author of *China: Alive in the Bitter Sea*

"Generalizations about China and its struggle for meaningful reform can be corrected with this work about the life of one man. An Wei has witnessed the most traumatic and important events of twentieth-century China and has become a visionary fighter for grassroots democracy at the village level. Nancy Pine's excellent book enables us to delve into the inner world of this modest yet effective survivor-reformer. After four decades of writing and teaching about China, I would recommend Pine's scrupulous research and vivid focus on An Wei to anyone interested in understanding the jagged landscape of change in China today."

—Vera Schwarcz, Wesleyan University; author of *Colors of Veracity: A Quest for Truth in China, and Beyond*

"Through the life of an ordinary man in China, Pine tells an extraordinary saga of struggle, perseverance, fortitude, and joy. Her subject matter, Mr. An Wei, has not held high positions nor is he wealthy, but his work has affected many lives in China and the United States. He continues to bring the two peoples closer to each other despite their many political and ideological differences. His story will inspire others to stand up and persist in doing what's right."

—Peter Chan, Brigham Young University

"An Wei's personal history is interwoven with China's history as it grew from dynasty to chaos to unified country. Nancy Pine's book makes the 'image' of China more than a superficial Communist behemoth—it gives an insider's perspective to the experiences of people who lived there throughout these transitions and who live there now."

—Elizabeth Tatum, social justice activist

"It is rare when an individual's life so perfectly parallels a revolutionary era in a vast nation's history. It is even rarer when that individual tells his story in fascinating detail to an American. That American is China scholar, Nancy Pine. The individual is An Wei, born in 1942, synchronized to catch the wave of Mao's Cultural Revolution, Great Leap Forward, and the oppression and corruption that followed. Chinese history is revealed in the details of a boy's life; a boy who caught and killed sparrows to protect his family's crops; who gathered fake money so he could use the paper three times over to practice his writing; a young man who grew up to challenge government corruption with the skill of a tightrope walker. Ms. Pine's writing is clear, concise, and swift moving; never upstaging a remarkable man's story. In *One in a Billion* the complex history of a complex country unrolls with the ease of a deeply textured Chinese scroll. To read this book is to absorb Chinese history through one person's unforgettable life story."

—Val Zavala, KCET award-winning journalist

"An Wei's story of courage and dedication deserves to be better known in both China and the United States."

—Robert Farnsworth, author of *From Vagabond to Journalist: Edgar Snow in Asia, 1928–1941*

"The friendship between An Wei and Helen Foster Snow must be one of the great friendships of the twentieth century. Symposiums, schools, scholarships, exhibits, and exchanges between China and the United States—all organized by An Wei over a period of nearly forty years, carry the US-China connection of friendship to the coming generations. How did a man with such entrepreneurial ability emerge out of the Cultural Revolution? Nancy Pine's book is the remarkable answer."

—Sheril Foster Bischoff, Helen Foster Snow Literary Trust

"This one book could change your opinion about what you think of China, its government, and its people."

—Debra Foster, niece of Helen Snow

"An invaluable read for anyone seeking a deeper understanding of modern China and the benefits and burdens endured by its people. Nancy Pine masterfully reveals the personal aspirations of one man who struggled to establish grassroots democracy in the countryside, stood up for truth within the provincial bureaucracy, and built substantial bridges for US-China relations. His is a compelling life story about the crucial issues facing China today."

—Sharon Crain, Shaanxi Teachers University

"Nancy Pine tells a delightfully readable and inspiring story about China through the life of An Wei. Readers will be fascinated by how he overcame setbacks, pursued education, and persevered through tumultuous governmental changes to become an interpreter for presidents and creator of democracy in his village. I look forward to encouraging all my contacts to read this book."
—Greta Nagel, Museum of Teaching and Learning

"A vivid and gripping account of the hardships overcome by a poor boy in rural China on the path to becoming a major force in the promotion of education and English language learning. An Wei seized the opportunity to get an education and used it aggressively to get that opportunity for the most underserved of China's children.

It is the story of China in turbulent times; from farm subsistence living to the city, from nothing to becoming the link to expanding knowledge among villages in Central China.

A true story of courage, determination, and the drive of an individual on a never-ending quest for the betterment of community. A story of altruism that depicts overcoming obstacles and the harshness of life. *One in a Billion* is a personal story with a universal theme. A story of triumph against overwhelming odds told through one man's journey."
—Peter H. Antoniou, California State University San Marcos

"More than just another account of an individual involved in US-China relations, this fascinating account tells the story of a man who is an exemplar of global citizenship and whose actions have shown the younger generation on both sides of the globe how to interact in selfless ways that benefit others."
—Kelly Long, Colorado State University

"China matters. But how can American readers possibly grasp the complexities of that world power whose fate and ours are inextricably bound? The best way may be to read Nancy Pine's superb biography of one extraordinary man whose odyssey through modern China is the closest we can come to a complete explanation of what makes China tick."
—Eric Maisel, author of *Coaching the Artist Within*

"From the very beginning of Nancy Pine's book *One in a Billion*, I was drawn to the personal childhood stories of An Wei and the parallel historical events behind them. Especially for me—an immigrant from China who went through similar vicissitudes during those early decades of modern China's development—An Wei's experiences resonate with me and bring back many memories. Dr. Pine gives his rural and primitive daily life a distinctive regional flavor, her descriptions of local peasants and indigenous agriculture in An Shang village are vivid and true to character. In addition, Dr. Pine introduces many historical events such as the Great Leap Forward and foot-binding. This is a great story of one man's long journey from a Chinese village to becoming a bridge between China and America. I found the book not only entertaining but also informative."

—Joan Huang, freelance composer

"It is oh-so-true that most Americans know China solely through quick commercial tours and media propaganda. Nancy Pine's biography of a single man and his fascinating career gives a glimpse of what has and can happen to make a difference in so many lives—one person at a time. After many years of being associated with An Wei and his colleagues and mentees through work, I can attest to his commitment and his enduring legacy. Nancy Pine portrays my friend as a man who has successfully spanned a gap and made the world better for those around him and for those of us on the other side of the global bridge. Enjoy the read!"

—Mary Warpeha, US-China Peoples Friendship Association of Minnesota

One in a Billion

One Man's Remarkable Odyssey through Modern-Day China

Nancy Pine

ROWMAN & LITTLEFIELD
Lanham · Boulder · New York · London

Published by Rowman & Littlefield
An imprint of The Rowman & Littlefield Publishing Group, Inc.
4501 Forbes Boulevard, Suite 200, Lanham, Maryland 20706
www.rowman.com

6 Tinworth Street, London SE11 5AL, United Kingdom

British Library Cataloguing in Publication Information Available

Library of Congress Cataloging-in-Publication Data
Names: Pine, Nancy, author.
Title: One in a billion : one man's remarkable odyssey through modern-day China /
    Nancy Pine.
Description: Lanham : Rowman & Littlefield, 2020. | Includes bibliographical
    references and index.
Identifiers: LCCN 2020030027 (print) | LCCN 2020030028 (ebook) | ISBN
    9781538143407 (cloth) | ISBN 9781538143414 (epub)
Subjects: LCSH: An, Wei (Translator) | Translators—China—Biography.
Classification: LCC P306.92.A46 P56 2020 (print) | LCC P306.92.A46 (ebook) |
    DDC 951.06092 [B]—dc23
LC record available at https://lccn.loc.gov/2020030027
LC ebook record available at https://lccn.loc.gov/2020030028

Contents

viii   *Contents*

Acknowledgments

First, I wish to express my deepest gratitude to An Wei who has, for over a decade, meticulously answered myriad questions during long interviews and in numerous emails. With his thorough explanations, he has helped me to better understand village life and the complex dynamics of development in modern China. If there are inaccuracies, the fault lies with me. A special thanks also to An Wei's family, especially his wife, Niu Jianhua, for their generous hospitality and willingness to show me their cultural ways; to his colleagues who shared their experiences working with An Wei; and to his good friend Sharon Crain, who has supported this book from the beginning and shared wonderful details of her collaborations with An Wei and Helen Snow.

My deep appreciation goes to my agent, Carol Mann, for her belief in this book and her persistence in helping bring it to its current form; to my Rowman & Littlefield editor, Susan McEachern, for her enthusiasm for An Wei's story; and to her assistant editor, Katelyn Turner. Over many years, I have benefited from Eric Maisel's wise book-writing consultation and Gordon Grice's skillful writing advice. By now they probably know An Wei better than I do. Finally, a hearty thanks to my editor, Kris Lindgren, for her way with words and perceptive understanding of An Wei's life.

Talented friends have given hours to read drafts. Barbara Madden and George Van Alstine have read and critiqued stacks of drafts, demanding clarity and asking probing questions. Elizabeth Tatum read for what needed clarifying about life in China, and Claire Gorfinkel and Irene Phillips read a near final draft with critical and skilled eyes. A special thanks for these gifts.

Over the years, Elizabeth Campbell has egged me on to write about China and has raised difficult and important questions; my creativity group has believed in me; and my sisters, Carol and Shirley, have been my supporters from the beginning.

Finally, a thousand thanks to my family: to my children who have always asked questions, probed for answers, and put up with my many trips to China; and to my late husband, Jerry Pine, whose unflagging enthusiasm for this project has kept me going for over the decade it has taken to bring An Wei's story to print.

Author's Note

A word about Chinese names.

The family name comes first; the given name follows. For An Wei, his family name is An, and his given name is Wei. He grew up in the village of An Shang, which means the home of the An clan. Many people in the village have the family name of An. Everyone, even children, are known by their full names and addressed as such. An Wei is known and addressed as An Wei, not as Wei; his daughter, as An Lin, not Lin.

On occasion, Chinese friends who have spent considerable time in the United States will sign emails with only their given name in the Western manner, but more typically full names are used.

Prologue

China 2004

I clutched the seat in front of me as our minibus turned off the macadam and lurched across deep ruts toward An Shang, the obscure village in central China where my host, An Wei, grew up and where his siblings still lived.

The wheels hit a deep rut and toppled a funeral arrangement An Wei was taking to a village family. The two young Chinese women with us jumped up and caught it before it hit the floor. With the intact flower arrangement clasped safely on their laps, they convulsed in laughter while in the front seat An Wei—oblivious to what was happening behind him—continued nonstop conversations on his two cell phones.

I was one of three American volunteers beginning a several-week assignment in the village to help rural high school teachers of English strengthen their language skills. I had been studying education in China for two decades, organizing programs between my university in California and those in China and enjoying hours in the homes of Chinese friends in Nanjing and Beijing. It was nearly impossible for foreigners to spend substantive time in the countryside, however, so these weeks were golden.

We were hosted by an American organization that An Wei had introduced to China in an effort to create a bridge between our two countries. While we taught, the villagers brought in a harvest of breathtakingly deep-yellow corn and then planted winter wheat. An Wei, who made our schedules, believed a day off should be filled with additional work, so seven days a week we planned lessons late into the night, learned about rural living from the teachers, and helped them with their conversational English. As I left An Shang village that autumn, I knew I would return. I longed to feel the rhythm of the seasons that permeated every part of rural life.

Subsequent trips took me deeper into peasant life. And on each trip I watched An Wei move from one village project to the next—negotiating, cajoling, and organizing. Now having become an educated professional in the city of Xi'an, he was building a bridge not only between villagers and American volunteers but also between rural existence and modern China.

I continued to do research on Chinese education methods, returning a couple of times a year. In addition, I began to spend several days during my visits with An Wei and his wife, learning as much as I could from him about the complex beginnings of the People's Republic of China and how they affected the lives of individuals. When he began primary school in 1950, the new nation was a year old.

An Wei belongs to the generation born in the old society that grew up under the Communism of Mao Zedong. For decades he has been buffeted by the dramatic changes in China. In a recent letter to me, he wrote, "As the Chinese saying goes, 'A small sign can indicate a great trend.' Just like a tiny leaf on a huge tree, I went through all the seasons and endured all the storms along with my tree."

Beyond the sweep of headlines and massive social, political, and economic changes, beyond the Confucian *Analects* and the *Dao Dejing*, millions of Chinese people carry their own stories of their life's travails and dreams. An Wei is one of them—in some ways like everyone else, yet he stands out from the crowd.

His story is one of survival in ever-shifting and sometimes dangerous times. It is a compelling story of a resourceful individual determined to work toward a goal despite myriad compromises that he accepted to survive. Resilient to the core, he continued to fight injustice when others gave up. He saw defeat as a chance to battle again. In the process, he has become a guiding light for young Chinese who want to improve their homeland.

• *1* •

Beginnings

April 2006

In a strong gravelly voice, An Wei enthralled us with stories of his childhood. Once again I was in the village of An Shang, seated with a group of US volunteers at the large table in his brother's home.

After a long day teaching teachers of English from remote areas around An Shang, we were exhausted, yet we leaned in, captivated. An Wei talked of attending the first primary school in the village temple, of how he outwitted the commune's cattle herder, and of incomprehensible starvation. As we listened, his brother, known in the family as Brother Number Five, plied us with Maotai, a potent Chinese liquor, and cheap red wine I'd bought in the county seat a day earlier.

When An Wei and I had met several years earlier, we were both working toward better communication between China and the United States. I had spent years studying elementary school education in both countries; he had created programs to bring Americans to China to teach English. Now in spring 2006, it was my second visit to An Shang, the home of the An clan. This time the village was surrounded by brilliant, light-green fields of ripening winter wheat.

I'd wondered during my first trip if it would be possible to learn about An Wei's life here in the remote world of the Loess Plateau, but he seemed unapproachable, even imperious at times. He frequently left the village in his efforts to get a new school built. When he was around, he was involved in negotiations with one person after another, too busy for interruptions.

That night, though, An Wei had agreed to volunteers' requests to tell them village history. As he continued his tale, a normally mild-mannered, retired American Airlines pilot interrupted. "Someone has got to do a PhD on this history before it's lost. On your history."

Even as my voice filled the silence, I wondered what I was committing myself to do: "I'm not going to do a PhD, but I could write an article."

1

An Wei said neither yes nor no. He merely nodded slightly and continued talk-ing about enduring years of starvation when he was in high school and how it left him with little energy for studying.

The next morning, with my toes curled to keep on outsized plastic slippers, I navigated the concrete stairs from the third-floor balcony of Brother Number Five's house, where I had been hanging my dripping laundry. The sing-song call of the tofu merchant announced his wares as he putt-putted along the small lane on his motorcycle. From my laundry perch, I had watched our neighbor's grand-mother lift a damp cloth off freshly made soybean curd to show the merchant how much she needed.

In the courtyard, An Wei sat at a wobbly little table writing intently. I walked across the dusty space, trying not to disturb him.

He looked up. "I'm making a list for you of my brothers, my sister, and their children, and what they all do." I looked over his shoulder, surprised. He had clearly agreed to have me write about his life.

During my remaining days in the village, An Wei gave me a tour of its five neighborhoods (each had been a subsection of a former commune). From the roof of Number Five's house, he pointed out his grandfather's old homestead, where he and his brothers had grown up and where the commune cattle shed had been.

Six months later I returned to China. I stayed in a cheap hotel in Xi'an, a two-hour drive from An Shang along a new expressway, and interviewed An Wei for three days straight. He didn't stop talking, except when he was drowned out by wedding firecrackers bursting outside my window. I took notes so intently that by the end of the second day during an evening walk through a nearby park, I saw throngs of Chinese families and multicolored balloons in double vision. In those three days, he spoke of his early years in school at the beginning of the People's Republic of China, of the Cultural Revolution, and of his various jobs, successes, and failures. This was obviously going to be more than an article. His life and the story of modern China were unfolding before me.

An Wei was born in October 1942 in An Shang, a village on the southern edge of the great Loess Plateau, where for millennia fierce winds laid down layer upon layer of yellow silt from the Gobi Desert to create a vast fertile region that would become the cradle of Chinese civilization. Named for its distinctive yellow clay soil, or loess, the plateau sustained the building of the Great Wall that marched across its northern reaches. And nearby, the monu-mental terra cotta army, crafted for the first Qin dynasty emperor, lay buried beneath layers of loess for more than two thousand years.

This sprawling region in north-central China was once home to forests, rushing rivers, wild animals, and thriving agrarian societies. But by the time An Wei's ancestors had settled An Shang, centuries of farmers had cut down all the trees and grazed sheep and goats, denuding the plateau and sending eroding soil into the rivers below. Twentieth-century villagers eked out a bare existence on the arid land.

From An Wei's crowded family homestead, fields stretched out to distant mountains that turned purple-blue in the evening haze. The land was expansive, inviting the children of the village to run along field edges and dirt tracks that led toward other villages. Young An Wei chased sparrows across the fields to see how many he could scare into flight. No roads entered the small community, just footpaths and ruts from farm carts. No one owned even a bicycle.

During the long, dry summers, dust permeated every nook of their homestead. Water stored in underground caches was cherished even though it was mixed with dirt and straw. Each fall and spring, cascades of rainfall threatened to melt the rammed-earth walls of homestead buildings and turned the dusty ground into sticky mud that was glorious for a young boy to walk through. In deepest winter, temperatures dropped and snow blanketed the fields.[1]

The third of seven children, An Wei slept with his brothers and parents on a large *kang*, a clay platform warmed from below in cold weather with burning grasses and cornstalks. A shock of black hair framed his square face, and his eyes danced with mischief. He loved to explore and play hard, but by age four he, like all village children, began taking on farm chores. He cared for the chickens, gathered wood and grasses for the fire, cleaned the courtyard, and carried water to his father and older brothers while they threshed wheat. Though he worked willingly, he showed the fierce temper and stubborn nature that would accompany him throughout his life. As a toddler, he cried and rolled his way through temper tantrums, obeying no one. He stopped only when he exhausted himself.

In January 1949, while seven-year-old An Wei was huddled against his siblings to find warmth under the tattered family quilt, the troops of rebel leader Mao Zedong entered distant Beijing to rout the Nationalist Army of President Chiang Kai-shek. During the coming months, as seasonal cycles controlled An Shang, Mao Zedong's troops continued south, occupying the presidential palace of Chiang Kai-shek in April. By October, the People's Republic of China was founded.

Chaos had long been the rule in China—servitude to Western powers during the nineteenth and early twentieth centuries, the overthrow of the last dynasty in 1911, occupation and devastation at the hands of the Japanese, and finally civil war between the Chinese Nationalists and Communists.

For centuries, farmers across China had struggled to stay alive. Buffeted by the weather, by warlords and fractious armies, and by terrible bouts of starvation, they survived with farming methods used for generations. Landlords and a few rich peasants owned most of the land in rural China; most farmers owned little or none. An Shang had a few rich peasants, but most villagers were desperately poor, their landholdings too meager to support their needs. They ate meat only once a year, for Spring Festival. An Wei's family resorted to eating wild grasses when food was short. His greatest childhood fear was going hungry.

Mao Zedong's Communist Party aimed to end starvation and overturn many other inequities in China. Within a few months of forming the new country, universal schooling was introduced and An Shang got its first school. Foot-binding and childhood marriages were outlawed, the end of child labor was declared, and opium addiction was attacked. In An Wei's home, the excruciatingly painful binding cloths were removed from his teenage sister's feet, and her partially broken bones, though deformed, began to heal.

In the fall of 1950, clusters of youngsters began passing the family homestead on the way to the north side of An Shang, where the government had turned a Buddhist temple into the village school. An Wei stood in the entryway to the family homestead, his curiosity piqued as he watched his obedient older brother join the small flock of children.

Their grandfather had chosen gentle-eyed Brother Number Two to be the one family member to attend school. An Haonian, unlike naughty An Wei, was their grandfather's favorite.

School cost a few coins a semester—less than one yuan, but the family could not afford to send six sons. Besides, despite emerging labor laws, the other children needed to work in the fields for the family to eat.

One morning during the first week of school, as An Wei began his homestead chores, he wondered what his brother was doing. When lunchtime neared, he caught the aroma of his favorite dish, wheat noodle soup with a few vegetables. He ran to the kitchen shed, filled his bowl, and squatted in the courtyard with his cousins and uncles to slurp in every noodle. As he sucked in the last one, An Haonian stormed through the gate and threw his books on the ground.

"I'm not going anymore," he declared, his eyes flashing with anger. "You people just stay at home and want *me* to study for you. I won't do it!"

Stunned silence enveloped the courtyard. After what seemed like many long minutes, An Wei walked over to the dusty textbooks, picked them up, and said, "Well, if you won't go, I want to." A thrill coursed through him as his fingers touched the soft paper pages.

His grandfather hesitated. An Wei was younger and strong willed. But the textbooks had been paid for, so he agreed. The next morning An Wei almost hugged the thin books as he followed the other children along the dirt track to the old temple.

* * *

About fifty boys crowded into the one-room building where the teacher, Mr. Zhang, taught grades 1 through 4 in turn. The oldest students, fourth graders, shared the few desks, which were made from adobe. An Wei and the rest of the younger students sat on large clay bricks, cool in dry hot weather but painfully cold in winter. He used his lap and books to write on.

Teacher Zhang taught them to write Chinese characters, read stories, and calculate math problems. On rainy days they all crowded into the classroom, the odor of old damp clothes mixing with the musty temple smell. In winter they never changed their one set of quilted, lice-filled clothing.

When it was not raining, some of the children studied outside. In the dirt courtyard, they would use a sharp stick to practice writing characters. Sometimes, though, they got to write on paper, which thrilled An Wei.

He loved school. The different subjects fed his insatiable curiosity. When Mr. Zhang was teaching other students, most of the boys fooled around, but An Wei practiced reading stories again and again, reviewed math problems, and wrote characters.

They had no homework because all the children did chores from the time they got home until they went to bed. In the morning, though, before the light touched the paper window of the family's room, An Wei lay awake on the kang and practiced characters.

"Shù, héngzhé, héng, héng, shùwangou," he said to himself. He repeated the names of the strokes used to make up characters, while he wrote each one in the air to memorize them.

The strokes had to be perfect to satisfy Teacher Zhang.

Most village boys dropped out after a year or two, but An Wei excelled. By the end of four grades, he passed tests that qualified him for fifth and sixth grades in the small town of Wujing, five kilometers away. Weekdays he slept at the school and ate meals with relatives who lived in the town. On weekends he returned home to help with family chores.

Peasant life was backbreaking, the rewards meager. Villagers constructed their buildings and walls from rammed earth and roofs from locally made clay tiles. An Wei learned to plant. He fed the pigs and, as soon as he was strong enough, helped carry tiles. Men worked long hours in the fields. During planting and harvesting time, they toiled into the night. Women stayed near home, given that many—including An Wei's mother—were crippled by "perfect bound feet" three inches long. They made noodles and vinegar from grain ground in the homestead, spun thread from cotton they grew, wove the material for clothes and quilts, and made everyone's shoes with thick layers of cloth.

Rats, lice, and hunger were constant companions. Rats got into the grain stored above their kang, lice bit them, and hunger tormented An Wei after most meals.

There were pleasures too. Market days in small towns meant tools and other goods for barter and traveling entertainers. An Wei and other village children loved the opera troupes that performed ancient moralizing tales accompanied by soulful music. Their elegant costumes and masks, rich in mystery and vibrant colors, captured the children's imaginations so much that they would act out parts of operas for months afterward. An Wei painted their pictures using a writing brush and some watercolors from school.

His family of nine lived in his grandfather's noisy, crowded homestead along with three uncles and their ever-increasing families. They all cooked in the communal kitchen shed. Adults called back and forth, children ran around and yelled, the chickens squawked, and the rasping brays of the donkey cut through it all. Each family had one room that opened onto the courtyard.

In keeping with Chinese tradition, An Wei's grandfather controlled every decision. The children were terrified of him. Sometimes An Wei and the others tried to stay with relatives in a neighboring village to escape him. Tough and serious, he cursed continuously, yelling at the children and threatening to beat them.

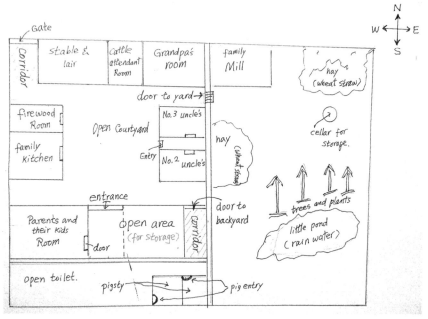

An Wei's family homestead in the 1950s. *Source:* Drawn by An Wei, July 2016.

An Wei's father, on the other hand, was called "Good Man" by the An Shang villagers because of his quiet sincerity and work ethic. Though kind-hearted to the core, he was a slow talker and could not express himself well. Unlike many parents, who hit their children to discipline them, he would look at them and sigh deeply. That was all it took to make An Wei and his brothers behave.

His mother, with a kind face and large, attentive eyes, was raised by a widow in a neighboring village and learned at an early age to sidestep taunts. Widows were considered bad luck and therefore ostracized. She knew how to get along with other villagers and was often the neighborhood peacemaker.

An Wei's father. *Source*: An Wei.   An Wei's mother. *Source*: An Wei.

When beggars came through An Shang village, An Wei and his brothers tried to shoo them away. "Go away. We don't have anything for you," they shouted.

But their mother stopped them and offered the beggars anything she could find—a piece of bread or a bowl of cornmeal, even though their grandfather did not approve.

She lectured An Wei and his siblings: "The only difference between us and the beggars is that now they have great difficulties. Once they get over them, maybe they will be better than us. Maybe we'll need their help. They are as good human beings as we are."

October 2007

Back in the same Xi'an hotel in China, I heard my doorbell ring at precisely 10:00 a.m.

Like most Chinese, An Wei was prompt. I wondered if he stood outside my door until the second hand on his watch hit the exact moment to push the bell.

He entered in typical style—briskly, with a smile, as if ready to conquer what lay ahead with enthusiasm. Balding a little on top, An Wei had combed his thinning hair neatly back against his head. He wore his usual heavy gray wool jacket, rumpled around the edges and always left unbuttoned, over an unpressed button-down yellow shirt, open at the neck.

He walked across the room talking about his wife and projects in An Shang village; then he laid his jacket on the bed and settled into the room's only chair. As the water boiler rumbled to a stop, I shook some tea leaves into cups and poured steaming water over them, watching them rise to the top. We chatted about his projects for a few moments as he sucked in the hot tea between clenched teeth to keep out the leaves.

This time I wanted to explore his childhood in An Shang. I knew it had been full of travail, but I wanted details. I asked what they did for fun. He began hesitantly to describe a few games, though he could not remember the rules. Then he let out a small chuckle and looked more eager to talk. "The mud ladders." He smiled as he slapped his leg.

"When it rained, the earth turned to thick mud."

Yes, I remembered walking in that clinging mud in An Shang. I'd taken a photo of my boots as I walked because I could not believe how much was stuck to my feet.

"Well, we used to strap stilt-like contraptions onto our cloth shoes. We called them 'mud ladders.' They were made of wood and raised us about six inches off the ground." He took my notebook and pen and drew a picture of them.

"Everyone used them. They helped us walk." He got up and trudged around the small room, lifting his feet as if they had heavy loads of mud on them. "Every step made a sucking noise and pulled at our feet." He laughed. "I even learned to run in them."

Soon, stories of his village life began to flow.

The 1950s

Tired of watching the chickens scratch for food, An Wei ran into the open fields. He had the day off from school, and there were not many farm jobs this time of winter.

He ran along the edge of the family field, stopping to inspect the footprints his homemade shoes left in the snow. His breath dragons curled into the morning sun. He charged at a group of sparrows. They rose in unison and landed in another part of the field.

But, he wondered, could he catch one of those sparrows? The previous night, Uncle Number One said they ate the family's precious food.

He ran back to their courtyard, an idea beginning to form. He found a shallow bamboo basket and fished a long bit of string from his pocket. Now all he needed was a strong stick to prop up the overturned basket. On the way back to the field he rummaged under the snow and leaves of a neighbor's apple tree and came up with a stick thick enough to do the job.

At the field's edge, he watched. It seemed a hundred sparrows flew together at a time. He needed to practice first and perfect how to use the trap. He tied the string around the bottom end of the stick, propped up the overturned basket, and practiced pulling on the string until he succeeded in getting the basket to drop.

When he was satisfied, An Wei walked slowly to where he thought the birds landed most. He set up the trap and dug under the snow for seeds and old grain stalks to entice the birds. He propped up the basket with the stick and crept backward, laying the string out on the ground and squirming into a nearby ditch to wait patiently.

He was glad for the sun on his back to counter the cold of the snowy ground seeping through his padded pants. As he tried to remain still, his sockless feet began to tingle inside his cloth shoes. It would be great to be rich enough to have socks, he thought.

A few sparrows ventured close to peck at stubble exposed by An Wei's footprints. One hopped closer to the basket. He fingered the string and held his breath. Come on. Just a few more inches. Another joined it. They scratched and hopped while An Wei disciplined himself to stay still. The first went all the way under the raised basket, finding the grain morsels he had put there. The other hopped half in and half out. He jerked the string fast. Puffs of loose snow rose as the basket fell. The first bird was trapped. An Wei snaked his hand underneath it until his fingers closed on the warm feathers. He had it. He lifted the basket and deftly hit the bird's head on a rock to kill it.

Pleased, he headed down the field to a new location. A shout made him turn his head. His younger brother, Number Four, and a neighbor were running toward him.

"What are you doing?" He had been enjoying his invention, but maybe they could help him catch more, if he could keep them quiet. He explained his trap and showed them the bird he had caught. Excited, they headed toward an area An Wei promised would be good.

As the afternoon began to wane, with three sparrows in hand, they headed down a bank into another field and collected dry grasses and a few sticks to build a small fire. In their hands they mixed the yellow clay soil with snow, covering the birds with the resulting mud, and baked them—a treat to be savored.

When nine-year-old An Wei was partway through second grade, the government sent work teams into villages across China. With painstaking effort, they attempted to distribute the limited supply of arable land equally. They categorized everyone by wealth: landlord, rich peasant, rich middle peasant, middle peasant, and so on. Slogans on the village walls and buildings declared, "Down with the landlord and rich peasant." "Distribute the land to the poor farmers." The more meager a family's wealth and landholdings, the more prestigious its members. Land was confiscated from An Shang's rich peasants and distributed to poorer villagers. Because they were designated "middle peasants," An Wei's large family did not need to give up land.

Within a year, it became obvious that this equalization plan did not work. Across rural China, tensions erupted between clans and between richer and poorer peasants. As a result, when An Wei was in third grade, new government propaganda teams arrived in An Shang to show farmers how to create Mutual Aid Teams. They told his family that they needed to band together with three to five families at planting and harvest time to help each other. If one had a donkey or an ox, another a cart, and another a plow, they should share them. Many An Shang farmers liked this new arrangement.

An Wei in sixth grade, 1956.
Source: An Wei.

But by the time he went to fifth grade in the town of Wujing, An Wei saw new slogans painted on village walls: "Move toward collectivization." "Join together to produce more." His family was assigned to a newly formed agricultural cooperative of nearly twenty families, and their oxen and donkey, as well as their tools, were to be used by everyone on a permanent basis. His parents and their neighbors complained. It was too complicated for them to get the right tools and animals when they needed them in their own fields. Yet the new grouping helped the village produce even more food, and once again they were thankful for the new government's determination to improve their lives.

Mutual Aid Teams

To improve agricultural output, especially grain, China launched a series of collectivization reforms. In 1952, the government had villages form Mutual Aid Teams on a seasonal basis to help peasant families pool their tools and animals and work together. Within two years, these family groups were converted into permanent agricultural cooperatives, in which everyone in the village shared their animals, carts, and tools. By 1956, the government formed Advanced Producers' Cooperatives, which grouped many more families together and took ownership of the land. Now, benefits such as food were distributed on the basis of a family's labor. What had started as a cooperative of a few families in 1952 became collectives of about 170 families by 1956. Between 1953 and 1957, grain output may have increased nationwide to an improved 3.5 percent a year.[2]

June 1953

The early morning sun pierced the dust-laden air as An Wei helped pile baskets and rope onto wheelbarrows while older brothers Numbers One and Two sharpened the family's curved sickles. Despite government changes, village life still followed the rhythm of the seasons. School closed for the June harvest so that children could join the adults to gather every kernel.

The winter snows and rains had been good, and as his family headed for their fields beyond the village, An Wei studied the full grain heads that drooped on golden stalks. It would take long days to harvest this crop, but all that grain meant their bellies would be full most of the year.

In the fields, An Wei shooed away sparrows while his father and brothers bent over the stalks and cut, bent, and cut. Rivulets of sweat ran through the stalk bits clinging to the men's faces. When they called for water, An Wei ran to them, carrying a ceramic container by its rope handle, careful to let no water spill. During brief idle periods, An Wei and his friends sang their favorite songs. He especially loved the one about the brave Chinese soldiers crossing the Yalu River into North Korea to drive away the American enemy. How he hated the Americans.

Another of An Wei's tasks was to lug bundles of wheat stalks to the family threshing ground where the long process of breaking the grain loose from the plants would begin. Brother Number Two hitched one of their oxen to a large stone roller and plodded around and around the threshing circle. An Wei watched intently, trying to figure out how the ridges on the roller knocked grain from the stalks. He needed to pay attention to his main task, though, which was to pick up the animal's fresh droppings before it could track them through the grain. He and his cousins thought it was great fun to dart behind the ox, scoop up the droppings in their hands, and pile them to one side.

To retrieve the last kernels, the farmers cut off the stalks and threw the grain heads into the air for winnowing. An Wei loved to watch as the western breeze lifted lighter husks into the air, allowing the grain to drop into a pile by grade—the heaviest and highest quality on the west side. The remaining hay, the animals' winter feed, was then stacked in a huge mound on the threshing ground.

August 31, 1956

An Wei, his thick hair combed back, set off for Fufeng Junior High School, elated and a little nervous. For the first time he would be attending a school without an An Shang classmate. But at age thirteen, he told himself, he was ready for new adventures. At Wujing Elementary School, he had excelled on exams and now was the first in An Shang village to go on to higher education. His parents were proud of him, but his dour grandfather just scowled, dubious that schooling would ever be useful.

Since An Shang was the village farthest from the school, his eldest brother went with him on this first trip so An Wei would know which dirt tracks to follow. An Wei threw the required sack of wheat flour weighing twenty-five kilos over his shoulder, and they headed for the paths that led across fields, through villages and down into the valley where Fufeng lay. As the sack got heavier, his brother took turns carrying it. Next time, An Wei realized, he would have to carry it himself.

In Fufeng, An Wei said good-bye to his brother and then joined the other students to register, get his food coupons in exchange for the sack of grain, and learn about his classes that would start the next day. The school was bigger than any An Wei had seen. The school gate, set in a high brick wall that extended around the periphery of the school, stood higher than three grown men. Several hundred students from all over the county were housed here, with a cafeteria, classrooms, dormitories, teachers' offices, and a large sports area.

Excited and exhausted, he spent that first night in the dormitory sandwiched together with fifteen boys on a slatted wooden sleeping platform. Their talking, noises, and smells were hard to deal with, and when he tried to turn over, he found he was wedged between the two on either side of him. What he wouldn't give to feel the warmth of his brothers on the familiar family kang, giggling and poking each other.

Classes carried An Wei into worlds he did not know existed. Teachers talked of how to negotiate the outside world beyond the village; he and the other students knew nothing about life in the cities. The teachers demanded that the students study much harder than before and talked of the possibility of college.

An Wei dove into the new lessons with his usual determination, making himself learn difficult characters and memorize increasingly complex texts and mathematical algorithms. When other boys horsed around in the yard or slept, An Wei sat in the low brick classroom building or paced back and forth on the sports ground trying to understand and memorize texts.

Learning was not easy for him. He needed to go over material again and again before he understood and remembered it, but he loved it. Once again he became a top student and was selected a class leader, taking on responsibilities assigned by the teachers.

With great enthusiasm, An Wei joined the school propaganda singing troupe, learning songs about the country. One of his favorite songs was the national anthem, "The March of the Volunteers."

> Arise, we who refuse to be slaves;
> With our very flesh and blood
> Let us build our new Great Wall!
> The peoples of China are at their most critical time,
> Everybody must roar defiance.
> Arise! Arise! Arise!

During one school vacation, they toured different townships, staying in people's homes and teaching songs to the villagers to encourage them to adopt new ways. It was the best way he could think of to help China.

Classes were held six days a week. Then on Saturday afternoons, An Wei trekked out of the valley toward An Shang. He walked past farmers bent to the soil, the fields turning from green to gold with the passing seasons. As he trudged up the final hill of the ten-kilometer walk, the low earth-colored buildings of An Shang came into view. Home.

Chores awaited him. Now a teenager, An Wei was expected to help his brothers plow, thresh, and grind flour. Although he hoped his future would take him far from these grueling demands, he joined in, but also invented new things. For a while he had a small business mass-producing paper window decorations for village dwellings, which did not have glass. He first sketched designs and simple pictures on his family's paper panes but soon realized a stencil would speed the process. With ink and school watercolors he began to paint the pages in just a few seconds and then sold them to villagers.

Once, terrified to ask his grandfather for the pennies to buy notebooks for schoolwork, An Wei devised a scheme he knew his parents would abhor. At the beginning of Spring Festival, villagers walked to the gravesites and held a ceremony to invite deceased family members to their homes for the festivities. On the last day, every family burned papers, candles, and incense at the gravesites to help the spirits back. Free-roaming ancestors could cause a lot of trouble. As a precaution, on top of the grave mounds, they left candles burning and imitation paper money in case the spirits needed it.

After everyone left the graveyard and the candles burned out, An Wei dared a few friends and Brother Number Four to return to the cemetery while the adults gathered for festivities in the village center. They ran behind buildings and sneaked to the track leading toward the bluffs. Once out of the village, they raced each other through the dark to the graveyard.

An Wei had to urge them into the side path to the grave mounds where trees cast eerie shadows. While the others ran around scaring each other, An Wei picked up one large piece of imitation money after another. He folded each carefully and tucked it inside his quilted jacket. Back in the homestead later, he hid the thick stack under the mat of their kang to press it. When others were busy the next few days, he cut the large pieces with a knife. Each one made several pages. He sewed them together with a needle and thread, creating notebooks. Back at school, quite proud of his work, he used the makeshift notebooks carefully. First he wrote in them with pencil. Next time he wrote over that work in ink. Finally he used them to practice writing characters with a brush.

1958

Waving large red flags that billowed in the open breezes and singing as loudly as they could, An Wei and the other class leaders of Fufeng Junior High School led the long march to the Wei River. "Across the mountains, across the plains," they sang.

Over the turbulent Yellow and Yangtze Rivers;
This vast and beautiful land,
Is our dear homeland;
The heroic people have stood up!
Our unity and fraternity is as strong as steel.

The words to "Ode to the Motherland," often called the second national anthem of the People's Republic of China, thrilled An Wei. He turned around to look at the long line of students singing behind him. It was 1958 and his final year of junior high school. Chairman Mao had just launched the Great Leap Forward, a determined effort to outpace the West. One initiative exhorted citizens to help build China's new factories by making steel in backyard furnaces.

For a month, the students dug up all the iron-bearing black sand they could find in the riverbed and hauled it to the school's backyard furnace. Their enthusiasm to outpace the British in steel production and help build a strong country was unbeatable.

An Wei loved the colorful posters outside the school gate. One showed happy villagers harvesting bountiful crops. In another, drumming workers on the backs of dragons rushed forward while the British were left behind. "Go all out and aim high," it read. "The East leaps forward; the West is worried."

An Wei next threw himself into the Four Pests Campaign to eradicate sparrows and other pests. He helped form teams to battle them. All night he and other students banged pots, scaring the crop-eating birds so they could not land. When the sparrows dropped from exhaustion, he raced other students to kill them. An Wei loved the excitement, but the hours of physical labor meant classes met irregularly, and he missed studying.

At the end of ninth grade, the exam to qualify for senior high school loomed. Although his chances of passing seemed slim because of his illiterate village origins, An Wei's teachers urged him to try. No one from An Shang village had even attended junior high school let alone gone further.

His father hoped he could avoid the backbreaking work of a peasant by becoming the village teacher. To qualify for that, he wanted An Wei to attend a special teacher-training high school. But An Wei loved drawing and dreamed of attending the Xi'an Fine Arts Academy high school. Then, a distant relative who was a school principal said he would do better at a regular high school, which could lead to college. That fascinated An Wei. It could offer him new ideas and satisfy his ever-growing curiosity.

With renewed purpose, he studied hard and passed the exam to enter Fufeng Senior High School with top scores.

Ecstatic, An Wei headed home for summer vacation. As he climbed out of the valley, he hummed his way across the fields to An Shang. He was

The Great Leap Forward

The Great Leap Forward, a name given to China's second Five-Year Plan of 1958–1963, pushed the country to increase agricultural output, build up industry, and collectivize society. Lacking modern amenities such as tractors and fertilizer, Mao Zedong relied on revolutionary zeal and the energy of farmers. Initiatives included increasing grain production, forming large communes, eliminating the pests (rats, mosquitoes, flies, and sparrows), and increasing steel production. Communes—where property, food, and work responsibility were shared—spread quickly across the country to help make production more efficient. Urged to outpace British production, backyard furnaces were created across China. Citizens went into overdrive, melting down tools, temple incense burners, cooking pots, and any other metal they could find to make steel. Farmers left their fields to keep the furnaces burning around the clock and, in a frenzy of competition, denuded hillsides of trees. But to no avail. The poor-quality steel was useless. The effort was quietly abandoned in 1959.

Some public works projects—including flood control, railroads, bridges, and reservoirs—succeeded in improving China's infrastructure. However, many others were carried out in haste with almost no engineering or other expertise since most educated Chinese had lost their jobs during Anti-Rightest Movements.[3]

The economic failure and starvation associated with the Great Leap Forward led to Mao Zedong's resignation as the country's chairman, but he retained his position as head of the Communist Party of China. Collectivization was fully dismantled nearly twenty years later when Deng Xiaoping came to power and moved the country toward a market economy.

already forming a picture of the future. He could not wait to attend school in the fall.

All summer vacation he thought about high school, but he was paralyzed at the prospect of asking his grandfather for tuition money. Many times while bending to farm chores, he thought about asking. Each time he lost his nerve.

The last week before school was to begin, An Wei walked slowly up to his grandfather, who was fixing a shovel.

He stood in front of the grim-faced patriarch, his hands clenching and unclenching with anxiety. His grandfather waited. An Wei told him how useful school was and how much he had already learned.

"Well, then, just go," his grandfather said.

"I need to pay seven yuan tuition."

The elder exploded. "No! You will get nothing from me. I have no money for that waste."

Seventeen-year-old An Wei drew his strong frame up to its full five feet ten inches. He was not going to show how humiliated he felt.

His grandfather yelled louder. "I spend food and money on all you grandchildren. And I spend it on your parents. They give me nothing. How dare you ask me for money for a useless school."

An Wei left. He asked his mother and father if they would talk to his grandfather. They were pleased about his acceptance to the high school, but they would never ask An Wei's stingy grandfather for anything.

Desperate, with three days remaining before school started, An Wei swallowed his pride and returned to his grandfather. He told him how important school was. Attending would bring honor to his grandfather and the family.

Unmoved, he yelled at An Wei again. "I have said it already. I will give you nothing. School is a waste of money."

An Wei walked out. He was not just desperate now; he was furious. He had labored long hours to get into senior high school. His parents, his teachers, and other villagers were proud of him, and his grandfather was destroying it all.

By evening he had a plan.

The following morning An Wei and Brother Number Four, his adventuresome younger brother, snuck into the backyard of the homestead that was shared by the pigs and the family toilet. Dry, packed loess walls surrounded it. The boys shoved the warped wooden entrance door closed and angled a strong stick against it so no one could get in. Their grandfather was out in the fields and not likely to come around the women's part of the house this time of day.

The brothers eyed the family's five piglets in the large open area. They had grown well during the summer months. An Wei set the woven-willow harvesting basket they had taken from the homestead against the rammed-earth wall. Anger consumed him. His grandfather had always been tough to deal with, but now An Wei hated him.

He and Number Four exchanged glances and slowly began to herd the piglets into one side of the yard. They had to keep them from running into the pigsty.

After the animals settled down, An Wei lunged for one, but it ran the other way. Diving at it again, he just missed the pink body dusted with dirt and manure. The yard was too big. While his brother tried to block its escape route, An Wei got up and crept toward the wary piglet. He launched himself once more and, sliding across the ground, managed to close his hands around the wriggling body. Number Four pulled its legs together with rope, and they wrestled the squealing creature into the tall basket.

By now they suspected the women in the homestead had heard the pigs and had figured out what was happening. The barricaded door would keep them out, but at one time or another everyone had suffered from the family patriarch's heavy hand. An Wei suspected the women were probably rooting for them.

The next piglet was even harder to catch, forcing them to run this way and that. The brothers tried to remain calm enough to avoid exciting the remaining piglets any further. An Wei crept toward his next victim and dove. He missed. Dirt and manure matted his thick hair and fell inside his shirt. His face was powdered with loess. On the fourth try he caught a piglet's back leg. It struggled and let out a piercing squeal, but An Wei held on, pulling himself toward the squirming mass. It was strong, but anger gave him the strength he needed. He held on while his brother tied its feet, and they stuffed it into the basket.

There was no doubt that everyone in the homestead had heard the ruckus. They gave up the plan to take all the piglets. Two would have to be enough. An Wei brushed himself off, shook out his shirt, and swung the deep basket onto his back, balancing the heavy load. The brothers shared a conspiratorial look and let themselves out the door. Quietly leaving the homestead, they headed along the path that led from An Shang to the nearest market town.

They passed the village houses clustered along dirt tracks and cave dwellings dug into the loess where some of their relatives lived. Chickens pecked the dust for bugs near a mud house, and an ox lowed from behind a courtyard wall. Leaving the village, they spirited their cargo past tilled fields that grudgingly yielded crops of corn and sorghum. A few neighbors were bent over plants in outlying fields.

The land stretched out on all sides as they trudged along, the late summer dust stirring around their feet. Although the sun beat down on them and the usual hunger gnawed at their insides, they felt an expansiveness about the land. Giant mountain ranges capped with snow rose in the distance beyond the Wei River valley, hinting of cool breezes and faraway dreams. With strong bodies, hardened from grueling farmwork since early childhood, they swung along toward the town.

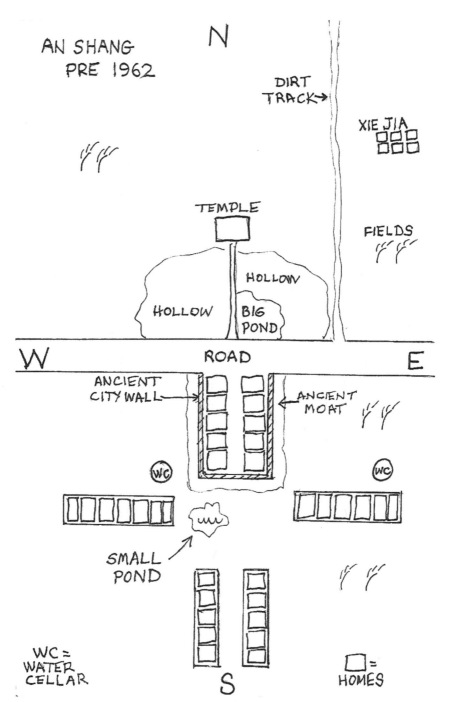

An Shang village, pre-1962. *Artist*: Christina Johnson.

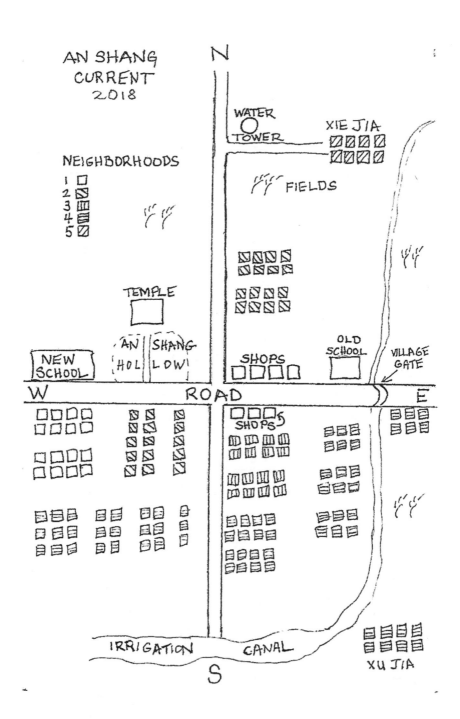

An Shang village, 2018. *Artist*: Christina Johnson.

A System Unraveling

"Pigs for sale. Pigs for sale. Strong pigs for sale," An Wei and Brother Number Four called out as they walked down the sloping path into the town market.

A few peasant farmers peered into the basket and felt the piglets. Others came to look. An Wei did not bother to bargain. He sold them for the seven yuan he needed for school.

Two days later, on August 31, 1959, he set off for Fufeng. A defiant edge to his stride, he settled the flour sack of twenty-five kilos on his shoulder. He felt for the yuan from the sale tucked safely inside his clothes. He had just turned seventeen, and he was going to senior high school no matter what his grandfather said or did.

The family patriarch had said nothing about the stolen piglets, but the evening before, An Wei's tall Number Three Uncle sought him out. He looked down at An Wei and asked what else he planned to steal from the family.

Unrepentant, An Wei looked back at him. "I need nothing right now. But if I can't get future tuition, I will sell whatever is necessary." Nobody was going to thwart his drive for more education.

By late afternoon, he strode through the school gate in Fufeng, traded his bag of grain for meal coupons, paid his tuition, and got ready for his first senior high school classes the next morning.

He worked harder than ever—Chinese language and literature, mathematics, English, physics, chemistry, biology, Chinese history, and political science. He loved them all. But they were a challenge. Because he wanted to be selected the class leader in charge of study, he was determined to be the best student.

The head teacher for their class, Teacher Bao, lectured them.

"You must study relentlessly to pass the college entrance exams you will take at the end of senior year." He warned that less than 10 percent of the students taking the exams would qualify for college, and most of them came from cities. Farmers, he said, had little chance to succeed because they had much less schooling and background to prepare them. Still they should try.

"University can change your lives," Teacher Bao said.

An Wei redoubled his efforts. In the evenings and during free time, he spent hours alone in the classroom where they studied, making sure he understood every portion of the lessons. When he did not grasp concepts thoroughly, he would go back over the material several times to make sense of it. In class, he participated fully.

Once again An Wei was selected class study monitor, the job he loved. He oversaw study habits and served as the liaison between students and teachers. He collected everyone's exercise books at the end of each class, delivered them to the teachers, and redistributed them the following day. He kept his classmates informed of the decisions made by the faculty and deans, such as midterm examination information and upcoming competitions. This meant he sometimes met privately with the teachers.

2004

A few other volunteers and I, working in An Shang with rural high school teachers, clambered into the dusty black four-door sedan of An Wei's nephew for an afternoon in Fufeng, the large town where An Wei had gone to junior and senior high school.

A light rain began as we started down the dirt road leading from An Shang. A few farmers walked along the edge, hauling cloth bags of planting materials, their shoulders hunched against the drizzle. As we passed village after village, the rain increased, and An Wei's nephew eased through small lakes that had filled dips in the road, sending muddy water spraying in all directions.

I imagined a barefoot An Wei and his schoolmates walking to Fufeng High School many years earlier when these roads were just dirt tracks. When it rained, they carried their handmade cloth shoes the ten kilometers because the mud would have ruined them.

Through rain-washed car windows, I could see the rich yellow of flowering rapeseed fields and the bright green of rain-soaked wheat. The road bent along the edge of a valley and curved down into Fufeng, along the same route students had trekked for years. In the large town, tan and gray in the dreary weather, the other volunteers set off to explore the shops and use the internet café if the connections were working. I had my own plan. An Wei had drawn a map of where the high school was located.

Leaving the main part of town, I headed up hill in a light drizzle. The storefront shops petered out, and the street widened. The map An Wei had given me put

Fufeng High School on top of the hill. Weaving among a horde of parents and students leaving an elementary school, some clad in reds and oranges that brightened the landscape, I stepped up my pace.

At the top, the scene appeared quite different from An Wei's descriptions. Perhaps the piece of wall that ran along the high school's current five-story dormitories was left from the days when he attended, but that may have been all that survived from the 1950s and 60s. The main white tile buildings with red trim were the most modern I had seen in Fufeng, and a graceful concrete sculpture of a woman and child stood at the entranceway. Two students on bicycles sauntered over to ask me questions and practice their English. They told me of life in their outlying villages and the long bike ride home every few weeks.

As I walked back to town, I tried to imagine An Wei and his classmates at the school fifty years earlier studying in their ragged clothes in single-story brick buildings and sleeping with large numbers of classmates on slatted wood pallets. The school still provided a high school education for a large rural area, but it seemed to have modernized much more than the villages from which the students came.

Fall 1959

At the top of the long climb out of Fufeng, An Wei stopped for a moment and then turned onto the track for home, singing and humming as he went. School had closed for the October harvest. Students and their teachers were on their way home to help bring in crops of corn, millet, sorghum, and soybean and to plant the winter wheat. The previous year's wheat crop had been scant, and summer plantings were disappointingly meager. Food was rationed. Yet An Wei headed home brimming with enthusiasm. He was sure shortages would end with this new season. Under Mao Zedong's leadership, crops had improved almost every year since 1949, the founding of the new country, and now the Great Leap Forward would create a better life.

As part of new China's first generation, An Wei and his peers believed deeply in the government's reforms. They sang about the country's achievements and encouraged each other to work hard to build a better China and beat Western countries.

During junior high school, An Wei had seen his family go from working in small aid groups to being part of a large cooperative where all property was shared. The front of their family homestead, where his grandparents slept, had become the co-op's communal cattle shed.

Now they were part of a huge commune, headquartered in the town of Wujing. An Shang village was a production brigade of the Wujing People's Commune, and his family's neighborhood had become Production Team 1. Their land, their animals and tools, their homes, and their labor now belonged

---

Communes

The Great Leap Forward introduced not only steel production in backyard furnaces and the Four Pests Campaign but also a new level of collectivization, which gathered twenty to thirty thousand people together into each People's Commune. Chinese farmers were in awe of what the new government had accomplished with the early collectives, such as the Mutual Aid Teams, and willingly followed Chairman Mao's directives.

In its continuous effort to turn its huge rural population into efficient production units, the Communist Party leaders experimented with a variety of arrangements. In the summer of 1958, a trial project did away with private plots in a portion of Henan Province and joined twenty-seven cooperatives into one very large commune. Viewed as wildly successful, the leaders decided by the end of the year to create communes across China. This rapid change was driven by a belief that harnessing the will and energy of the population would guarantee China's continuous growth.[1]

Land that had been parceled out to peasants in the early days of new China was now assigned to communes. Farmers received food and other resources according to a formula based on what each family had contributed in cattle and tools plus labor, with elaborate systems for keeping track of everything. Within a year, China had formed twenty-five thousand communes.[2]

---

to the commune. An Wei thought all these new improvements were certain to improve their life.

A new slogan greeted him as he entered the village: "Dare to act. Aim high. Build socialism faster and better."

October 2007

"Yes. Our plow was exactly like that," An Wei said as he peered at a picture I'd found in an old book. He pored over other old photos.[3]

A millstone. "Yes, exactly." It was about a meter wide with ridges.

A metal pitchfork. "Not like that. Ours were made of wood with long prongs."

A large stone roller for threshing. "Exactly, with those grooves across it."

The photos opened a floodgate of detailed memories. He talked of the satisfying crack of wheat kernels as their ox pulled the millstone, of lugging scratchy cornstalks from the fields, and of the pressure to work late into the night to harvest one crop and then quickly plant seeds for the next one while the weather held.

I'd witnessed that same intensity during my first stay in An Shang.

One day I watched Brother Number Five strain against the canvas strap slung over his shoulder to gently pull an overloaded handcart into his courtyard where he tipped it back and let the ears of corn slide to the ground. That evening he and his wife sat on small stools under a bright light bulb, husking piles of dried corn long into the night.

The small village throbbed with work. Farmers passed me with handcarts laden with cornstalks. Occasional tractors pulled loaded flatbed trailers heaped with more cornstalks. I was mesmerized by the deep golden color of the husked corn that was tied into long yellow braids that hung from roof edges and drying racks.

Once the fields were cleared, the village men plowed and planted into the night, while women, children, and elderly men continued to husk. One woman told me how her mother had pinched her ear to keep her awake and on task. Others nodded in agreement. Their hands cracked from the dry husks, and they described how much they hated the worms they'd find feasting on some of the kernels.

Fall 1959

From the first morning after An Wei arrived home for the October harvest, he joined in the backbreaking work. His labor helped the family earn additional work points that they traded for food and other essentials from the commune.

Each night, by the time he fell onto the kang, exhaustion numbed him, yet he knew they had to continue for many days to stave off hunger and build a prosperous country. The commune had promised to turn over a large amount of corn and grain to the government, so they must meet that goal.

As the family prepared to plant the winter wheat, his father directed An Wei to plow. He already knew how to steady the heavy wood and iron plow and keep it and the ox or donkey moving, but he had never completed a field by himself. That required both skill and strength. He was honored his father thought he could do it, yet he hated to learn new farm chores. He was going to be a college student, not a farmer. His father, however, insisted that he master the plowing technique. He had to admit, his father was right. There was no guarantee he would pass the college entrance exams.

The next morning as dawn arrived and a tan mist hung over the fields, his father led the ox from the commune shed. Damp, musty dust saturated the courtyard. An Wei and his brothers fitted the patient animal with the harness, lifted seed bags onto their shoulders, and headed out to plant. Neighbors were walking to other sections of the large communal fields. After the brothers fitted the plow to the harness, An Wei maneuvered the ox into place and tipped the plow into the earth. He snapped the bamboo-and-rope whip, prompting the ox to take several steps forward. To his chagrin, the plow pulled out of the furrow. He knew his father was watching. Trying to remain calm, An Wei tilted the plow at a better angle and cracked the whip lightly. The ox strained and the plow caught. They moved forward, but his hand slipped on the handle and it nosed down too deep.

Whoa. He stopped the ox. He had to get this right. Resetting the plow, he started again, willing himself to focus hard on the hand and arm that guided it.

Once An Wei got it into the soil at the right depth and angle, the heavy plow head slid along smoothly. It was a matter of keeping it there, of paying attention. He flicked the whip, reminding the ox to keep plodding steadily. It was slow work, but he had to admit feeling satisfaction in knowing he was succeeding. He did not dare look back at the furrow, though, for fear of losing his grip. He was sure it was not as straight as the ones his father or brothers made. His plow hand slipped a little as he tried to stretch his cramped fingers. The head dipped. He reached quickly and pulled it up to the right depth. Focus. He had to focus, but he realized he was beginning to sense how it felt when it was right. He moved the animal into a better line with the furrow and settled into a comfortable pace.

At the end of the long row, he turned the ox and plow, opened and shut his hand a few times, and began back the other way. Eyeing the size of the field, he tried to calculate the number of furrows. It would take a long time, but he knew the reward of a bountiful crop in spring would be worth it.

Once the wheat was planted, students and teachers headed back to school, pleased that they had started a new crop on its way, even though they knew food rationing continued.

Walking through the school gate, An Wei felt renewed energy. He wanted to learn all he could. Right away he reviewed everything they had learned before the harvest. Then, as usual, he turned to making sure he understood every lesson in all his subjects. His favorite subjects were Chinese literature, English, physics, and history. He read as much as he could from the school library—mostly modern literature. His teachers said older books like *Dream of Red Mansions* and Chinese classics would mislead young people. They should read new ones such as *The Song of Youth*, about the 1930s student movement opposing the Japanese invaders. That book made a deep impression on him.

He also loved to write. For years he had wanted to become a writer, and in junior high school he had even written a short story about his family's life. An Wei and his classmates who read a lot became followers of a talented teacher who was an expert on Chinese literature and spent hours alone in his office writing stories. He was too serious to approach, so they admired him from a distance and even hand-copied a story of his that had inspired them. Then one day they learned that their idol was accused of abusing the government-mandated beliefs of Mao Zedong Thought. With the Anti-Bourgeois Writers' Movement gaining strength, the teacher was forbidden to teach, publicly criticized in struggle sessions, and forced to burn his manuscripts.

Seeing his teacher sent off to be instructed by illiterate farmers, probably for years, An Wei buried his writer's dream.

The Anti-Bourgeois Rightest Campaign

In 1956, Mao Zedong launched a movement asking citizens to criticize the country's problems. "Let a hundred flowers bloom; let a hundred schools of thought contend," he said. In cities across the country, they responded, criticizing policy and making suggestions for improvement. Spontaneous groups of literate men and women engaged in serious conversations about how to improve the Communist Party and the country. A year later, however, a new directive came. Those who had criticized the government were labeled "Bourgeois Rightists," and tens of thousands of intellectuals and scientists who had participated in the earlier public discussions were sent to labor camps, prisons, and the countryside to learn from the peasants. Stripped of their official jobs and positions and forced to live in unbearably harsh conditions, many were broken physically and psychologically.[4]

The Anti-Bourgeois Writers' Movement gained strength. Throughout the country, writers were labeled rightists, often for the flimsiest reasons, with nearly one million condemned. However slight their criticism, writers including Ding Ling, one of the most famous women writers in China, were abused in mass meetings, and most were sent far away to do manual labor for years. By 1958 and the beginning of the Great Leap Forward, criticism from the educated classes had been silenced.

---

*   *   *

An Wei had begun senior high school toting the required twenty-five kilos of grain to school every month, but as the year progressed, the bags grew lighter and the school cut back on food. Students lost weight, their hunger increased, and yet they kept studying.

Despite the difficulties, teachers sometimes entertained the students. During one memorable assembly, An Wei was awestruck when two teachers pretended to speak different languages. One said something in a pretend language; the other interpreted the "foreign language." It was hilarious. It also introduced a new idea. He had just begun to study English. What if he became an interpreter between Chinese and English or another language? It would be safer than being a writer. Writing your own ideas was dangerous, but maybe translating someone else's would be safer.

Back home for weekend chores, An Wei followed the cattle attendant down the row of animals in the communal cattle shed. He hated this attendant, who always gave him the slowest ox. It added hours to grinding corn or wheat.

An Wei glanced at the good animals as they passed them. Then, without thinking twice, he stepped in beside a good ox, pushed it into the open area of the shed, and walked toward the exit. The attendant, who was about to back the slowest one out, wheeled around.

"Hey. You can't do that," he yelled.

An Wei said nothing and led the ox to the family grinding mill, his fury dissipating as he urged the ox into the harness. The predawn sky began to lighten, accompanied by the coos of mourning doves. He dumped grain onto the bottom stone, he flicked his whip, and the ox began to pull. It moved steadily around the circle, the deep rumble of the stones taking on a repetitive rhythm. From time to time he extracted partially ground grain from the sieve below the stone and put it back for further grinding.

When he was younger, An Wei used to laugh at his father and older brothers because when they finished grinding they were covered with flour. Now he realized this was a waste of food. He experimented with different techniques as he ground. If he moved the little door underneath the grinding stone gently, he found the flour would drop from the stone and only leave a little on one of his arms. When he moved it back and forth violently, the way most people did, flour flew all over the place. He realized he should show the others how they could save flour this way.

An Wei settled into the long grinding routine. He loved the sound of the heavy stone cracking the kernels as the millstone moved at an even pace. He thought about the problem of the cattle attendant; solving that was not going to be easy. If he did not, the man could make life difficult for An Wei by reporting him to the commune or, maybe worse, bullying him constantly. The attendant seemed to think highly of himself because he was classified as a "poor peasant" and therefore was considered better than An Wei's "middle peasant" family, which had greater resources. The poorer you were, the more status you had.

He wondered if the man hated him because he was going to school and could read. Or maybe he just liked tormenting An Wei and his family because the shed and feedlot used to belong to them.

Chairman Mao and the commune leaders said they needed to rely on the poor and the lower middle peasants. An Wei knew that was policy, but the cattle attendant did not have to give him the worst ox every time he ground grain.

How could he stop this unfair behavior since the man held all the power over the production team's animals? The more he thought about it, the more he was sure he needed to act. If he did not speak out, this man and maybe others in the cattle shed would treat him worse and worse. But An Wei knew enough about life and politics in new China to realize he had to get back at the man within a narrow range between personal insult and public loss of face. He had to fight for his own rights cleverly—and now.

He dumped the remaining grain onto the stone, sifted the flour into the box, and quickly returned the half ground kernels. As the last of the flour fell into the box, he slowed the ox and untied it from the stone. Giving the gentle-eyed animal several pats, he led it toward the cattle shed and hoped he could respond just right to whatever the attendant said to him.

As they entered, the man was waiting. "How could you take the liberty to think you can have whichever ox you want? That's not right."

An Wei's anger rose, and his words flowed. "My family is a middle peasant family. We invested more than enough compared to many villagers."

He could not contain himself once he started.

"Why do you always assign that slow ox to me? It's not fair for you to punish me each time. Once in a while if you give me the slow ox, like everybody else, that's okay. But you give me the slow one every time. This is my demonstration against you. I took that hardworking ox on purpose because I want to teach you a lesson. You should be fair."

The man's jaw tightened, yet he remained speechless. An Wei knew that most farmers would not expose people like this; they avoided making them lose face. But An Wei felt proud. He had spoken his mind. He had done it in private, so the man was only embarrassed in private.

On the way back to school that afternoon, he mulled over the incident and was reminded of a story about his father's mother. She put up with her husband, An Wei's difficult grandfather, but one day she took on a larger challenge. It happened when An Wei was very young, before the People's Republic of China was formed.

In those days, because of the civil war between the Nationalists led by Chiang Kai-shek and the Communists, recruiters went to villages and made men "volunteer" to serve in their armies. When soldiers came to An Shang and said the village had to provide a certain number of men, An Wei's father was chosen because he was the oldest of four sons. He was forced to drive a horse cart and transport materials for half a year for one of the armies, though

An Wei does not know whether it was the Communists or the Nationalists. He was lucky to return since many never got back home.

The next year the opposing army arrived in the village and ordered the family to give them a cow. Because the family had already donated An Wei's father, his grandmother refused. When soldiers started to take the cow, his grandmother tied the cow's rope to her arm, declaring she would stay together with her cow forever. She refused to let them have it. An Wei chuckled at the image.

The soldiers tried to take it by force. His grandmother, with the rope still around her arm, lay down on the ground. Her actions shook the whole village.

An Wei did not remember whether the army took the cow or not, but the image of her spirited resistance reminded him that you cannot be tame. You have to be determined, and sometimes you have to teach some people a lesson, just as he had taught a lesson to the cattle attendant.

In mid-June 1960, school closed and all the students and teachers headed home for two weeks to bring in the most important crop, the winter wheat they had planted in October. They worked to beat the coming wind and rain that could destroy it, calling their feverish pace "grabbing the food from the dragon's mouth."

On his earlier weekend trips home, An Wei had noticed that the wheat was not growing well. Now as they piled the grain in the threshing grounds, the final results confirmed it. The crop they had planted with so much enthusiasm in the fall turned out to be terrible. The lack of rain had left the stalks stunted. Many had not developed grain heads, and those that had held few kernels. Their meals for the foreseeable future would be skimpier, especially since a large portion of the grain they harvested had to be given to the government.

An Wei had always been hungry growing up in their large family, but this was different. Now he was beginning to feel weak. Still he toiled with his family and the other villagers. They had to plow the fields and sow the summer crop quickly to give the new plants time to ripen before winter approached.

But that next harvest was terrible too, and again much of it was promised to the government. In the village, his younger brothers were getting thinner as family members spent hours foraging for wild vegetables. School had very little food, and hunger made the trek to and from home more difficult.

The following harvests repeated the pattern, and food allotments continuously decreased. Terrible stomach pains, gas, and diarrhea tormented students and teachers. Teacher Bao, their head teacher, said they had to tighten their belts as they survived on meals of one steamed bun and thin soup.

They did not know that harvests across the whole country were bad and that rural areas were suffering the most.

Hunger in the 1960s

Throughout 1960 to 1962, people died in Shaanxi Province, where An Shang village was located, but not as many as in other places. In Anhui and Hunan Provinces, thousands of people died of starvation every day. Family after family perished, and the living were too weak to bury the dead.[5]

History now records this period as the Bitter Years, which the Chinese government sometimes refers to as the Three Years of Natural Disaster. Government statistics say about fifteen million Chinese people starved to death,[6] though other estimates soar as high as forty-five million.

The causes, which are still debated, were varied. There were several years of severe drought, coupled with locust swarms that resulted from killing all the sparrows, their natural predators, during the Great Leap Forward. But there were other major causes. Commune leaders and production teams, trying to impress Chairman Mao, predicted wildly optimistic production output far greater than could be achieved. Lying became endemic. Revolutionary fervor remained high, and one boss tried to outdo the next. Across China, peasants were forced to meet these unrealistic quotas by ceding their own grain supplies to the government. Communes visited by Mao Zedong even borrowed grain from other areas to fabricate their production amounts. Some officials, including the minister of National Defense, saw what was happening and expressed concern about the unfolding disaster, but Chairman Mao labeled them traitors. Most people at all levels were afraid to speak the truth for fear of being imprisoned.

In 1957, the average amount of grain per person in rural areas was 205 kilos. By 1959, An Wei's first year of high school, it had dropped to 183 kilos per person. By 1961, his last year in high school, it plummeted to a disastrous 154 kilos. The median age of those dying dropped to 9.7 years of age.[7]

* * *

As people became more and more desperate, they did things that in normal times they would never consider. One day a ruckus erupted at An Wei's school. A student from northern Fufeng County said he was being cheated. The north was less populated than the south, where An Wei was from, which meant the farmers could find places up in the hills to plant extra vegetables. Each week when their children returned to school, the northern parents sent extra food in the form of a stack of pancakes to supplement the meager school diet. The student gave his cloth-wrapped stack of pancakes to a teacher to keep the food safe from his half-starved classmates. But the teacher, who was also half starved, kept cutting little pieces from each pancake, leaving the number the same, but smaller.

Situations like this multiplied. In the city of Fufeng, An Wei saw a man buy a pancake from a food vendor. As he began eating it, a boy grabbed it from behind and ran. The man chased him, the thief spit on the pancake, and then offered to return it. Desperately hungry people did not think much about morality or laws.

Even in An Shang, where An Wei never heard of hungry villagers stealing from each other, stealing from the commune became a normal way of life.

Once the whole village stole the alfalfa crop. Every one—parents, neighbors, and older children—snuck into the field one midnight. Illegal or not, it was edible. In the past, the watchman would hunt down thieves, but not now. He ignored the rustling of many people among the plants until they had collected a considerable amount of alfalfa.

Then the watchman walked slowly in their direction calling, "Who's there? Who's there?" It was his signal for them to leave.

The next morning when the village leader discovered that half the alfalfa was gone, he asked the watchman if he had seen anyone.

"I heard some people walking in the field and tried to catch them, but they ran away," he said. "I don't know who they were."

Stealing from the attendant who fed the commune cattle in An Wei's homestead was trickier. The man let no one near the cattle fodder, which consisted of hay, straw, and good grain. As An Wei and his little brothers got hungrier, they eyed the fodder spread out in boxes in their homestead.

If the attendant thought grain was missing, An Wei and his brothers would be the most obvious suspects. They studied the situation carefully and discovered the attendant was only clever to a point. After he took out fodder to feed the cattle, he carefully smoothed the top so he could tell if someone took any. But he did not mark how high it was on the side of the box.

For weeks when the attendant was dozing or out getting the cows from their tethers, the boys snuck in, took a handful of fodder, carefully smoothed the surface, and ran off to bake the stolen feed in a wok. The cattleman kept telling villagers that he did not think he had used much fodder, yet it ran out quickly. He never figured out what was happening, and An Wei and his brothers were able to fill some of the empty spaces in their bellies.

As the months went on, An Wei could barely stand his trips home. Everyone was numb from hunger. His parents and grandparents increasingly found their bodies swollen from edema. His brothers' bellies were distended, and when his father pressed his thumb into his thigh, the hole remained. His father's muscles were gone; his leg felt like tofu. Yet An Wei's parents still gave him grain for school. He knew they were keeping less for themselves and that every month their allotment from the commune was smaller.

1961

Back for their third and final year of senior high school, meals still consisted of one steamed bun, but now the buns were filled with straw and cornhusks, and the soup was mostly water. It seemed that starvation would never end. Their teachers told them to eat every crumb for nourishment, but it was hard to imagine there was much nutrition in what they were getting.

To save the students' energy for studying, the school stopped sports and enforced long naps. Often An Wei spent afternoons in the fields beyond the school hunting for wild vegetables. He and a few others fared better than many because they were willing to eat anything edible no matter how awful it tasted. When he found wild plants in out-of-the-way places, he gave them to his good friend, Sun Zhonglun, who had his mother cook them for An Wei. The Suns did not have enough food for themselves, but they had more than An Wei, so they prepared the vegetables for him and never kept any for themselves.

The hungry teenagers continued to study. An Wei's hope of passing the college entrance exam remained strong. Teacher Bao moved slowly like everyone else and was painfully thin from lack of food, but he worked to keep the students' spirits up. When he talked he still lit up with enthusiasm, his face animated. Crinkles around his eyes and at the edge of his lips hinted at his kindness. The students admired him. He talked differently and thought differently from other teachers or adults they knew. He had experience in the outside world and spent hours teaching these poor farm children how to negotiate their futures—not just how to study for exams but also how city people lived.

He also rescued their language studies. Though trained in mathematics, Teacher Bao stepped into the gap when their English teacher was dismissed for being a "Rightist." Determined to give the students the best education he could, he taught himself English, lesson by lesson, as they went along.

Every bit of An Wei's energy in his final year was aimed at earning a high-enough score on the college entrance exam to get a coveted place in a university.

Before taking the exam, students had to declare a college major. Their choice would determine some of their exam content and the grading of their exams. Teachers were invaluable in guiding them through this complicated thicket. Once again Teacher Bao stepped in. He convinced An Wei his best chance would be to select English as his major.

He said that because most high schools in Shaanxi Province taught Russian, and only a few, including theirs, taught English, An Wei would have much less competition if he took the exam for English majors.

"Just memorize the three years of English textbooks before the exam," Teacher Bao told him.

One Saturday in late spring, An Wei made his usual trip home to help with chores and collect his grain ration for school because he had no more food coupons. Though weak, his spirits rose as he walked past fields of healthy crops, the grain heads quite full. What a relief.

When he got home, however, he discovered that his large family had used all of its rations from the meager commune supplies and had borrowed as much grain as they could from the brigade emergency reserve. They could borrow no more. Even if the June harvest was better than previous ones, they would have to pay back what they owed immediately. Their food supply would not change dramatically even after the summer harvest.

The crushing truth slowly became clear to An Wei. There was no food.

His parents insisted on giving him their hopelessly small rations, but there was no way he could take them. They and his brothers would starve. He grew numb with the realization that he must stay home to help forage for food.

He had to give up his dream of finishing high school and passing the national college entrance examination. He could not abandon his family.

On Sunday afternoon, instead of heading for Fufeng High School to study, he walked slowly into the gullies near their homestead to help hunt for bark and wild plants.

• 3 •

Moving On

An Wei plodded a distance, hoping to find some morsels overlooked by the other starving peasants. But every edible plant and most tree leaves and bark near the village had been eaten—everything except the ripening crops.

When he returned to their homestead, he used what little energy he had for farm chores, trying to erase his disappointment at giving up a life's dream. At night, thoughts of all his wasted study haunted him, as hunger pains racked his body.

Back at school, Teacher Bao noticed that An Wei had not returned. After a few days he realized that one of the few students who might have a chance at passing the college entrance exams must be having difficulty. If An Wei was going to get a high-enough score to be admitted to university, he had to be studying day and night.

Teacher Bao pointed his battered bicycle up the dirt track toward An Shang, the steep, rutted path forcing him to carry it partway. Several hours later, the teacher arrived dusty and exhausted, for he too was starving.

An Wei was sitting in the courtyard when he heard someone come through the open gate. Teacher Bao.

It was like seeing a mirage. Why was he here?

An Wei's father and mother emerged from their room, barely able to walk. Despite their weakness, they greeted him cordially and shyly as he introduced himself.

Teacher Bao got to the point quickly.

"Why hasn't your son returned to school?"

They explained their hopeless situation and their inability to send grain back to school with An Wei. The disappointment showed on their tired, gaunt faces. Although the summer harvest looked promising, they must pay most of their share back to the commune.

Teacher Bao knew peasant life was difficult in the extreme, especially now. Yet he also believed deeply in the importance of farmers' children getting the education their parents and grandparents never dreamed of. He persisted.

"Well, it doesn't matter what you owe." He would find food for An Wei at the high school. He would borrow food coupons from the students from the north, where food was not as scarce. They could pay them back later.

Although uneasy about more debt, his mother and father agreed to the arrangement. They were intensely proud of An Wei's school accomplishments.

Without wasting a minute, An Wei gathered what he needed and followed his teacher down the dirt track leading back to school to continue his exam preparation, incredulous that life had taken yet another dramatic turn.

2007

As I walked back to Brother Number Five's house from the An Shang village school, soaking up the spring warmth and taking in the sweep of fields where ripening winter wheat rippled light green in the spring breeze, a dusty car passed and turned into Brother Number Five's home.

I was in An Shang for another few weeks of volunteer teaching, and Teacher Bao was a passenger in that car. A few weeks earlier, An Wei's impish Brother Number Five had come back from the large town of Baoji bursting with news. He had run into An Wei's former head teacher who had agreed to visit. An Wei and his revered teacher had not seen each other for thirty years.

I ducked through the plastic strips in the doorway that served to keep the dust and flies out of the house, washed my hands, and served myself from the delectable dishes Brother Number Five's wife and another villager had prepared for us: cut-up vegetables with bits of chicken, wheat noodles in broth, potatoes with onions,

Teacher Bao, An Wei's high school teacher, at the 2007 interview in An Shang village.

and lotus roots—some of my favorites. I poured a cup of tea and sat with the other volunteers at the laminate table, chatting about the morning's teaching.

Through the large window that looked out on the courtyard, I caught a glimpse of An Wei and his teacher emerging from the little living room area of Number Five's house. Tall and erect, seventy-seven-year-old Teacher Bao walked easily in his gray jacket and pants, which were almost the same color as his short-cropped hair. An Wei, his strong voice preceding him, pulled the plastic strips to one side and followed his teacher into the room. He introduced Teacher Bao, and we all leaned forward in anticipation.

Relaxed and amiable, and without urging, he talked of An Wei's high school years, of the terrible starvation, and of urging An Wei to study English since almost all the high school students in the county studied Russian. I had heard this from An Wei, but I was pleased to have unsolicited verification. Primarily, however, I marveled at the resilience and obvious kindness of this man who had done so much for An Wei and other students. Energy and enthusiasm spread across his face as he talked. I could imagine him in front of fifty or so serious, starving teenagers, urging them on and using humor to keep their spirits up.

The more stories he told us, the more animated he became. Though he taught English to An Wei's class, he was really a math teacher. Every night he studied the next English lesson, keeping just ahead of the class and working toward approximate pronunciation. As he smiled quietly, crinkles forming around his eyes, he joked about An Wei's constant talking, but also volunteered that he was an excellent student.

With a heartfelt tribute to his teacher, An Wei brought the sharing to an end. Seldom one to talk about his own feelings, he said with considerable emotion that Teacher Bao changed his life. On that, they said good-bye to us and went off to have lunch together and allow his teacher to relax before returning home.

Late Spring 1962

As soon as An Wei reached school with Teacher Bao, he went right to his books. He was driven now—not just by his teacher's commitment and his parents' belief in him but also by a raw determination to escape a Chinese farmer's poverty and starvation. His jaw tightened as he set himself a rigid schedule.

He would begin each study session with English, since it would count the most. He had memorized the first book and studied half of the next one. But he still had a book and a half of English to memorize, plus math, physics, chemistry, history, and Chinese.

Each morning he got up from the wooden slats as the first light crept into the big dormitory. He straightened his clothes, slipped on his shoes, and headed outside to exercise a little, but not so much that he would wear himself

An Wei in 1962, his last year of high school, after three years of starvation. *Source*: An Wei.

out. He needed to keep his brain clear in order to get a perfect score on the exam. If he aimed lower than 100, others might beat him, and he would end up a poor farmer for life.

Hour after hour, English ran through his head. *The man ran around the track. Three mans ran around the tree.* No, *mens.* No, *men. Three men ran. I am, you are, he is.* Why couldn't it be consistent? Why did it have to have plurals, he/she, and past tense? Chinese was so much easier.

Each night he crawled exhausted onto the platform with the rest of the students and tried to sleep, his body, like everyone else's, crying for more than the meager buns they were allotted.

When he tired of sitting in the classroom, he went to the sports ground and sometimes walked south of the school to the river where it was quieter. Days turned to weeks. He was edgy, and sleep was difficult. Mid-June brought the summer harvest, and though students and teachers had little energy, they all trudged home to help bring in the grain and plant the next crops.

This time—finally—they had a good harvest. An Wei's family had to give a lot back to the commune, but they were better off than before. Starvation began to ebb, and though still painfully thin, An Wei could feel his energy increase a little.

Back at school for the final weeks of exam preparation, pressure mounted. With only a month to go, every minute counted.

At one point a friend suggested they go to the famous Famen Temple to study. They could have a good time walking there, and it would be quiet. An Wei worried about taking time from studying but decided it might do him good.

Several of them set off the next day, heading up the dirt track looking for the turnoff that would take them to the ancient temple with its high pagoda. As they walked and joked, An Wei relaxed.

This outing might even help him think better. The exam was not all memorization. He needed to think and write well and support arguments with good facts. And if he did not pass? He pushed the prospect of spending his life in An Shang from his thoughts and walked a little faster toward the temple.

An Wei had never seen anything like the pagoda. So tall and complex. Who built it? he wondered. How did you create something like that?

He knew Chairman Mao said Buddhist beliefs were superstitions, but he hoped that if there were any good spirits around, they would bless him and help him through his exam.

He found a shady spot and tugged the last of the English books out of his shirt to work on two difficult passages. If he repeated them enough times, maybe they would make sense. The teachers had told him about learning from ancient texts: *Du shu bai bian, Qi yi zi xian.* (If you read or recite a book one hundred times, the meaning of the book will come out naturally; 读书百遍, 其义自见.) Maybe this method would work for English too.

At school, An Wei continued his routine. Study in the fields near the school made it easier to memorize the English textbooks as well as Chinese passages and grammar. He tried to envision this exam as just one more, like the others he had taken.

One week before the exam, school authorities sent the students home. They told them that if they crammed until the last minute, they would get nervous and might fail even if they knew the material.

"Go home and do your normal chores," the school director said.

Teacher Bao gave them final instructions: "You must report to the examination school in Xingping County by four o'clock, July 22." Each student needed to take light bedding and enough food to last for the three-day exam. That was it.

An Wei and his classmates headed up the long grade from Fufeng and along the summer-dusty paths. Twelve years of schooling were over.

July 1962

An Wei boarded the train for Xingping, the neighboring county, clutching his bedding and a bundle of cloth-wrapped pancakes for his meals. About two hundred students from Fufeng High School and other areas milled around the exam school until a teacher directed them to where they would sleep.

Slowly, An Wei ate the two pancakes he had allotted for supper and washed them down with boiled drinking water the school provided. The rest he tucked away—one for each breakfast and two each for lunch and supper. Being a little hungry, he thought, would keep him alert.

The next morning, he found his assigned seat and carefully placed his registration card on the desk, making sure he had the correct seat number. Surrounded by other students, he willed himself to remain calm while they waited for the proctors to give out the first section. At least they were starting with a subject he loved, Chinese.

As his hands touched the papers, his limbs went cold. He shut his eyes for a minute, took a deep breath, and said to himself, "Remember, it is just another exam. Just like the ones you have taken in every grade."

An Wei checked to make sure the exam number matched his registration number and then looked through the pages. It had three parts: classical Chinese to translate into modern Chinese, Chinese language and grammar, and a composition. He flexed his hands and began. If he kept up a steady pace, he could finish easily within the two-hour limit.

Classical Chinese was a challenge, but he figured out the passages. It was like solving a puzzle, and the language part was easy for him. The composition took thought, though.

There were two options. One was "After a Rain"; the other asked why they should not be afraid of ghosts. An Wei pondered the choices. Since the new government said belief in ghosts was superstitious, he felt they wanted students to state the official belief. But older villagers, like his grandparents, and maybe even his parents, still believed in ghosts. It would be hard to ignore their beliefs as he wrote. So he chose "After the Rain."

Ideas began to flow. He described life in a dry land where water was precious, and how, when the rains came, villagers rejoiced, savoring the moist soil, the blue skies, and fresh air. Although this was an exam, he loved putting these words together to create a vivid picture.

The next day, An Wei's heart pounded when he looked at the English exam handed to him. It would count the most.

As he leafed through its five pages, a rush of confidence surged through him. At first glance, at least, it did not look difficult; his studying had paid off. He just had to remember everything he had memorized from those textbooks. He picked up his pen and began, knowing that his answers needed to be perfect for a high score. First he had to correct error-ridden sentences. He read each one with care, double-checking to be sure he was not making mistakes.

Next came definite and indefinite articles—*the* and *a* and *an*—which always gave him trouble. To arm himself, he had memorized every example and rule in the textbooks. He paused and told himself the definitions.

"The definite article—*the*—tells the listener a noun is specific." He remembered some examples. "I am going to the library." "Do you want the book on the table?"

"The indefinite articles—*a* and *an*—are for general use." "I need a pen." "I want a notebook."

He wrote each answer carefully, making sure to use the articles correctly.

After stretching a little, he went on to translate English sentences into Chinese. He read each several times and worked on them slowly and steadily, making sure to translate whole phrases, not just word by word.

Finally, the last section required writing a passage using a given set of English words and phrases. He wrote slowly, making sure to dot *i*'s and use capital letters correctly. As he added the last period, he put his pen down, sat up straight, and reread his work, making sure all the letters were formed well.

As he turned in his completed exam, he felt he had done well, but all the energy had drained from his body.

After three grueling days that also included exams in math, chemistry, physics, and politics, An Wei returned home and fell back into the rhythm of the countryside, wondering what lay ahead. About three or four hundred students in the province took the English exam. Teacher Bao predicted that only a third of them were better at English than An Wei, but that was a lot of competition.

As he helped repair roof leaks and worked in the commune fields, he vowed that no matter what, he would not live like this forever. Not one to sit idly, he knew he must make plans in case he did not pass the exam. His father had often urged him to become a village teacher, and that seemed a realistic possibility. Though it would keep him tied to poverty since teachers often did not get paid, at least his father would be pleased that one of his six sons had escaped farm life.

The next available morning he walked to the township and asked the officials if there were any teaching jobs. Though he had not attended a teacher preparation high school, he qualified to teach elementary school and some positions remained. He selected one and registered to teach there. Although depressed by the prospect, he had at least ensured his future.

Following several weeks of fieldwork, his father sent him to buy white construction lime in Fufeng to repair the homestead walls. As An Wei swung down the familiar track, he thought about that year of hard study and wondered about the exam, but it was too early for results. At the bottom of the long grade, he turned into the village of his good friend, Sun Zhonglun, whose family had cooked his wild vegetables when he was starving at school. Their village produced the lime.

He got the lime and walked to Sun's homestead. Their loud greetings erupted. Like everyone, they talked about the improved harvest and their hopes for good crops.

Then Sun startled him, saying, "The final exam notice is at the school."

An Wei stood rooted to the spot. This was it. What if he failed? He would need to keep his face unemotional; he could not show his crushing disappointment if he failed.

Finally he got the words out. "And . . . what did they say? Do you know?"

"Nearly twenty are enrolled into *college!*"

"How about you?" An Wei asked cautiously.

"Well, I failed, and *you* are enrolled—*into college.*"

He could not believe it was true. He felt terrible for his friend, and yet An Wei knew Sun had not spent as much time studying. No one had.

An Wei managed to keep his demeanor calm as his insides churned. But maybe Sun had made an error.

He hoisted the lime, said good-bye, and left the homestead. The school was close by. When he got there he looked for a way to sneak in along a side building. He did not have the courage to go through the school gate. If he had failed, he did not want anyone to see him.

Quietly he went to the place where he thought the list would be, his fear growing with every step.

There it was. He glanced at the list quickly, and then away. Was his name really there? He stared at it.

Name: An Wei. Score: 97.

Ninety-seven. Ninety-seven out of 100. He had aimed high, and it had worked.

He stood there transfixed. He was accepted into college!

He hoisted the full bag of lime onto his shoulder and headed home. Usually he stopped at least twice when he carried a heavy sack the ten kilometers between Fufeng and An Shang village. This time his body sprang from step to step without stopping.

Neighbors came to greet him as he approached his village.

"There's a *letter* for you. An official letter."

He steadied his nerves to open it and slowly read the notice. He was to enter Xi'an Foreign Languages Institute in September.[1]

September 1962

As September 1, 1962, neared, An Wei gathered what he needed for college. His mother and sister, who wove the material for all of their clothes, made An Wei new pants and a shirt, plus new black cloth shoes that had to be broken in. He put together his bedding, a few English books, his small dictionary, pens, an eating bowl, and a washbasin. On the appointed day, as the sun rose, he pulled on his new shirt of carefully woven cloth, pushed his feet into the stiff new shoes, and hiked down the steep cliff from the loess plateau to the train track that ran along the Wei River. His thick black hair neatly trimmed, he carried his few belongings in a bag and his quilt on his back. The clothes he wore were all he had.

Finally, a steam engine ground to a stop, and he climbed onto the train for the four-hour ride to Xi'an. Arriving about noon and not wanting to spend money on bus fare, An Wei decided to walk to the university in the southern part of the city despite the end-of-summer heat. He followed the directions sent by the university, wending his way south through the noisy, crowded streets filled with handcarts and fuming buses. At one intersection he asked directions from a tea merchant lining up ceramic mugs on a low sidewalk table. At another point he paused to read colorful film and book notices pasted on a large board. But mostly, he kept moving at a steady pace.

South of the ancient city walls, fewer trucks and buses rumbled past and the area seemed quieter. Sweat was rolling down his face when he saw the university sign. He gazed at the archway overhead and rested for a moment. What was it going to be like?

Older students greeted An Wei and led him to the registration area. Numb with exhilaration, he stood tall, brushed his sweaty hair to one side, and unfolded his acceptance notification for the administrators. The upper classmen helped him fill out the necessary papers and then showed him to his room. He dumped his belongings on his assigned bed and looked around. One, two, three, four—he could hardly believe it. There were four separate wooden beds. That was all. So different from high school with fifteen to twenty packed onto a wooden platform.

Once he caught his breath, the students showed him around the small campus, the three-story classroom building, and large library. Then they made their way to the cafeteria for a dinner of corn soup made with noodles and a few vegetables. He was ecstatic. The food was so much better than at home. For the first time he thought he could say good-bye to hunger.

2008, Xi'an

"There's the auditorium where we had meetings," An Wei said. He and his wife, Niu Jianhua, were showing me around the college they had both attended in the 1960s, now named the Xi'an International Studies University.

Niu Jianhua beckoned me to follow her around the corner to a door that opened onto a huge low-ceiled room filled with tables and red stools. The cafeteria. It was empty except for a few stray pink and green thermoses for hot water sitting on a table.

"I remember, I would come through this door with my friends and put my coat over there," she said, laughing heartily. "You could eat anything, three meals a day."

I asked her how many others from her Xi'an high school had gone to college. She said hers was the top-performing school in the city, with a senior class of two hundred students. Of those, only thirty-five passed the college entrance exam and were accepted to university.

An Wei joined us. *"From 6:30 to late evening, you could come here and eat anytime."*

Niu Jianhua nodded.

Their enthusiasm reminded me that they had come to college just after the years of hunger. For An Wei the starvation in the village and at school had been awful. Niu Jianhua, who lived in the city, had not suffered as much, but her family still went hungry.

An Wei pointed.

"We used to have lots of posters on that wall," he said.

Niu Jianhua nodded again.

"And a stage was over there."

She nodded.

"We picked up our food there. It was delicious."

Niu Jianhua and I meandered outside to a tree-lined walkway and a three-story stucco building with a hint of pink trim under the windows. An Wei followed.

She pointed. *"That was my classroom. An Wei was in that one."* He was a year ahead of her. *"It was a very small college. We all fit into this one classroom building."*

"Yes," An Wei said, catching up with us. *"Eighteen classrooms. Students all studying different languages."*

We passed the library, which looked almost the same as it had when they were students. I followed Niu Jianhua through the keystone-shaped entrance to the stone-paved courtyard of the original gray brick administration building. She stood in silence, looking around, her thoughts private. Old single-story buildings edged the courtyard where the college administrators worked.

"We spent a lot of time here," An Wei said. He had his first job interview here. He pointed to a battered red door in a side building where a casement window had been flung open. *"That's the original office of the publicity department. We worked there collecting and editing posters and newsletters during the beginning of the Cultural Revolution."*

Niu Jianhua had worked a couple of rooms down.

While I took photos, they lingered there before we sauntered on. I wondered what they must be thinking. So much had happened in China over the next forty years.

Fall 1962

At university, it turned out An Wei's food situation was not as good as he had hoped. Although tuition was free, students needed to pay twelve yuan and fifty cents a month for food, an enormous amount for a farmer in those days. When the first-year students went to collect their food cards, the poor rural students showed their required documentation to get free meals. Like the others, An Wei was supposed to present a letter from his village brigade chief saying his parents and grandparents did not earn cash and he needed a subsidy. However, during high school An Wei had infuriated the An Shang leader.

Empty-handed, he stood before the political commissar for his class. Should he tell him what really happened?

"You don't have a letter from the village leader?" asked the commissar.

"No. I offended him, and he would not write me one." He did not know how much he should add. "I asked several times, but he refused."

In fact, his mother had found out the brigade chief was stealing from the commune. When An Wei heard this, he was furious. Villagers were starving. Everyone was supposed to follow Chairman Mao to make a strong country, but their leader was stealing from them. An Wei reported everything to the county government and asked them to sue the brigade chief.

The county forwarded An Wei's letter to the authorities of the People's Commune. They, in turn, sent inspectors to An Shang, who showed the letter to the village leader. An Wei had not signed it, but it was easy to figure out who wrote it. He was the only one in An Shang who was that literate.

Two years later, when An Wei asked the brigade chief for his food subsidy letter, the leader stalled.

"Come back later," he said.

In a few days, An Wei returned.

"I need to decide if you qualify," the leader said. An Wei knew he was using a timeworn Chinese technique to avoid an answer. He was never going to say *yes* or *no*.

He was sure the brigade chief wanted him to retract his accusation, but he would not do such a thing. He stood as tall as he could and left. He would rather go to university with no letter than lie to that crook.

An Wei waited for the political commissar to respond. He was looking at An Wei's high school records and turned a page thoughtfully.

"In school you were honest, and we know you are from a poor farmer's family," he said as he looked at a few more papers.

"Without the leader's letter we cannot offer you the full grant. But because we know your background, we can give you eight yuan a month." Dispirited, An Wei thanked the commissar. Four yuan and fifty cents was an impossible amount for a poor student to make up. He was going to be hungry again, though not starving.

The first day of classes, nervous and excited, An Wei walked with the other new English majors to their classroom on the ground floor of the three-story building that housed the English Department. It was a comfortably sized room with ample light from large windows. They would have all their classes plus their evening study period here for the next four years.

Their English teacher asked the twenty students to introduce themselves. It turned out only a few had studied English in high school; the rest had studied Russian.

"No matter which language you studied, you will all have to learn English from the very beginning, starting with the letters and sounds," the teacher said. If they had studied English, they needed to learn near-perfect pronunciation and intonation; if they had studied Russian, they needed to forget all of its pronunciation and learn English sounds.

The teachers were impressed with An Wei's academic abilities. He and one other student had earned the highest scores in the National Entrance Examination. But they warned that his local dialect was so pronounced that it might severely hamper his English. His speech was nearly incomprehensible to his classmates and teachers. He had never learned to speak Mandarin.

However, to An Wei's relief, English pronunciation was difficult for almost all the students. They spent hours on tedious exercises. "To pronounce the sound *eh* make the shape of your mouth like a smile," the teacher said. "You will never say 'eh' correctly if you close your mouth or open your mouth too wide. No."

He had the students keep their mouths in that unnatural smiling position for over a minute, and then made them practice it again and again. For every vowel and consonant on the classroom wall chart, he made meticulous demands of how to position their tongues and the width of their mouths.

"For the *th* sound, you have to push your tongue between your teeth and then pull it back."

"It is 'Thank you, thank you.' Not 'sank you, sank you.'"

Pulling out their pocket-sized mirror pieces, they practiced over and over, trying to put their tongues in the right position and making sure their mouths were opened wide enough.

Eh, eh, eh. Thank, thank, thank. Th, th, th. The sounds drifting through their open classroom windows must have been comical.

An Wei spent hours trying to find the right way to pronounce sounds like the *f* in *telephone*. Was his mouth opened wide enough? Was the sound far enough back in his throat? Adhering to a stringent regimen, he rose from his bed long before others, left his sleeping roommates undisturbed, took a half-hour run, and returned as the wake-up bell rang. While the others struggled to get up, he was already studying. Some students memorized lists of words, but An Wei memorized complete English passages so he would learn content, grammar, and vocabulary all at once. Just as in high school, he found a quiet place on the campus and read passages aloud again and again. It was grueling, tedious work.

The only relief was literature class, where they read short pieces by British and American authors. On his own he also read translations of Theodore Dreiser's *American Tragedy*, Mark Twain and Charles Dickens, and important Chinese writing. They all fueled his ever-growing love of literature and good writing.

By the end of first semester, An Wei had made remarkable progress in English pronunciation and intonation. Even though his Mandarin was improving, his fellow students complained about his Chinese and began asking him to speak to them in English because it was easier for them to understand.

Meanwhile his stomach sometimes cried for food. Though he was getting much more than in high school, memories of those starvation years haunted him. In the daytime he drove himself to study as hard as possible, but at night his hungry belly kept him awake.

Spring 1963

By the second semester An Wei began to read voraciously in his spare time. Biographies caught his interest. Because Russia had helped set China on the course to world Communism, he read about Marx, Engels, and Lenin. He was also intrigued by American culture. The United States was China's number one enemy, and An Wei and other students attended anti-American rallies. Rhetoric continued to heat up as the US became increasingly involved in Vietnam.

He learned about slavery and read Harriet Beecher Stowe's *Uncle Tom's Cabin*. Later he was appalled by photos of dogs and fire hoses attacking civil rights demonstrators in Birmingham, Alabama. Chairman Mao said the African American rebellion was part of a worldwide class struggle, and An Wei realized he needed to know more.

His determination to do well began to pay off. He again became one of the top students in his class and was elected secretary of the Communist Youth League for the English majors. He loved to spend time serving others. He worked on the campus newspaper, and he was asked to counsel students who did not study hard enough or follow rules.

Afternoons were often devoted to Student Union leadership meetings and to organizing sports competitions, festival performances, and marching practice for celebrations. Because this all took time, An Wei used every evening, weekend, and holiday to study. On Saturday evenings, the college showed a movie, but he could not afford to attend, so he spent that time reviewing everything from the previous week. He felt college was a unique opportunity for someone from An Shang village, and he had to excel. From his viewpoint, he was in a constant race to compete against himself.

Despite the terrible starvation years, the university students followed Mao Zedong's directives with open hearts. Important quotes from him were everywhere—on thermos bottles, glasses, and mugs, and painted on walls.

> "Carry the revolution through to the end."
> "Serve the people by preparing for natural calamities and war."
> "Promote production by accelerating the revolution."
> "Serve the people."
> "Study Mao Zedong Thought and work for Communism."

Chairman Mao was like a father to them. During An Wei's junior high school years, Mao Zedong had given a speech that still inspired him. Using eloquent language, the chairman had placed great hope in young people and helped them envision paths to the future. No one in An Shang had ever done that for An Wei. They could not see the potential an education could provide.

The government had also begun a campaign to have young people learn from the example of Comrade Lei Feng, a People's Liberation Army soldier who had lost his life in service. Large, colorful posters exhorted them to follow Lei Feng's example to "Love the Party, love Socialism, and love the People." Lei Feng's diary was published so they could follow his selfless ways.[2] An Wei was deeply moved, saying that the diary spoke to him more profoundly than any teachers or friends.

An Wei poured his energy into emulating his new hero in every act he performed. He focused daily on the idea that he should love his country and its people, and should work hard to defeat their enemies.

He and other members of the Chinese Communist Youth League—to which he had belonged since high school—competed to see who could be the most perfect in ideology, work and study, physical strength, and behavior. They became increasingly polite, particularly to their elders and to women and children, giving them their seats on buses and helping them to cross streets and carry heavy items. Even when An Wei was alone, he tried to live up to these standards by studying hard, exercising, and improving his thoughts.

Except for his limited food allotment, An Wei's life was good. Not only was he attending college, but also the country as a whole seemed to be better

---

Antagonism between China and the Soviet Union

In the 1960s, China and the Soviet Union, which had ideological disagreements dating back to the 1950s, began airing their differences publicly. For nearly a decade, the Soviet Union had assisted China with considerable numbers of technicians and loans. However, Nikita Khrushchev, the premier of the Union of Soviet Socialist Republics (USSR), and Mao Zedong began moving in different foreign policy directions. Khrushchev started working toward "peaceful coexistence" with the West, including arms-control discussions with the United States. Mao Zedong was adamantly opposed to this, and by 1960, while An Wei and his family were starving, the two leaders insulted each other at international Communist Party congresses. In response, Khrushchev withdrew all 1,400 Soviet experts and technical advisors from China, taking their blueprints with them, including those for nuclear weapons development.

Following the 1962 Cuban missile crisis, which brought the US and USSR close to nuclear war, the Soviet Union, Britain, and the United States signed a test-ban treaty. China, working to develop nuclear weapons, viewed the treaty and the Soviets' withdrawal of experts as a direct affront. Between September 1963 and July 1964, Mao Zedong published nine letters openly criticizing Khrushchev's leadership. The Russian leader responded with a retaliatory public statement. So ended any direct collaboration between the two countries for many years.

---

off. And because of growing disagreements with the Soviet Union, everyone was being drawn together to work even harder for China.

In the fall of 1963, An Wei and his second-year classmates felt proud to show new freshmen around the campus. The university's political commissar decided to give An Wei the full food grant because he was so poor and worked hard.

The new class of English students was about the same size as An Wei's, with a few young women. The new government's 1950 requirement that girls get an education had begun to increase their numbers in colleges, even though many families still did not think girls needed an education. To An Wei's delight, the new class also included his high school friend, Sun Zhonglun, who had retaken the college-entrance exam and passed.

With the heavy work of precise pronunciation under his belt, An Wei went on to much more comprehensive speaking, reading, and writing of English, as well as studying Chinese literature, classical Chinese, political economy, philosophy, and history. (Language majors did not need to study science or math.) To these he added a second language—Esperanto. Though only a few students took it, An Wei found it intriguing.

Their new English teacher was a tiny woman from Shanghai who lived in a Xi'an monastery. An Wei was fascinated that she had been raised in a Western church where she learned fluent English but could barely speak Chinese. In class she spoke almost entirely in English, which An Wei and nearly every one else found very difficult, but by the end of the year they loved her.

Besides following Lei Feng, students were enlisted to rid the Communist Party and society in general of "reactionary elements." Called the Four Clean-Ups, the Socialist Education Movement was meant to reform politics, the economy, government organization, and ideology. Student leaders, including An Wei, were sent to clean up a commune near Xi'an, where the party had discovered bosses abusing their power. Assigned to uncover the facts, An Wei realized he was learning how to help people understand new points of view and to use knowledge and persuasion to influence change.

When he returned to the university, he picked up his studies with even more vigor. One Saturday evening while most students were at the weekly movie and he was studying alone in a classroom, the college president walked in. Startled by An Wei's presence, he asked his name and what he was learning. A month later, while inspecting dormitories, the president met An Wei returning from his morning run while the other students were still asleep. Later, much to his surprise at an all-campus meeting, the president lauded An Wei as an exceptionally hardworking student who studied and exercised while others played or slept. Overnight, everyone at the university knew his name.

By his third year An Wei had a distinct advantage. Because of his high school studies and his extra work at college, he had a much better foundation in written Chinese and literature than most. It was a major asset for interpreting and translating from one language to another. And the more they studied English grammar, composition, and translation in depth, the easier it became for him.

The idea of becoming a translator grew more intriguing. He began to think of translation as a literary effort, and he assumed a translator would not become a political target like his high school teacher. If he translated a book that was later condemned, it would be the writer's fault. If it were thought valuable, people would say, "Oh, this translator is wonderful."

The year filled up with opportunities. An Wei was one of three picked to meet with a British group visiting Xi'an. He began practicing English every available hour, and the night before the meeting, he washed his one shirt so he would make a good impression. He had never been to a hotel, let alone talked with foreigners. The British delegation president welcomed them warmly, and conversation flowed easily as the students described their college life, what they studied, and how they lived. An Wei was amazed that he could respond to the visitors' questions in English and, when necessary, even interpret difficult phrases for the other students.

Next came the greatest honor he could imagine. He was admitted to the Communist Party as an introductory member. He was one of only three students who were accepted to serve as party role models for the student body.

Finally, in late spring, he was chosen to represent the college at a provincial congress for youth. It was his first chance to meet government leaders, learn how various organizations were connected, and become acquainted with student leaders from across the province.

Then his final year of college began. One day their political advisor, Mr. Li, sent for him. An Wei walked through the entranceway of the administrative courtyard and crossed the uneven paving stones to his office. Always serious, Mr. Li leaned forward, his arms resting on the desk.

"Your instructors and the college authorities have selected you to study in England after you graduate." An Wei was not sure he was hearing correctly. Mr. Li continued. He would spend two years perfecting his English and learning literature in more depth. "If you do well, you will return as a new instructor at this university."

Too overwhelmed to speak, An Wei thanked Mr. Li and left his office.

An Wei studied even harder and used all the school's interpreting opportunities to perfect his skills. By April he had completed his graduation papers, and in early May 1966, with a mixture of confidence and nervousness, he took the graduation examinations, passing with high scores and completing the requirements for a graduation certificate.

Following tradition, the graduates stayed at the college during June to receive their certificates and await their job assignments. They were all eager to join the adult world. An Wei's thoughts turned toward preparations for his two years in England. He would depart in August.

The new graduates knew nothing about what Chairman Mao had in store for them.

· 4 ·

Into the Maelstrom

> What was the world coming to? In those fantastic times, truth
> and falsehood, good and evil, right and wrong had all been mixed
> up in one simmering witches' cauldron. The innocent had to put
> up with humiliation and drag out a wretched existence. Bitter
> factionalism led to wild excesses.
>
> —Gu Hua, *A Small Town Called Hibiscus*[1]

In early June 1966, An Wei sat in his dormitory room at Xi'an Foreign Languages Institute scanning his well-worn texts. He pulled out his beloved English-Chinese dictionary and leafed through the pages, remembering how he had skimped on meals to save money for it. He set it to one side. It was definitely going to England with him.

In another part of the country, though, Mao Zedong had called a secret meeting to set a new course for the People's Republic of China that would dramatically affect An Wei.

When, five years earlier, it had become obvious the Great Leap Forward was crippling the country's economy, Mao Zedong relinquished his leadership to others such as Liu Shaoqi and Deng Xiaoping. With some success, they worked to restore the economy, especially through heavy industry and market activity. But while An Wei was finishing his college classes, Chairman Mao was intent on returning the young country to its ideological origins. He accused Liu and Deng, along with other high-ranking government workers, party members, and intellectuals, of advocating capitalism. Mao Zedong wanted the workers to retain political and economic power and promote continuous class struggle.

His new plan was to re-ignite the revolution by unleashing the nation's youth against established party members and any who deviated from "Mao

Zedong Thought." In May, he had called the secret meeting while his pre-mier, Zhou Enlai, was away. Although little is known about what transpired, afterward it became obvious that a major power struggle had started between the president of China, Liu Shaoqi, and Party Chairman Mao. The Cultural Revolution had begun.

A week later, the ruling politburo formalized Mao Zedong's decrees, dismissed officials he had accused, and warned party committees at all levels that the government and party were riddled with enemies of the Communist cause. The guilty were to be sent to the countryside to work with their hands, live in poverty, and restudy the chairman's writings on Communist ideology.[2]

An Wei and his friends lingered in the college cafeteria one evening, relish-ing the luxury of no more schoolwork and discussing the jobs they hoped for. Graduation was a week away, and they could hardly believe their good fortune, having finished four demanding years of college. The cafeteria loud-speakers crackled to life. An Wei ran his fingers along a crack in the tabletop.

An announcer began, "Enemies inside China threaten her existence." All students, even those about to finish, must stay at their college and help eliminate traitors. To save the country they must join the Great Cultural Revolution and weed out bad elements.

An Wei pushed his empty bowl and chopsticks to one side and leaned closer to his friends. In hushed voices they talked about what this might mean. What about graduation? When would they get jobs?

Circulars printed the next day and passed out all over China said they must wait for further instructions.

Then came the first directive. "Attack Communist Party members who have deviated from Mao Zedong's interpretation of Marxism."

But how could they do that?

An Wei struggled to understand the order, but if Chairman Mao said you must do something, then you must obey. For now, at least, he must stay at the college. Mao Zedong had led them through the glorious revolution against Chiang Kai-shek's troops, and he would lead them through this. Ex-cept for the great hunger, the chairman had led the country to a place it was proud of. But what about his year in England? Surely graduates would be able to go to their jobs and help China.

Soon An Wei learned of college student uprisings in Beijing. Some were running around screaming to smash the old education system. At one university, students burned all the recently completed exam papers in large brass urns while others, horrified, watched from dormitory windows. The suddenness terrified many—and exhilarated others.[3] When party leaders like

Liu Shaoqi moved to quell the extremism, Mao Zedong denounced them and lauded the student activists. A few weeks later, the chairman removed Liu Shaoqi from his national post as deputy chairman of the Communist Party.

Like wind-driven fire, the student revolt spread across the country, fanned by segments of the government. Huge posters went up on walls and buildings exhorting citizens to launch a new revolution. These images of billowing red flags and determined young people marching into the future were emblazoned with slogans.

"Criticize the old world. Build a new one. Mao Zedong Thought is your weapon."

"Cherish the great red banner of Mao Zedong Thought. Fight the Great Proletarian Revolution to the end."

At the Xi'an Foreign Languages Institute, students began to publicly accuse college officials of incorrect policies, which distressed An Wei. He had worked with these administrators as a student leader and as a new Communist Party member who believed in Mao Zedong's theories. Yes, there were things the administration could improve, but they did not deserve abusive public shaming. An Wei abhorred unfair treatment.

Throughout the summer, Xi'an students were sucked deeper into the fray. An Wei, like the majority of the students known as the Conservatives, felt they must follow Chairman Mao's orders and carry out the Cultural Revolution. Certainly, they believed, this new reform could be accomplished through reason and by taking their strong beliefs in Mao Zedong Thought to their new jobs.

A smaller group, the Revolutionary Rebels, consisting of students who had always been loud and critical, condemned administrators and professors. They called for their ouster and also began to hurl invective at the college Communist Party committee. All the Foreign Languages Institute leaders should be shamed and dismissed for wrong thinking. Only Mao Zedong deserved support.

The campus—and the city—became tense.

On August 8, while An Wei was reading in his dormitory room, the Political Bureau of the Communist Party Central Committee blared an official decision through the campus loudspeakers. All students, including An Wei's class of 1966, must stay at their universities and join in the Cultural Revolution. They could not graduate. Chairman Mao called on everyone in the country to engage in this revolution with open hearts for China's future.

For An Wei, a searing reality sank in. Eighteen years of work. Eighteen years of effort to escape a farmer's poverty. All for naught. Two years of study in England had become a mirage.

*   *   *

Extremists took over the country. Earlier movements such as the Anti-Rightest Campaign had attacked professionals, such as An Wei's high school English teacher. This was a broader, more furious attack on everything everywhere. Everyone was exhorted to "Destroy the 'Four Olds'"—the old customs, old cultures, old habits, and old ideas.

Chairman Mao encouraged young people to travel freely, to destroy relics such as temples, and to connect with each other around this great revolution. An Wei heard reports that on August 18, mobs of students flocked to Tiananmen Square in Beijing for an audience with their beloved leader. At the north end of the square, Mao Zedong and his newly designated heir, Lin Biao, stood atop the huge ceremonial gate to welcome an estimated million or more young people committed to his revolution.[4] They clutched copies of the little red book, *Quotations from Chairman Mao*, raising them high toward the leader they revered. Included in its pages was a message they cherished: "The world is yours, as well as ours, but in the last analysis, it is yours. You young people, full of vigour and vitality, are in the bloom of life, like the sun at eight or nine in the morning. Our hope is placed on you."[5]

At the rally, Mao Zedong threw his support behind the student group known as the Revolutionary Rebels. In response, many Conservatives abandoned their beliefs and joined them. Now a majority, they were increasingly accusatory and imperious, going after anyone. The Rebels trumped up crimes. At the Xi'an Foreign Languages Institute, they began to abuse all Communist Party members, including An Wei.

The school president had praised An Wei, and that proved he was a counterrevolutionary and should be punished. One day he saw his name emblazoned on huge big-character posters that were all the rage for criticizing enemies. They were plastered all over the classroom building, one on top of the other, and in many other places on campus.

The Rebels called An Wei "a running dog" of the school administrators, an apologist for their "incorrect behaviors." An Wei sensed that many who attacked him were students who had done poorly, who were jealous because he had worked hard and had become a successful student and leader. But it did not matter. They were after him, and they were dangerous. Sometimes they beat their victims until they were crippled or died. Even if they did not injure or kill him, he knew they could use their passion and cunning to humiliate and destroy him.

Disturbing reports arrived daily. How could people behave like this? he wondered. Some high school students went after one of their senior teachers. She had been the school principal, but during the Anti-Rightest Campaign, she was labeled a "Rightest" and forced to become the janitor. Now the students forced her to "confess" her crimes. They stuffed garlic into her mouth until she could not bear it. Then they mixed the garlic with shoe polish and forced her to swallow that. Finally they stuffed her mouth with grape leaves wrapped around mud. The students saw themselves as true revolutionaries because they were punishing someone who, they said, went against Mao Zedong's ideas.[6] Often those who repeatedly endured such abuse resorted to suicide to end their humiliation.

To save himself, An Wei quit the Conservatives and decided not to participate in anything. But he was harassed for that. Even though he hated the Revolutionary Rebels' violent tactics, he decided to shift to their side. Chairman Mao now supported them, and An Wei must obey him. He tried to lay low.

The Rebels called him a coward, but they stopped abusing him. Some said he was not a real revolutionary; others, that he was a spy from the Conservatives. The Conservatives were furious because he had switched sides.

Although he cherished the journals he had filled with his thoughts since the first day of college, An Wei burned them all. He watched the paper scorch, turn brown, and his words vanish into flames—how college was different from high school, what he hoped to learn, ideas about what he was reading, and how hard it was to learn English pronunciation. The acrid smoke was nauseating. He burned his translations too. He felt as though he was betraying old friends, but he needed to protect himself. Any of his words could become a reason for brutal attacks.

Chinese cities resounded with rallies and parades. Workers and young people sang, yelled slogans, and carried huge red flags and giant posters of the Great Helmsman, Mao Zedong. Adults joined to protect themselves from being labeled traitors. Truckloads of the little red book of Mao Zedong's quotations were given out to everyone. Throughout the country, citizens gathered to study new government decisions and Mao Zedong's quotations during factory breaks and middle school classes, office meetings, and preschool teacher training. University gatherings were used to study his quotations or to harangue those accused of anti-revolutionary behavior.[7] Thousands were humiliated and tortured daily.

The Languages Institute required all students, faculty, and workers to attend mass rallies held by the Revolutionary Rebels to criticize the so-called wrong ideas of the president and professors, who were accused of leaning toward capitalism. Professors were labeled "bourgeois authorities" because they were experts in their fields. Forced to stand on the auditorium stage for what were called "struggle sessions," they waited, heads bowed, to silently endure the humiliation.

The meeting chairman would declare their "crime," then Rebel representatives yelled at them, describing why their actions went against the revolutionary ideas of Chairman Mao. After each accuser, a student on stage led the audience in slogan shouting. Everyone, including An Wei, roared:

"Down with capitalist roaders!"
"Down with bourgeois authorities."
"We must carry the Cultural Revolution through to the end."

If An Wei were quiet, he knew he would be attacked.

Then another speaker would hurl criticisms at each of the professors and administrators. The accused wore tall paper hats, like dunce caps. Heavy signs that bore their names obliterated by red slashes hung around their necks on chains.

One of the student leaders would yell for them to lower their heads. Next someone would yell, "Don't act like a dead pig." That meant they should now raise their heads. Back and forth, the torment continued. Sometimes they had to stand with their arms held back in painful positions or kneel for long periods on narrow benches.

It did not matter if those being attacked were actually guilty of anything. The government encouraged the students to expose anyone. The Rebels would take a phrase from a speech or article and declare it wrong. Someone like the university president might have said, "We must make a big effort to achieve our goal." Then the Rebels would ask, "Why didn't you mention the leadership of the party? How could you achieve your goal by relying on your own efforts?" They would pick absurd holes in any statement. An Wei realized that if they wanted to criticize someone, they could find a thousand reasons.

During the many years I have done research and consulted in China, I have heard Chinese adults mention the Cultural Revolution, but only in snippets. A comment here, a small example there. A department chair of a famous university told me in frustration one evening, "China was set back ten years by that movement. My only accomplishment during those years was to produce two children." A professor at another university said, "It was terrible. Even wives and husbands turned against each other." An army officer told me, "My wife was in high school and turned against her grandfather. To this day she cries when she remembers how cruel she was to him." But few have gone into more detail.

In my experience, the Cultural Revolution is not a place Chinese adults want to revisit. Many lived in hell for ten years. Those who felt it was wrong and survived do not want to relive it.

When I have asked An Wei about this period, especially about the time immediately after college, he has usually given me a few factual details about rallies or big-character posters denouncing professors or administrators, and then veered off to other topics. One of his classic comments was that the Cultural Revolution gave him a lot of time to practice his calligraphy by writing big-character posters. "That was really good," he said. When I responded, "Really?" he just laughed, that inscrutable Chinese laugh that is hard for Westerners to understand and, as far as I can tell, covers up feelings. It certainly has nothing to do with humor.

An Wei once mentioned briefly that he attended events of the Revolutionary Rebels and tried not to participate in anything physically abusive, but then he shifted the topic to political trends. He pointed out that Mao Zedong said you could call people names and accuse them, but you should not beat, smash, or fight. However, when I asked him if there was anything that made him afraid during his life, he named only two: as a child, being afraid they would starve, and the Cultural Revolution, especially the first year.

Younger people often do not want to believe the excesses of the Cultural Revolution even happened. One young translator was working for me on a life history of a preschool teacher. The teacher had accomplished many things but was forced to live in a pigsty for a couple of years during the Cultural Revolution. The translator was shocked that any respectable professional would talk about such things. She said it should not be included in the woman's history, and when I asked her to translate it anyway, she "lost" the computer file and refused to work on it.

1966–1967

An Wei developed a new view of life. Survival in China was like swimming in a vast and turbulent ocean. His first task was to figure out how to keep himself alive. Then, if he had any leftover energy, he could try swimming to the opposite shore. If he made a small mistake, if he ended up in prison or was tortured, he would accomplish nothing.

He attended Revolutionary Rebels' meetings and, like many others, began to create the big-character posters that Chairman Mao encouraged to spread his ideas. To protect his identity, An Wei needed a penname. Others chose mundane names, but he hungered for one with deep meaning.

Maybe he could connect it to the name his parents gave him, An Kezhong. He ran through combinations of characters. *An* (安), his family and clan name, meant "peace." He wanted to keep that. It would make up for living surrounded by so much danger.

He wrote lists of all the popular phrases that included *an*. There were a lot. Many alluded to danger *and* peace or safety. He selected 危 (*wei*), the character for danger, to make 安危 (*An Wei*). He liked that. Together they meant "peace and danger." That was exactly what life seemed to be like. Yet he felt his penname needed more. He tried out more character combinations. Then knowing he couldn't tarry, he made his choice. His penname would be 安危战斗队 (An Wei Zhandou Dui), An Wei Fighting Group.

He began to write as many posters as possible, signing his new name with a flourish. He tried to be quick in responding to new events or policies and saying where he agreed or disagreed and why. It became like a religious fever. He *wanted* to do it. Even though he hated what his group did, he felt driven to support this new revolution and the need to make China better. He wrote about the bad bourgeois tendencies in society, the need to follow Mao Zedong Thought, and the importance of supporting new directives from Chairman Mao. He did not attack individuals. His posters caught students' attention: whoever this one-person fighting group was, he could write well.

An Wei's class was required to stay at the college indefinitely. There were no courses; they studied only Mao Zedong quotations. Frenzied activities dominated their lives. The students venerated Chairman Mao, calling him "The Red Sun in Our Lives," and they even performed a "Dance of Loyalty" to him.

The Rebels, in control of the college, took over the buildings in the administrative courtyard for their operations. Assigned to the propaganda department, An Wei edited their newspaper about the achievements of the Cultural Revolution and about Rebel events. It included information from other parts of the country, letting everyone know the great victories that had been accomplished through Mao Zedong's political ideas. He learned to cut wordy articles and edit awkward material, but he was excruciatingly careful not to change the meaning, regardless of what he thought of it. He also served as secretary at meetings.

Although he did not like public demonstrations, he attended them. Otherwise he would be accused of not being a revolutionary. At rallies he joined hundreds of thousands of people to yell slogans, and in parades he marched carrying huge posters of the Great Helmsman, while others used bullhorns to celebrate Mao Zedong Thought.

He went with the Rebels to outlying areas to hold rallies among workers and peasants and tell them about the new revolution. It was a relief to leave the city for a few hours. They lugged heavy microphone equipment, banners, and outsized portraits of Chairman Mao to villages and towns. Taking tables from nearby buildings, they set up their loudspeakers and demanded that villagers and factory workers attend the rally. An Wei was good at delivering harangues. He and the other Rebels shouted directives and slogans at the top of their lungs. Their volume proved they were true revolutionaries.

An Wei speaking at a village rally organized by the Revolutionary Rebels, about 1967. *Source*: An Wei.

During these months one good thing happened to An Wei. In the main Rebel office, a few doors along the courtyard, he noticed a young woman, Niu Jianhua, who directed activities. When she talked, her dark attentive eyes told of her serious nature, and he enjoyed watching her braids bounce as she walked along.

They attended meetings where, as secretary, he took notes and from time to time would hand her official papers. As she reached for them, she would look directly at him. Although demonstrating feelings was inappropriate, he felt warmed by her gaze.

Niu Jianhua was an English major one class behind An Wei. Although their courses met in the same building, their paths had never crossed before. The college had very strict rules about girls and boys getting to know each other. In fact, as a student leader, one of An Wei's jobs had been to caution students who were interested in a girlfriend or boyfriend. If they became seriously involved, they could be expelled. Despite these rules, after the college president highlighted An Wei's exemplary study habits in a college speech and he became well known among students, Niu Jianhua and some classmates surreptitiously meandered past the first-floor classroom trying to figure out which student was An Wei.

By December, violence between various factions increased across China. Lei Feng, the model soldier everyone had emulated in college, was forgotten;

students as well as workers grew more uncontrolled. In some cities, the Rebels stole guns and ammunition from the army, and battles ensued. By spring 1967, the Central Committee of the Communist Party sent army representatives to campuses to stop the struggle between factions and form alliances. When men from the army propaganda team arrived at the Foreign Languages Institute, An Wei was surprised that they asked him and other former student leaders to meet with them. The men, thinking these leaders could influence the younger students, urged them to help resolve differences and stop the fighting. But that effort did not succeed, not at the college or in other cities. Those dedicated to violence would not give up.

During this time, one of his college English teachers was continuously humiliated, accused of being an enemy of the people merely because his father had been a warlord in old China and had two wives. Students who had never had Mr. Sun as a teacher beat him, spit on him, and yelled in his face. An Wei felt awful. Mr. Sun was a wonderful teacher who had done nothing wrong. It was not his fault that his father had behaved that way. But An Wei, and other students who loved Mr. Sun, had to pretend they hated him. At rallies when he was being humiliated, they yelled taunts and accusations.

"Down with Sun Tianyi."
"Down with the son of a warlord."

They shunned him whenever they happened to get near him on campus. If they befriended him, they would endanger Mr. Sun as well as themselves.

In June, though, amid the chaos, An Wei had the rare chance to help Mr. Sun. He went with a group of students to the countryside to help farmers bring in the crops. As punishment, Mr. Sun was sent with them to do physical labor. Almost like a family during those few weeks, Mr. Sun and the students who admired him worked and ate together and could even talk a little. Gradually the students were able to show their respect for him. Most touching to An Wei, they all quietly took over Mr. Sun's arduous tasks. He seemed pleased that they still valued him, and they were relieved he was not humiliated for those few weeks. On their return, the spitting and beating resumed, and Mr. Sun, as usual, was polite to his tormentors. Amazed at his capacity for forgiveness, An Wei has said that he valued him as the most noble person he had ever known.

By summer 1967, the government began to gain more control. Provincial officials formed a committee made up of equal numbers of student rebels (now usually called Red Guards), government cadres, and revolutionary workers and laborers. The committee took over the Rebel offices. Although the attacks of the Cultural Revolution continued undiminished across the country, the Languages Institute was no longer controlled by the Revolutionary Rebels.

An Wei and Niu Jianhua retained their jobs and saw each other often. He found her quiet confidence refreshing in these awful times. At rallies they managed to be near each other. Their attraction was mutual, and he enjoyed seeing the few stray hairs that came loose from her two neat braids.

They became good friends and together wrote posters and attended criticism meetings. One memorable day, An Wei climbed into a truck with a pack of other Red Guards, headed for a rally. He watched as Niu Jianhua organized the rest and got them on the truck. As the engine started, she was the last one to climb aboard. An Wei extended his hand and pulled her up. It was an electric moment, for young men and women in China never touched each other or even shook hands.

The accusations against An Wei had not scared Niu Jianhua. As a student he had stood tall with a confident expression. He had drive and was serious about life. Even in these difficult times, although he looked haggard and his eyes were sometimes sullen, she still saw those qualities.

In August 1967, to their vast relief, the students of the class of 1966 were notified by the central government that they could graduate and be assigned jobs. Finally he had completed college. An Wei eagerly read his graduation certificate. His name on the paper startled him, though. It was not his given name, An Ke-zhong. The Revolutionary Committee had recorded it as An Wei, but he certainly was not going to say anything about that. Besides, he liked that new name.

The new governing committee selected An Wei to teach at the Foreign Languages Institute. Although it had once been his dream to be an instructor there after studying in England, the college remained in disarray. There were still no classes, and teachers continued to be abused. Who knew what the future would hold for him there.

But then Niu Jianhua, who had been directing activities in the main office, told him that representatives from the provincial Foreign Affairs Office had arrived to look through student records for an English interpreter. They were going to interview several English majors in An Wei's class. In secret, he reviewed his English, practicing answers to all the possible questions they might ask him: his family background, descriptions of the Chinese revolution, Mao Zedong Thought, and important elements of Chinese history. He practiced pronouncing difficult English sounds again and again. He didn't want to stumble over the difficult *th* and the pronouns.

He could feel each paving stone through his thin shoes as he headed to the room for his interview in the administrative courtyard. Two grave-looking officials sat behind a well-worn wooden desk.

"Ni hao," he nodded to greet them, standing as tall as possible to look professional. He hoped his Mao Zedong pin lay flat on his dark blue jacket. The men nodded, and the most senior motioned to a bench.

An Wei took his place gingerly.

"Where are you from, and what do your parents do?" began the older official.

An Wei, surprised he was hearing Chinese, not English, leaned forward a little and began a brief description of life in An Shang village. Questions followed about school activities, again all in Chinese. He wondered if he should use a little English but decided against it. Follow their lead, he told himself.

His hands were sweating. He thought he was answering with enough, though not too much, politically acceptable information. He began to realize that the men might not speak English. The senior official, who An Wei later learned had been Chairman Mao's secretary for more than twenty years and had arrived in Xi'an only recently, shifted some papers on the desk. He looked at his notes and began to ask questions about the job. Did An Wei want to stay at the Foreign Languages Institute, or would he rather be an interpreter? This was a politically difficult question since the Rebels remained a powerful group at the college.

An Wei thought fast.

"I believe I've been in school long enough," he answered. "I should experience a different part of our society. Being an interpreter would be a good opportunity." He omitted the fact that he was sure too many at the institute distrusted him and his life there would be miserable.

The official continued. "To be an interpreter, you have to keep on learning all kinds of knowledge. You will be very busy if you are an interpreter with no time for entertainment. Do you like to work that hard?" An Wei felt comfortable with this one. He had worked as hard as possible all his life.

More questions followed about strict work codes and being professional at all times. Finally the older man said they knew he had been a top student and met all their basic requirements.

As he left, he could feel his shoulders relax a little as he crossed the paving stone courtyard. Once beyond the entranceway, he wiped his sweaty hands on his trousers and hoped for the best. They had several candidates to interview.

Several days later, An Wei learned that he had been selected as the English interpreter for the Foreign Affairs Office of Shaanxi Province. The prospect of leaving school was thrilling, and getting away from the Revolutionary Rebels a great relief.

In October, An Wei packed his few belongings and boarded a city bus to the office in the middle of Xi'an. The unique two-story, brick structure built in a somewhat Western style surprised him. In the early twentieth century it had been a well-known guesthouse for foreigners.

He stood outside several minutes, soaking in the moment and humming a little. After years of schooling, his life was about to change enormously. He felt excited but unsettled. What would it be like? What would he need to learn? What was the staff like?

The gatekeeper examined his papers and directed him where to register, down a dark hall where he introduced himself to the official sitting at a desk laden with stacks of paper.

The official asked for his college graduation certificate. With care, An Wei pulled the cherished document from his belongings, handing it to the man as if it were fragile. The official read it, and An Wei watched as he copied down his name—An Wei. An interesting twist, An Wei thought. From now on, that would be his official name. Well, he would still be An Ke-zhong in his village.

Most important, he was no longer being tormented by the Red Guard. He had a job, and he would get his first salary ever—forty-eight yuan and fifty cents a month, plus food and housing. Plenty for a poor farm boy, especially as there was almost nothing to buy.

After registering and putting his belongings in his room, he tried to settle into his new life.

Like all the staff, he sat in his bedroom office at his plain wooden desk studying government documents and editorials in the *People's Daily*, the government mouthpiece. That was it, except for meetings in the conference room. After breakfast, the staff met to study Mao Zedong's works and government policies. They were free the rest of the morning. He kept waiting for something to happen, for someone to give a new directive. The only change of pace came when he wandered to the kitchen for meals.

An Wei was not used to managing himself or being idle. College had taught him how to study, guided by the teachers' assignments, and he was also kept busy as class leader. Now at the Foreign Affairs Office, his eighteen-year goal of getting an education had ended, but nothing much had replaced it. He studied the papers and policies seriously, but he longed to *do* something. He wanted to help his young country become stronger, but how?

On some afternoons they all gathered to criticize and curse those who followed a capitalist path and other popular enemies, known as Capitalist

Roaders. They were the number one enemy, of whom the former leaders Deng Xiaoping and Liu Shaoqi were the most famous. Although they had led the country out of economic ruin, Mao Zedong had accused them of moving it toward capitalism. Stripped of their titles, Liu Shaoqi was arrested and beaten regularly by the Red Guard; Deng Xiaoping was sent to labor in a tractor factory, and his family members were tortured.

Enemy number two was the bourgeois academic authority: college professors and experts in science, technology, and education. Enemy number three was the landlord class; number four, rich peasants; five, counterrevolutionaries; and six, bad elements. Number seven was bourgeois Rightists; and number eight, ghosts of the past (meaning people with bad backgrounds such as Mr. Sun). Number nine was the intellectuals. They were often called the "stinking number nine" because knowledge was useless, and they were like a smelly turd in the toilet.

The cycle of violence and suicides continued. A few months after An Wei joined the Foreign Affairs Office, a segment of the government mounted the "Cleanse the Class Ranks" movement, subjecting millions more to struggle sessions and abuse, and claiming an estimated half million lives.[8] Things became so chaotic that Chairman Mao was alarmed. He and the party's Central Committee issued nationwide notices to end armed conflict and reduce extortion of confessions, but to no avail.[9]

For An Wei, each workday was a repeat of the previous, with occasional breaks to participate in a big rally in the center of Xi'an or to watch students demonstrate in the streets. After group study, though, An Wei found he could read and work on anything he liked, as long as it was politically acceptable. Another respite came when he was assigned to a state farm for several months to feed cows and clean their sheds. As much as he hated farmwork, it was more desirable than sitting in the office all day and worrying that he might say something politically wrong.

Come spring, members of a few embassies visited Xi'an, and An Wei joined older staff members to arrange the visitors' trips to different organizations, factories, and the people's communes. The People's Republic of China had been recognized by the Soviet bloc countries, as well as by India, Great Britain, Sweden, and others. But most of those who visited spoke Chinese, so he was called on to interpret only a few times.

1968–1969

An Wei had always vowed he would not marry until he had a job. Now he could consider it. He and Niu Jianhua became more serious and were with each other whenever possible. They spent their time talking and sometimes picnicking in a nearby park. She should have graduated in June 1967, but because of the Cultural Revolution, her last year of college was devoted to political activities. As a result, she and her classmates had to remain at the college for an additional year to carry on the increasingly chaotic revolution.

In spring 1968, An Wei visited Niu Jianhua's parents who lived in Xi'an. Proud of new shoes his mother had made for him, he cleaned them carefully for the occasion. However, Niu Jianhua said they were so stiff and peculiar looking with their thick white, hand-stitched cloth soles that he should not wear them in the city. They looked too much like peasant shoes. He bought a new pair, but he was sad to leave his mother's unused, and the new ones squeaked when he walked.

As he and her family became better acquainted, they gathered in a park to have a family photo taken, including An Wei. All serious in their rumpled pants and warm jackets, they stood tall, Mao buttons pinned over their hearts, with Niu Jianhua's younger brother clasping the little red book of Chairman Mao quotations. An engagement photo soon followed. Young and serious, they wore dark jackets. Their black hair framed their youthful faces, with Niu Jianhua's parted down the middle and neatly set into two braids, as required by the Cultural Revolution. Her soft features contrasted with the determined light in her eyes. An Wei's shock of hair accentuated his square face and angular jaw, and being a government employee, he sported a fashionable Mao Zedong pin in the shape of a five-pointed star. Her parents gave him his first wristwatch to celebrate the occasion, and Niu Jianhua and An Wei visited them about once a month, often for Sunday dinner.

A few months later Niu Jianhua received her assignment to work in an industrial production district, a two-hour bus ride from Xi'an. She was to collect and translate technical materials for the information office of the largest aircraft manufacturer in China. She had grown up under Mao Zedong and was sure that what he said was right and that his directives should be followed enthusiastically. However, even though her father was a laborer, she was considered an intellectual because she had finished college. She was told that her most important job was to learn from the workers. Living in a dormitory with them, she was supposed to start every meeting with the words "I need to learn from the workers."

For the October 1968 national holiday, celebrating the founding of the People's Republic of China, An Wei and Niu Jianhua headed for An Shang village to introduce his fiancée to his family. As the westbound train ran along the Wei River valley, the bluffs of the Loess Plateau rose beside them. Since Niu Jianhua was from the city, An Wei explained a little about life in the village where he grew up. He was sure she would not be shocked by An Shang because during college she had worked in rural areas.

From the train station they walked to the path that led up the steep loess bluff to An Shang. It was an arduous trek, and An Wei realized city living had softened him. As they climbed over the edge of the bluff, a village of caves stretched east and west in front of them. They greeted the families there and walked up the track past newly planted fields toward An Shang.

An Wei's mother and father greeted them in their small crowded room, while several of his brothers hung around the edges looking. The kang, the family's clay bed, became the gathering place for everyone to sit, including his brothers' children.

Though Brother Number Two with the gentle eyes was away working, his wife made every effort to welcome Niu Jianhua. She prepared a special meal for the family that started with a small dish of pickled onions for a vegetable, followed by noodles and some bread to cut their appetites. Though Niu Jianhua had worked in other villages, this one was by far the poorest she had ever seen.

They chatted about changes in farming, crops, the family, and a little about the Cultural Revolution and their new jobs. An Wei's very elderly grandmother tugged on Niu Jianhua's jacket, teasing her that it felt like material for grain sacks. Niu Jianhua blushed, but that was all city cloth rationing allowed.

She slept on a kang with Number Two's wife, who brought her a small basin of heated water to wash her feet. As Niu Jianhua went to throw it out, her host stopped her. She needed it to clean her children.

The next day the skies darkened, and by afternoon heavy drops hit the dust in the courtyard. They retreated to the kang, and there they stayed for hours as sheets of rain turned the homestead, paths, and fields to sticky mud.

In the morning, with the possibility of rain getting worse and the prospect of a day crammed on the kang, they left for Xi'an. They slogged along the track accompanied by Brother Number Five, who had often been An Wei's helper. At the edge of the bluff, the slippery thousand-foot descent was daunting. Number Five began by cutting a footstep into the path. Then with An Wei's support, Niu Jianhua took a step and waited while he cut the next one. Step by slippery step, they descended to the bottom.

Their wedding day arrived Thursday, March 27, 1969, the tenth day of the second month of the Chinese lunar calendar. They selected the date to take advantage of Niu Jianhua's day off. If she left for Xi'an after work Wednesday, they could have a four-day holiday.

They were married in the Foreign Affairs Office meeting room joined by Niu Jianhua's family, two of their closest neighbors, and the leaders and

Niu Jianhua and An Wei at their wedding, Xi'an Foreign Affairs Office, 1969. *Source*: An Wei.

staff members from An Wei's office. An Wei's family was much too poor to travel so far.

The nervous couple wore dark clothes, the fashion of the day. An Wei was in his government jacket and Niu Jianhua in a new jacket and sweater. Both wore Chairman Mao pins. The wedding photo, taken in An Wei's Foreign Affairs Office room, showed a shy-looking Niu Jianhua and An Wei nearly smiling and looking satisfied. On the wall behind them were Mao Zedong posters and quotations, and on a table were the ubiquitous thermoses of boiled water, symbols of a modernizing China.

Mr. Meng Zhaobin, one of the office directors, served as host. Everyone sang the popular song "The East Is Red," in praise of Chairman Mao, followed by Mr. Meng reading a Mao Zedong quotation: "We hail from all corners of the country and have joined together for a common revolutionary objective. . . . Our cadres must show concern for every soldier, and all people in the revolutionary ranks must care for each other, must love and help each other."

He then proclaimed, "An Wei and Niu Jianhua are married today, and I feel very excited." Another director asked, "Why are you excited when others get married?" Their exchange caused a roar of laughter.

Mr. Meng and Niu Jianhua's father congratulated them and wished them the best. After this, she and An Wei gave their thanks to all and expressed their determination to work hard, love and help each other, and show filial piety to their parents. They offered everyone a handful of candies An Wei had bought for thirty yuan along with a gift of one cigarette for each of the men. Neighborhood children sang and danced for them, and friends gave them several sets of Mao Zedong's works plus the little red book.

After a four-day honeymoon, An Wei said good-bye to Niu Jianhua, and she boarded a bus back to the aircraft factory. She would be able to visit An Wei for a day once or twice a month.

The Cultural Revolution continued unabated, and few foreigners visited China. Breaking from its earlier attempts to calm violence between groups, the Chinese Communist Party was calling for the masses to "purify" the party through criticism. Rather than urging peaceful change, it praised those who purged the party of enemy agents and capitalist roaders. Chaos was ramped up.

In December 1969, the Foreign Affairs Office director called a meeting. A new order had arrived.

An Wei froze. What now?

"Two-thirds of the staff must be sent away for reeducation through physical labor," the director began. They would be split into three groups: one would go to a cadre school in a northern suburb, one group would stay in the office, and a few were to be sent to a cadre school in the far north.[10]

An Wei and three others were in the last group, assigned to Nanniwan, a well-known labor school in northern Shaanxi Province. It had been established by Mao Zedong after the Long March to prove that the Communists could sustain themselves in difficult terrain and survive Chiang Kai-shek's constant bombardments. Along with a few other camps, it was now labeled a "May 7th Cadre School," designated for government officials and intellectuals to learn from workers and peasants.[11] Although government policy said that those assigned to cadre schools would eventually return to work, in Chinese the term "May 7th" (*wu chi*) sounds the same as "a school without end." An Wei was not optimistic.

He and Niu Jianhua had been married nine months.

· 5 ·

Clinging to Shattered Dreams

On December 12, 1969, as early morning light filtered through fine dust blowing from the great Loess Plateau, An Wei waited with dozens of fellow government workers at a designated meeting place in Xi'an. They eyed five parked trucks ready to haul them north to the reeducation school in Nanniwan. A hundred cadres—the term used for government workers active in the revolution—were leaving immediately, and several hundred more would follow in coming months. The school there was just being built to accommodate the new arrivals, and the group was needed to help finish it.[1]

A winter breeze caught the edges of tattered posters, while new ones plastered on nearby walls and buildings exhorted citizens to create revolution. The posters showed enthusiastic workers striding off to the fields with banners flying and radiant expressions. An Wei and his fellow "recruits" could find nothing worth smiling about. They were prisoners of the reeducation movement and the Cultural Revolution.

Talking in subdued tones, the men shifted their weight from one foot to the other or leaned against the nearby buildings, keeping their thoughts and fears to themselves. An Wei paced back and forth. This was the final blow to his dreams. The last three years had dashed all possibility of studying in England. Now he was leaving his new wife and his job. After all he had worked for, what would become of him?

No one had any idea how long they would be at this school created by Mao Zedong to reform them through physical labor. Many people who had been sent to the countryside never returned. For those who did come back, so much time had passed that their professional skills had eroded. They had become deadwood in the new Chinese society.

When the drivers appeared, An Wei and the other cadres climbed onto the open truck beds. He pushed his bundle of belongings into a corner of one truck as they all jostled to make room for each other. He had wrapped a few changes of clothes, toothpaste, a pad, and writing implements inside his warm cotton quilt and tied it tight. Also tucked in were four required volumes of Mao Zedong's writings and An Wei's treasured English translations of Mao's works. They had better not take those away from him.

The truck vibrated as the engine started and heaved forward into the street. An Wei grabbed a side slat to steady himself. Soon the city's buildings faded into the dust as they crossed the Wei River, where An Wei swam as a child. As the line of trucks lumbered up the steep road to the plateau, the men settled in for the long, cold three-hundred-kilometer trip. An Wei pulled on a winter hat and wrapped his scarf tightly around his neck to protect himself from the stinging chill. Taking turns, the men sat on their bundles or stood to see the tan gullies and scrub-covered hills pass by. Every hour took them farther from their homes and loved ones. He wondered if he and Niu Jianhua would even have a future together.

Being sent to a farm to learn from peasants seemed like a cruel joke. According to Chairman Mao, the skills and knowledge An Wei had acquired in school were worthless. Only farmers had wisdom and knowledge. An Wei's world felt upside down.

As the trucks rumbled on, he vowed to hang onto English. He had labored hundreds of hours to learn it. Although he had burned his journals and translations out of fear they would be used against him, he would preserve what was inside him, and those English translations of Mao Zedong's writings in his bundle would help.

When the sun sank into darkness, the town of Yan'an came into view. The Communists had headquartered there for several years to regroup, plan, and theorize at the end of the Long March in the late 1930s. It was where Mao Zedong had done most of his writing. The trucks veered onto a small dirt road that climbed into the mountains, over ruts and stones as punishing as the cold that pierced their winter clothes.

No one spoke. They just hung on and tried to keep their balance. The caravan finally descended into a wide valley and swung onto another dirt road that ran along the low hills, where they could see a few distant lights in the pitch-black darkness.

The trucks ground to a halt near a cluster of single-story buildings. Stiff and cold, the men climbed down. An Wei looked beyond the dimly lit buildings, where few people stirred, to the silhouettes of hills rising toward the black night sky. They were a long way from city life. He knew that this valley had been cleared by the tough 395 Brigade to prove that they could create a self-sufficient community living on inhospitable land.

The housing, with its wooden sleeping platforms, reminded An Wei of Fufeng High School, only worse. Now he would share the room with a dozen or so adults whose cigarette smoke would fill the crowded quarters with noxious fumes, and loud talk would make it impossible to read. Each of them had just enough room to lie down, but not enough to turn over. From that first night, An Wei loathed it. He had come to love the independence of his little office bedroom in the Foreign Affairs building. To endure this place, he would need to blot out many things and keep focused on his work.

As usual, An Wei was up before dawn the next morning. He exercised—a good idea to warm himself in the frigid air—and surveyed this place so far from Niu Jianhua and the city he had come to call home. It was much colder than Xi'an. Behind the rough school buildings, steep tracks led into hills covered with winter-bare trees. In the other direction, he could see dried-up rice paddies and winter crops spreading north and south. Some small houses hugged the far side of the valley, and at the northern end he could see the few single-story buildings that made up Nanniwan village. Pigs snorted off to his right as he walked along the dirt tracks where patches of snow clung to frozen ruts. He knew he was stubborn enough and had the farming experience to survive here, but to what end?

The rest of the men straggled out for required calisthenics, followed by a barely edible breakfast. The food was dry and cooked with little oil. Within days everyone was constipated.

Breakfast was followed by an hour of studying Mao Zedong Thought. Someone usually read aloud a long passage of Chairman Mao's writing, and everyone followed along.

An Wei learned the routine quickly. Calisthenics and breakfast before sunup and then study sessions and chores—except on Sundays or when it rained or snowed. At those times they crowded into the dormitories to play cards, smoke, belch, and talk louder than An Wei could bear.

The goal of the reeducation school movement was to create a classless society. An Wei had heard rumors his stay could depend on someone's arbitrary assessment of his attitude.

The older men were the most apprehensive about their future. They had been accused of any number of political offenses, had been removed from leading positions, and had often endured the humiliation of ruthless struggle sessions, persecution, and sometimes torture. They had no idea if they would ever be permitted to return to their families, but they knew they would never be able to return to their jobs.

In some ways, An Wei considered himself fortunate. At Nanniwan, he was a "small potato" compared to the older cadres. He was no longer a prime target of struggle sessions, unlike during the year after college when he was a well-known student leader. In the eyes of the Xi'an Foreign Affairs Office, he had committed no major mistakes. He had been sent to the reeducation school, he was told, because he needed more revolutionary experience. Moreover, there was no longer anything for him to do at the office.

When they first arrived in Nanniwan, An Wei and some of the other younger cadres were assigned to perform heavy physical labor in a platoon called the Shock Brigade. One of their first jobs was to gather firewood in far-away valleys and mountains.

Winter temperatures at Nanniwan hovered well below freezing. Even An Wei's village of An Shang never got this cold. To keep the dormitories warm enough for survival, several times a week they set off on foot after a 6:00 a.m. breakfast. An Wei gritted his teeth against the bitter cold as they worked in pairs to pull two-wheeled carts.

He tried to pace himself for the fifteen-kilometer trip. On the valley floor, he took turns with his partner—one pulled, running, while the other rode or ran alongside to keep warm. Once they hit the mountains, one of them pulled and the other pushed, singing revolutionary songs as encouragement.

Deep in the woods, they hefted their axes and fanned out to hunt for dead trees and fallen branches. With each trip, they had to hunt farther into the forest to fill the carts. Cold from the snowy ground penetrated An Wei's lightweight shoes. To keep his hands from going numb, he beat them against his thighs. Although he was in good physical shape, his feet hurt with every step and his muscles burned from exhaustion.

Carts loaded, they broke for lunch—two pieces of corn bread, which had frozen during the morning, and handfuls of snow—then they began the long trip back to Nanniwan.

When they were not working, the cadres had to read Chairman Mao's works and criticize themselves in writing. An Wei and many others hated these repetitive activities. To his relief, the platoon's many firewood trips often spared him from the collective studies and gave him a chance to study on his own time. By the end of the Cultural Revolution, he could recite the essays in Mao Zedong's books from beginning to end.

In an attempt to add substance to the required readings and writings, An Wei began dipping into the English translations and learning from their footnotes that explained Chinese historical events to English-language readers. Because Mao Zedong was highly literate and had embedded many literary and historical references in his writings, the footnotes added richness. In fact, the English volumes sometimes helped An Wei understand the original Chinese better.

However, what he was doing was against school regulations, and soon his platoon leader, Commander Fan, a worker-peasant with little schooling, called him in.

"You are here to touch your soul and receive reeducation," the commander lectured. "How dare you read a foreign language? It's against all rules." He ordered An Wei to turn in his English volumes.

An Wei tensed with fury, but he willed himself to keep his tone respectful.

"Commander Fan, if a good citizen must spread Mao Zedong Thought to the rest of the world, isn't it imperative to read some of it in English? Otherwise, how can we convert foreigners?" Reading it in English, he added, helped him understand difficult Chinese passages.

Knowing that he was taking a risk, An Wei pushed Mr. Fan well beyond his meager education. He quoted a phrase from Chairman Mao's works that many Chinese people had difficulty understanding and asked him what it meant.

The commander responded, "It means that if a person does something bad that needs correcting, then we must correct him. If he corrects his mistakes, then we should just give him a warning. If he does not correct his mistakes, then he should go to prison."

An Wei, gloating inside, pointed out that the passage actually said that for someone to learn from his mistakes, he needed help to understand his errors. "The Chairman said it is best to cure the disease and save the patient," he continued. "I learned the correct interpretation because I read it in both English and Chinese."

Commander Fan's face showed frustration and humiliation, and he hesitated. Without comment, he dismissed An Wei, letting him keep the English volumes.

An Wei continued to read the English works often, though discreetly. He had been lucky with Mr. Fan, but he did not want to challenge other Nanniwan leaders or cadres who would not be so easily convinced.

The snow began to melt in the valley, and the barren trees took on a reddish tinge as sap began to flow and leaf buds formed. Spring had arrived, and An Wei was reassigned to a crew planting rice seedlings. Each morning, they strode off to the paddies in two lines. Because An Wei was younger, he carried the huge red flag that fluttered over their heads. Each crew had one, and as the cadres fanned out into the fields, the bright patches of color stood out against the drab landscape.

An Wei had never planted rice and found it painful to squat in the cold, flooded rice paddies hour after hour, planting one seedling at a time. Other crops were more familiar to him, but they were forced to use absurdly ancient farming methods. Why they needed to prepare the soil with hoes and shovels was beyond him. He was supposed to be learning from these peasants, but in his poor village of An Shang they used animals to plow the land, not their ancestors' backbreaking tools. The hours in the fields and paddies made him ache from head to toe. By mid-morning the cadres were all famished, and stomach pains gripped An Wei's body.

He kept in touch with Niu Jianhua by letter and rare phone calls since the nearest phone was a two-kilometer walk to the Nanniwan village post office. They wrote about their lives and tasks but also wondered when they might see each other again. Cadres were supposed to be allowed to visit their spouses fifteen days a year, but it was uncertain whether this would be allowed. The driving force of the Cultural Revolution was a strong commitment to the country and the denial of personal desires.

When summer came, An Wei was assigned to the food-processing workshop to grind wheat or corn into flour. Unlike An Shang village, where a grindstone and animals were used to process the grain, Nanniwan had a small electric mill. But the grinding still took a long time because of the volume of flour needed to feed several hundred mouths. He began early in the morning, when others were just getting up, and continued after supper until the electricity in the school was switched off at 10:00 p.m.

In July, Niu Jianhua got a two-week leave to visit Nanniwan. An Wei was ecstatic because the food-processing work kept him in one place, a much better situation than if he were collecting firewood. Once his wife arrived, he doubled his efforts to grind as much grain as possible in the morning so he could have more time in the evening with her, and other cadres helped him.

Some evenings they had several hours to themselves and would climb into the hills to enjoy the breeze and quiet conversation. They shared stories about how they tried to keep up their English. An Wei talked about his potentially disastrous altercation with Mr. Fan and how he continued to study the English volumes of Mao Zedong, often in the hills where he read them aloud and practiced speaking English.

Niu Jianhua said that the older intellectuals assigned to the aircraft factory where she had been sent urged her to keep her skills however she could. Though their own professional lives had been brought to a heartless end, they told her that someday she might be able to use her knowledge. An Wei was amazed to find out that she had bought a radio. In the early morning hours, she would drape her quilt over her head and turn the radio on very softly so she could listen to English broadcasts in the room she shared with five other women. She could understand only half of the words, but the radio programs from other countries helped her retain what she had learned.

One of her roommates, though, reported her to the director and accused her of being a spy. The director called her to his office and said the English broadcasts might include words that criticized the Communist Party, and he forbade her to listen anymore. Undaunted, she waited until she was alone to turn on the radio for the English-language programs.

Early Winter 1970

"Strip off your clothes and rub this on your arms and legs, hard," said Tian, a teacher from an agricultural college. He handed An Wei a bottle of Chinese liquor.

"Rub it up and down, up and down." Tian bent over and started stripping. It was early November, and they had rotated jobs again. He and Tian were assigned to clean the pigsties and feed the pigs. One of their tasks was to gather aquatic plants from a nearby pond to feed the swine.

"It will keep us from freezing while we're in the water," Tian explained. They rubbed hard, warming their legs. Tian then tipped the bottle and drank half, giving the rest to An Wei.

"Let's go!" Tian said as he plunged into the frigid water with a knife and sloshed toward the fish grass they had to cut for the pigs. An Wei took a deep breath and jumped in after him. The icy water left him momentarily breathless. It was the coldest he had ever felt. They both cut at the fish grass furiously until their bodies were numb and then emerged with armfuls of plants. The thought of doing this again was daunting. But they had no choice.

One bonus of their work, besides praise, was that An Wei and Tian got permission to live in a small cave, using the excuse that their differing work schedule disturbed others. Though unheated, it was not as cold as the thin-walled dormitory, and it was quiet. The isolation pleased An Wei. On cold days he sometimes sat on a stool outside the west-facing cave to soak up the sun. If he wanted to study, he could concentrate and make notes. If he wanted to sleep, he could do so. He finally had the privacy and silence he cherished.

Then he got a letter from Niu Jianhua, telling him that she was pregnant, and that the doctors thought the baby would arrive in April. An Wei celebrated the news quietly, imagining what it would be like to hold the tiny infant. But when would they be able to live together? Many young couples assigned to Cultural Revolution posts like An Wei and Niu Jianhua had to leave their infants with parents or other caretakers.

2008, Northern Shaanxi Province

I hung onto the back-seat door handle of an aged maroon sedan as the driver made a sharp left turn down an incline and onto a dirt track leading across the valley to the reeducation school.

Road into the Nanniwan reeducation school, 2008.

"There's Nanniwan," An Wei said from the front seat. "Not so different from when I was here. Thirty—no, forty years ago." He sounded surprised.

I strained to see, leaning out my window as far as I dared, taking one photo after another.

"Wait a minute," I said. "I want to get out and take some pictures." I also wanted to just stand there quietly for a few minutes.

I climbed out and took a deep breath. Here they were—the valley and reeducation camp I had heard so much about. I wanted to breathe in the brisk air, see the dried rice paddies and cornfields, and feel what it must have been like for An Wei when he was forced to live here.

I knew he had underplayed how hard life was at the school, because Niu Jianhua confided that An Wei suffered a lot here. They never got enough food to fuel their bodies for the strenuous labor, and what they did eat was of very poor quality. Early on, he developed a stomach ailment that produced severe pains before every meal, pains that he endured for years.

I took a moment to let the valley and surroundings soak in. Then, knocking the dirt from my feet, I clambered back into the car. We jolted along the track to the buildings, pulling up between old concrete rubble and a coal pile. We were parked near the hills An Wei must have climbed with his English volumes. I peppered him with questions. Had this building been a dormitory? A cafeteria? I got no answer. Instead, he took off down a rutted track of semi-frozen mud that ran parallel to the valley. Taking as many photos as possible while I tried to catch up with An Wei, I finally got within earshot.

"It's here somewhere."

"What?" I asked. But he had pulled ahead again.

"Maybe here," he said as he climbed up a path that soon leveled out.

By the time he returned to the main track, I finally managed to catch up.

We passed one farmer's house built into the loess hill and then another. All the one-story buildings had sod roofs of dried grass.

"These homes weren't here."

He was scanning the hill for his cave as we came to a third house. Its roof curved down and ended near the ground. At its highest point, it was attached to the hill. A short path led to a cave entrance.

"I'm sure that's it," An Wei said as he strode toward the house, a snarling dog running alongside, behind a flimsy stick fence. He was on a mission, dog or no dog. Quiet excitement seemed to propel him.

An Wei pointed to the iron grate across the entrance of the cave. "It must be used for grain storage," he said. I was still eyeing the dog, the hair bristling on its neck announcing that it did not like intruders.

An elderly peasant came from the house, looking inquisitive and friendly. He and An Wei talked, pointing to the cave. The man corralled his dog and invited us to climb onto the roof, helping An Wei, who slipped in his leather, loafer-like shoes.

"This is it," he announced.

We headed up the short path from the roof and peered into the small cave. It was just big enough for two cots with a tiny space between them. An Wei snapped photos. Then I took several of him at the cave's entrance, standing erect in his baseball cap, his snap-on sunglasses flipped up and a broad smile spreading across his face.

1970

Just as in Xi'an, Cultural Revolution slogans were everywhere in Nanniwan. The cafeteria, dormitories, and the courtyard were filled with huge posters exhorting everyone to carry out the revolution.

"To learn from the peasants is to wage revolution."

"Advance courageously along the glorious road of Chairman Mao's May 7th Directive."

"American imperialism must be beaten."

One whole wall was painted red, the symbol of China and Chairman Mao.

An Wei by his cave at the Nanniwan reeducation school, 2008.

The *Daily News* radio station in Beijing blared across Nanniwan through loudspeakers every evening, heralding the revolution's newest achievements. An Wei listened intently to learn what was happening. He and everyone else at the reeducation school knew it was essential to follow the twists and turns of the Cultural Revolution: government officials were being sent to the countryside or to jail, and more university presidents and teachers were being accused of terrible crimes—examples of how not to behave.

But how *should* one behave? An Wei could not figure it out. What should people like him believe? He was the son of a farmer. It had been extremely difficult for him to attend school and complete his education, which was now declared useless.

He could not accept this. The skills he had learned were important, regardless of the official doctrine. If he gave up what little capital he had gained through learning, then he really would have nothing. Yet teachers and professors were labeled stinking turds.

Why, he wondered, were some people the driving force of the revolution one day but its target the next? Throughout the country, as people turned against friends and families in their fervor to follow Chairman Mao's directives, many were asking the same questions. A talented preschool expert, who had been forced to live in a pigsty, said no one knew whom to follow. Even preschool teachers were terrified of saying the wrong thing in their classrooms. Maybe something they said to the young children had just been outlawed and could be used against them.

When An Wei was in college, Mao Zedong was like a god to him and his friends. The chairman's words were sacred, and his directives were building a new nation. Now, once again, everything was like a mirage. The only thing that remained constant was the English his teachers had taught him. No longer just a skill, English had become his anchor.

As An Wei's first year at the reeducation school ended, word arrived that the American journalist Edgar Snow would visit Nanniwan. Snow was famous for making a dangerous trip to Yan'an to interview Mao Zedong in 1936, when the Communist Party was sequestered there and under siege by Chiang Kai-shek's nationalist army. An Wei could barely contain his excitement. He had studied English for so many years, and now he would have a chance to hear this famous foreigner.

To An Wei's dismay, though, the Nanniwan leaders kept him and the others who knew some English so far away that they could not see the visitors' faces and had no idea which one was Edgar Snow.

Nevertheless, An Wei managed to learn about the visit through news items and interviews published in a confidential government newspaper, *Limited Information*, which was intended only for school leaders and senior cadres in good standing. But the information always leaked to others, allowing An Wei to absorb every little bit he could about Snow's visit.

What he learned suggested that Edgar Snow's style of interviewing and reporting differed from that of Chinese correspondents. He appeared to ask questions but never give his own opinion. Although An Wei did not see Snow's articles, from the morsels he heard about, he gleaned that Snow seemed to say nothing good or bad about the revolution or Chairman Mao while China's media declared repeatedly that the Cultural Revolution was achieving its aims and that Mao Zedong was a great leader and helmsman. Snow just reported what he had heard in the interviews. To An Wei, this type of writing was a revelation and piqued his curiosity.

Carrying on with his chores, An Wei tried to ignore his pain-filled body. Every day he wondered when his first child would arrive because then he was supposed to get a brief leave to visit Niu Jianhua. Meanwhile, he used his spare time to focus on the English volumes. When he could, he climbed into the hills with a volume tucked into his shirt. He found a quiet place to read passages aloud—sometimes sitting on a rock, other times pacing back and forth. No slogans assaulted him there. No one was around to report him. He was learning how to swim in this dangerous ocean, not just survive, and still keep his hard-earned English skills alive.

March 1971 brought a hint of spring into the valley. Over a year had passed since An Wei had arrived at Nanniwan. He hoped work would be less painful as the temperatures warmed. The loudspeaker blared big news that China had launched a satellite into orbit. An Wei was fascinated but had a hard time imagining it.

Each day he practiced what he could from his worn Mao Zedong volumes. He chatted with friends, enjoyed the solitude of the cave, and wrote letters to Niu Jianhua. He was both thrilled and worried about her forthcoming delivery. Things could go terribly wrong in childbirth.

Then, one day without warning, he was called to the small Nanniwan administrative office. Puzzled, he walked to the smoky room. Commander Fan, sitting at one of the few desks, announced that he had selected An Wei to write display descriptions for the Yan'an History Museum.

"Be ready to leave in the morning," Fan ordered.

For a week, rumors had been circulating that some cadres were being selected for the museum, but An Wei had ignored them, figuring that he was not a historian and had no ability for such work.

Perplexed, he stood before his semi-literate commander and said, "But I have no knowledge for that."

"Well, I have selected you," the commander responded. "Your record says you are good at writing."

An Wei hesitated. Would it be safer to stay with the physical labor at Nanniwan? Yan'an was where the Communists ended the Long March—the arduous military retreat they undertook in the 1930s to escape unremitting attacks from Chiang Kai-shek's nationalist army. An old museum in Yan'an was dedicated to that period. Now, in the middle of the Cultural Revolution, the government wanted to capture more of that revolutionary history and rewrite parts. That could be dangerous business.

The saying that haunted him when he was first sent to Nanniwan disturbed him once again: *Wu chi. Wu chi. The period that never ends.*

If he did not go to Yan'an, would he remain in the reeducation school forever? It was probably wiser to accept, so he agreed to go.

An Wei returned to his cave, pondering how he could write historical information. He sat down on his cot in the small space and slowly began to collect his belongings to be ready for the morning trip.

· *6* ·

Unshackled

March 1971

As a cold mist rose off the frost-covered land, An Wei climbed onto the school's small bus for the trip to Yan'an, where he was to work at the History Museum. Besides An Wei, Commander Fan had chosen two famous artists who had well-known paintings in public places, and a young man from the Xi'an Fine Arts Academy, which An Wei once dreamed of attending. Fan had also selected two historians, who An Wei knew were better equipped to adhere to the Cultural Revolution view of history than he was.

The bus engine coughed to a rough start. An Wei stared out the window at the crude Nanniwan buildings and the hills where he had found moments of solitude for reading English. He glimpsed the corner of his cave entrance, almost hidden from view. He would not miss working in the miserable rice paddies or collecting firewood, but he felt a pang of nostalgia for his peaceful cave.

The bus heaved over some rocks and then lumbered onto the rutted track and across the fields toward the road that climbed out of the valley. An Wei closed his jacket tighter against the cold breeze as they ascended into the forested areas. Relief seeped into his body when he realized he was leaving this forsaken place. For more than a year he had been laboring at Nanniwan with no end in sight. Now, suddenly, it was over.

As the driver navigated the rutted road, An Wei's fingers drummed on the hard seat. He had not been able to tell Niu Jianhua about his transfer. Would he still get a leave when the baby came? Lines of tension creased his face. He tried to put a positive spin on his upside-down world, but still he agonized about the future.

After what seemed like hours, they rumbled down into the next valley, passed Thirty-Li village, and entered the outskirts of Yan'an. Slogging along muddy streets past scattered low buildings, the bus turned onto the only bridge over the Yan River. Paved streets announcing the main part of the city drew An Wei's attention. Trucks and jeeps wove among donkeys and horses hauling vegetables. He saw only a few bicycles and one car. It was a far cry from bustling Xi'an but welcome nonetheless after being isolated in the Nanniwan valley.

The bus shuddered to a stop in front of a cluster of single-story buildings. Nearby stood a three-story hotel, the only one in Yan'an to admit foreign guests, and the museum. An Wei hefted his bedroll and followed a museum staff member to a courtyard where a few chickens scratched in the dirt. He would share a large room with four other men. It was much better than the Nanniwan dormitory with all the cadres packed together on wooden slats, but he missed his cave.

That night, after supper in the hotel cafeteria, which definitely served more nutritious food than Nanniwan, An Wei sat in the empty courtyard relishing the quiet. What a strange world: from starvation in high school to the honor of a college education, the life-threatening Cultural Revolution, and the forced education from the peasants at Nanniwan. Now this.

None of it made sense. He would just have to do whatever was demanded with utmost care to avoid making any political mistakes and hope that he, Niu Jianhua, and their family would someday live together.

Spring 1971, Yan'an

Finished with his early morning exercise, An Wei found his way to the small museum cafeteria in one of the low buildings that crowded around a dusty courtyard. Cloth mops and willow-branch brooms leaned haphazardly against walls. The museum, a group of buildings including An Wei's dorm room, sat at the base of Phoenix Mountain, known as Feng Huang Shan, which was peppered with low-growing trees and bushes that clung to the dry soil. Here Mao Zedong had established his first Yan'an headquarters.

After breakfast with the museum staff and the usual hour of reading from Mao Zedong's works, An Wei asked permission to call Niu Jianhua. She was happy to hear his voice but startled to learn he had been transferred to Yan'an. They talked about his anticipated visit after she had their baby, but he had to cut the call short because others were waiting for him.

The museum had formed two work groups: one to design new exhibits; the other, composed of the two experts and An Wei, to do research and write historical descriptions for the exhibits. His stomach tightened as he realized how much more party history the experts knew than he. One of them, a middle-aged man, had been a history lecturer in a provincial univer-

The Long March and the Yan'an Years

In 1934, about eighty thousand Communist soldiers, cadres, and followers broke through Chinese Nationalist troops surrounding their base in Jiangxi Province in southern China and headed west in search of a safer area. The trek—known as the Long March and a defining moment for the Chinese Communist Party—took a zigzagging route of more than six thousand miles that crossed twenty-four rivers and eighteen mountain ranges. They fought innumerable skirmishes and were chased by Nationalist troops and aerial bombardment much of the way. Only eight thousand people survived the march, including about fifty women. Its leaders were Mao Zedong, Zhou Enlai, Zhu De, and many others who became instrumental in forming and ruling the People's Republic of China in 1949.

The march ended in Shaanxi Province in north-central China, where the army first settled in Bao'an, and then found permanent headquarters in Yan'an. There the Communists took up a simple life in cave dwellings to recuperate and build their strength. They would remain in Yan'an for a decade.

During these years, Mao Zedong read voraciously, including Marx and Lenin, and he developed a communist theory based not on a Russian approach to revolution, which counted on enlisting urban areas, but rather on inspiring the rural population. Much of China was under the control of the Nationalists, led by Chiang Kai-shek, and increasingly by Japanese invaders. The Communists, meanwhile, were isolated enough to be able to develop policies. They spent considerable effort building support in rural areas. Instead of abusing the peasants and stealing from them as the Nationalist troops did, the Communist Party members and soldiers helped bring in their harvests and showed them respect. The Communists also fought against the Japanese and endured encirclement by Nationalist troops.

Perhaps the most important outcome of the Yan'an years was Mao Zedong's rise to leadership and consolidation of his followers into disciplined, obedient members of the Chinese Communist Party. He wrote extensively during this period, including most of the essays in the *Selected Works of Mao Zedong*. He also became a master at outwitting his opponents and eventually was elected chair of the Central Committee of the Politburo, the ruling body.[1]

sity for several years; the other was from the Party History Teaching Group of a political law institute.

From their first team meeting, An Wei was cautious. Writing Communist Party history was a delicate business. If you got it wrong, you could be punished unmercifully. He realized that these two experts, who had been sent for reeducation to Nanniwan, must be acutely aware of that. Many of the struggles that engulfed the country occurred when shifting power groups misinterpreted Mao Zedong's words.

When the two historians asked him to help write descriptions, An Wei demurred. He was not a history major, he said, and had no skills in this area. "I could help in small ways," he suggested. He modestly added that although his penmanship was poor, he could make final copies of their description—if that would help.

To his relief, they agreed. They explained the project they were to work on and said he needed to study the archives in the museum reading room. "Get yourself familiar with the history of Yan'an and our leaders while they were here from 1935 to 1947. Then you'll be able to help us more."

An Wei's head spun. They were sending him to a reading room? How could that be? The whole country was forbidden to read *anything* except government newspapers and Chairman Mao's words. The Cultural Revolution was still tearing China apart. Could they really be asking him to do this?

Except for occasional government documents, for the past five years he had been allowed to read only works of Mao Zedong and his little red book of quotations.

But the directive was clear: "Tomorrow, report to the reading room."

The next morning, An Wei slowly pushed open the reading room door. Sitting down on one of two benches, he stared, afraid to touch anything.

Where should he begin?

Several bookcases lining the walls of the small room were filled with magazines and books. On top of the shelves were stacks of newspapers published during the Yan'an days. In the 1930s, printing presses set up in caves had spun out the continuous writings, deliberations, and policies of the Communist Party. Newspapers reported resistance maneuvers against the Japanese and attacks by Chiang Kai-shek's troops on Mao Zedong's revolutionary forces.

His step tentative, An Wei approached a stack of yellowing newspapers and ran his fingers along their edges. Dust particles stuck to his fingers. With prickles of anticipation running along his scalp, he carried a paper to a table and began to read. The paper felt rougher than what he was used to. He wondered if any of the famous leaders had touched it.

Reading the front page carefully, he thought about what he knew from the footnotes in his English-language Mao Zedong volumes, as well as from college studies. Much of what he read was new to him. As he finished one paper he picked up the next, turning each page carefully so as not to damage it. The hours flew by. As dinner approached he folded the issue he had been reading, put it carefully back on the stack, and viewed the rest of the room with a smile. He felt like a cow let loose in a vegetable garden. He had to force himself to leave for the evening.

The following day An Wei surveyed all the books and then turned to his most important task of understanding the development of the Communist Party and what it had accomplished in Yan'an. He carefully read *The Brief History of the Chinese Communist Party*. Next, he began to page methodically through the *Liberation Daily*, the newspaper published during the Yan'an years. Strategy and theory had always been fundamental to the party's development, and during the Yan'an years, Mao Zedong wrote essay after essay, many of which An Wei had read repeatedly. They were all here, even drafts in the Great Helmsman's handwriting. It was thrilling.

He set to work learning details of this short, critical period: about military affairs, industry, agriculture, medicine, education, and art. For days he read and took notes, read and took notes. Dates, names, and events crowded his mind.

In the days to come, he continued to deflect the experts' requests to do substantive writing.

"No, no, you are the professionals, the experts in party history," he told them. He added, though, that he had learned enough to provide them with simple material like correct names, dates, and details about military maneuvers. They seemed content to let him do that and to make the final handwritten copy of their writing.

While continuing to study tirelessly in the reading room, An Wei also began to check out books overnight so he could read in his spare time. He was drawn to a bookcase that held an assortment of writings by people who visited Yan'an in the 1930s. Two books stood out. The first was *Red Star Over China* by Edgar Snow, the journalist who had recently visited Nanniwan. He had spent several months interviewing Mao Zedong and other leaders in their first encampment near Yan'an. Next to that book was *Inside Red China*, a book by Nym Wales. She had come to Yan'an shortly after Snow's trip, by escaping Chiang Kai-shek's Xi'an police patrols in the dead of night. An Wei was amazed at her courage. Her adventures were more breathtaking than any of the movies he had seen.

He fell in love with these works.[2] Living in rough circumstances, both writers were in daily contact with leaders, troops, and the local people. For years An Wei had been told that Americans were evil, that they were China's worst enemies, and that they had caused thousands of Chinese deaths in Korea. Yet these two Americans had risked their lives to travel through war zones and reach the northwest. Their writing brought to life the historic Yan'an sites he was now living among.[3]

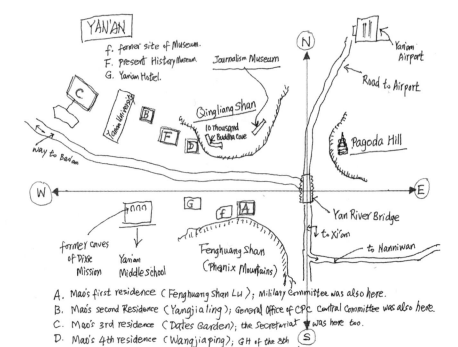

An Wei's drawing of Yan'an as it looked when he was sent there in the 1970s. Drawn from memory in 2014, An Wei later pointed out that he had omitted the Yan River that runs from west to east, although he included the bridge.

*   *   *

The call came too soon. On April 10, 1971, Niu Jianhua had given birth to their daughter. Excited and concerned, An Wei got clearance from his superiors to leave and climbed onto the next bus to Xi'an—a full day's trip south, plus extra hours to reach the aircraft factory.

An Qun, An Qun. He repeated her name to himself, liking the sound. They had carefully chosen her given name, *Qun*—meaning "the masses." It was appropriate for the Cultural Revolution, but also connected to their lives. Combined with *An*—peace, safe, to settle down—*An Qun* meant to settle peacefully among the masses. It was a way to recognize that Niu Jianhua had become an ordinary factory worker and An Wei was a laborer and farmer.

As the bus passed through towns and villages and across dry ravines, his mind was a jumble of thoughts and feelings. Excitement about the birth and worry that the infant and Niu Jianhua might not be well all merged with the facts and information about the 1930s in Yan'an that he was supposed to remember. Unconscious humming slipped through his lips, and he checked his watch too often. Hope stole into his thoughts. Now that he had a child in Xi'an, maybe he could transfer there.

By the time An Wei reached the factory, Niu Jianhua's mother had already arrived to help tend the baby. Niu Jianhua had been assigned a tiny room, with nothing in it. But the workers supplied her with everything she needed by "borrowing" from the factory. As she and An Qun settled into a routine, An Wei tried to assist with chores. They were all new to him. In An Shang, women did the housework and tended the babies. He was clumsy but was also sure he could help. One day when Niu Jianhua craved meat-stuffed dumplings, he offered to make them. The dough fell apart in the water as they cooked, and she was furious that he had ruined the valuable meat mixture.

Holding their precious little girl made up for his mistakes. Her tiny fingers clasped around his rough, weather-beaten hands. He loved to touch her wisps of black hair, and he spent long periods admiring her dark curious eyes. But her cries—An Wei could not believe how demanding they were.

Though a strong young woman, Niu Jianhua was exhausted from tending the infant. She was relieved to be granted the forty-day leave for new mothers and moved with their daughter to her parents' home in Xi'an. Once mother and infant were settled, An Wei looked longingly at his wife and daughter and headed for the bus station. The trip back to Yan'an seemed interminable. Images of An Qun flashed through his mind. Unless she or Niu Jianhua ended up in the hospital, he would not see them for a long time.

Back in Yan'an, An Wei continued to read voraciously, take notes, and copy final drafts. As the spring days lengthened, he explored the different locales Mao Zedong used as headquarters. The more he read about the Yan'an years, the more he understood what had happened in every gathering hall, cave, and courtyard. It was astounding to realize that Chairman Mao and his diplomatic negotiator, Zhou Enlai, had walked these very streets and courtyards. Everywhere An Wei went, the future leaders of the People's Republic of China had lived and worked. He also learned that he and his roommates were living in the cave house of Zhu De, who with Chairman Mao and Zhou Enlai, ruled China for decades.

2008

At a restaurant near my hotel in Xi'an, An Wei and I finished the corn soup and walked across a major intersection, navigating buses, cars, bicycles, motorbikes, and handcarts. The ancient city wall loomed above us. An Wei asked if I had been to Yan'an. I had not, but I knew I would need to visit the city since it was his home during an important period of his life. We left it at that.

Two days later, he emailed me that a friend at Yan'an University, a vice president, would like us to visit. If we gave a series of lectures for the students on Chinese and US culture and education, the university would reimburse us by providing a driver and car for several days. When could I go?

Six months later I was back in China following fast-moving An Wei into the high-ceilinged waiting room of the Xi'an train station.

Train K214 flipped up on the digital signboard, and tickets in hand, we joined the crowd pressing through a narrow opening and down the stairs to track 7 where we found our assigned compartment. As the sleek, modern train slid quietly from the station, An Wei pulled out lunch—a large bag of dense cookies he had taken from home. To add some nutrition, I rummaged for a bag of unshelled peanuts in my briefcase, and we found the hot water thermos under the table.

My hands wrapped around a hot mug of tea, I leaned back to watch the city and towns give way to barren gullies and occasional fields while An Wei carried on a string of conversations on his mobile phone.

It was dark when we pulled into the Yan'an station, where a driver in a battered university car was waiting to take us to a hotel. After An Wei made sure our rooms had functioning internet, we ate a good meal and hit the computers to finalize our first talks.

For the next days, we alternated between giving speeches and trekking to one important historical site after another. I nearly had to run to keep up with An Wei—a tape recorder in my jacket pocket, a microphone draped around my neck on a long wire, and my camera in the other pocket for easy access. We visited the museum reading room where he had soaked up his country's history, the site of Mao Zedong's first headquarters, the printing press caves, and the neighboring town of Bao'an, where the soldiers of the first Red Army Academy had studied in caves. It took me hours and hours to transcribe and double-check what I was learning.

Summer 1971

An Wei and Niu Jianhua stayed in touch by letter. He loved to read about how An Qun was growing and changing. She noticed everything and was making sounds in response to Niu Jianhua. He longed to hold his daughter in his arms and feel her tiny fingers grasping his.

When Niu Jianhua had to return to the aircraft factory and leave An Qun with her mother, An Wei applied for a transfer so they could be together. He hoped it would be approved, not caring what job the aircraft factory assigned him. Cultural Revolution policy focused entirely on modernizing China, often at the expense of home life, but he was determined to do everything he could to unite his family.

Frustrated by his Yan'an living arrangement with four other men, An Wei hunted for another place. He got up earlier than anyone else and had to creep around; when he wanted to read and take notes at night, their big room was dark and his roommates smoked, which he abhorred. On the opposite side of the courtyard, he found a tiny room, really a large closet with a window. With his supervisor's approval, An Wei soon moved his cot. Each night he was able to sit on his narrow bed and use a shelf by the window as a desk to read and take notes. It was perfect.

Despite the ongoing Cultural Revolution, An Wei felt that as long as he was careful, his current position was a safe bubble. In the rest of the country, however, terrible persecution continued. Citizens faced ever-changing government directives. Colleges remained closed; teachers were still being abused for having academic knowledge. Young people continued to perform the "Loyalty Dance" to show their unwavering dedication to Chairman Mao. Everyone—soldiers, peasants in the fields, and museum staff, including An Wei—continued to study *The Quotations of Chairman Mao* or other official writings at the beginning of every workday. Factory workers throughout China regularly wrote "good news letters" to Mao Zedong describing their accomplishments for the country.[4]

An Wei continued to devour the books in the information room. He could rattle off details about the reorganization of the Red Army, how the segments in north China became the Eighth Route Army, while those in south China were reorganized as the new Fourth Army. He learned about party policies and how artists throughout the country were organized to

An Wei in Yan'an, 1971. *Source*: An Wei.

inspire and educate the citizens. He could recite the contents of essays and doctrines and the dates when specific meetings were convened. He also learned that the author of *Inside Red China*, Nym Wales, was really Helen Foster Snow, wife of Edgar Snow.

Poring over the details in Helen Snow's book, he realized that she had conducted many conversations with Mao Zedong and other party leaders at the very site where he was working, with Phoenix Mountain rising behind them. As he sat in the courtyard reading, he could look at the low-growing trees and bushes climbing the steep slope and imagine their meetings.

As the documentarians of new China, An Wei and other staff members often joined tours for old revolutionaries as well as foreigners who had been associated with China during the Yan'an years. Their job was to jot down any historical information the visitors provided—where a photo was taken, who was in it, and stories about particular events.

The foreign groups were accompanied by interpreters from Beijing whose English was superb but who knew little revolutionary history. Terms that An Wei had learned from reading the English volumes of Mao Zedong's work—*guerilla warfare, Party Rectification Movement, tunnel warfare*, and *the Three Great Styles of how the party worked*—were strange to them. When they stumbled, An Wei supplied the correct English term silently in his head.

One autumn day as he jotted notes, an interpreter hesitated.

"Party Rectification Movement," An Wei murmured to himself.

The interpreter began again. Then paused, obviously agitated and embarrassed.

Without thinking, An Wei blurted out, "Party Rectification Movement." The other staff in the room stared at him.

Startled at what he had done, An Wei waited. What would happen to him? Until that minute, no one at the museum knew he spoke English. Well-mannered young people kept their knowledge to themselves. They were expected to do what others requested and not mention their skills. All over the country people were still punished for knowing English.

He was soon relieved when the director of the Yan'an Foreign Affairs Office asked him if he could interpret for them. Gradually, the Beijing interpreters also began asking him to interpret for them in the museum since he knew the Yan'an history and vocabulary better than anyone else.

As winter neared and visitor tours stopped, An Wei was allowed to travel to Xi'an and see Niu Jianhua and An Qun, now a healthy, energetic seven-month-old, eating well, cooing, and babbling. But his request for a transfer had been turned down, and all too soon he was back in Yan'an as temperatures dropped.

Along with other staff, he was sent to the countryside to help the dreadfully poor peasants who lived in scattered villages and were enduring a severe drought. Before they left, morning readings focused on facing hard times, and the director told them, if they armed their minds with Mao Zedong Thought, they could do what was needed of them.

Once in the countryside, An Wei was appalled by the conditions. Though he had grown up in a terribly poor village, his austere life in An Shang had been good when compared to how these people lived. He stayed with a family that was better off than many, yet even the caves they lived in were dark and filthy, and the food was terrible. No meat, no vegetables, no steamed bread. Just corn bread, corn soup, and inedible pickled vegetables. More than once during the long weeks, he drew on Chairman Mao's words to face the bleak conditions with a positive attitude.

He helped the farmers make terraced fields and carry water to stressed crops. He tried to help them understand some of the government's new policies, and he and his colleagues held small meetings where they read documents to the farmers and explained how to improve production. Goodhearted and illiterate, the people did not know about radios and had no contact with the outside world.

Once he returned to Yan'an, he called Niu Jianhua. He laughed when she described how An Qun was trying to walk and talk. But the best news was that she was pregnant again, and their second child was due in early August. Though frustrated and sad about their pulled-apart lives, An Wei was exhilarated with anticipation for their second child, and he dug deeper into his work.

Summer 1972, Yan'an

Sap rose in the bushes on Phoenix Mountain, signaling warm weather and renewed visits from groups that included more English speakers. By summer An Wei had become a full-time interpreter of the Yan'an Foreign Affairs Office and had a bedroom office in the low-slung buildings in front of the hotel. Elegant by Yan'an standards, the hotel had three floors, a large banquet hall, and the luxury of private bathrooms that he and others sometimes used to bathe.

What a difference from life in Nanniwan. In Yan'an he was able to improve his English, develop more organizational skills, and meet people from many cultures. Elsewhere most Chinese people were still being limited to myopic and ever-shifting government views.

An Wei dove into this new job. Everything required detailed attention. Each day, dressed in a jacket in the style worn by the father of modern China,

Sun Yatsen, and dark trousers, he was determined to meet the expectations of the Foreign Affairs Office director. He planned schedules, took care of all the guests' arrangements, and made sure he understood every protocol.

On the way to the small Yan'an airport to meet his first British group, worries plagued him. Would he be polite enough? Would his English be understood? He had spent hours practicing vocabulary the guests might use, but what if he did not understand them? Taking a deep breath, he climbed out of the staff car and crossed the tarmac with the director.

"Good day," the Englishman said, sticking out his hand. The director reached out and shook it. What a strange gesture, An Wei thought. It was much better to bow a little. He moved into the position beside the director, and as the two men began to talk, relief coursed through his limbs when his English words came easily.

At the hotel he lugged the group's baggage up to the rooms and answered endless questions.

"If we need extra towels, how do we get them?"

"You will need to let me know. But these should be enough," An Wei answered.

One of them ran the water in the bathroom. It was cold. "Will there be hot water some time?"

"Yes, hot water is from 7:00 to 8:00 p.m."

Once the guests were settled, he scurried to the dining room to make sure it was set up properly for the opening banquet. Then back up to the rooms to escort the guests to the dining room.

During the meal, he interpreted conversations between the group leader and local officials. Formal speeches followed. He had read them ahead of time, looking up unfamiliar language. Still he feared the speakers would go off script and he would be lost.

With each new group, An Wei gained confidence. Soon the leaders of the revolutionary sites and the museum asked him to take over as their host, guide, and interpreter. That was fine when the guests just listened and didn't ask questions. He could go on at length: "This is the office building of the Political Bureau of the Party Central Committee. All the major decisions during the Anti-Japanese War were discussed and adopted here. Also the Yan'an Forum on Literature and Art was held here for forty-three days . . ."

But casual situations mortified him. He spoke English much better than he comprehended it, so visitors assumed he understood everything. When they began conversations on an unfamiliar topic, he often had no idea what they were talking about and had to ask them to repeat what they were saying, which was humiliating.

*   *   *

"Look," a staff member said to An Wei, pointing at an open hotel window one summer evening.

An Wei walked across the courtyard and stood beside him. He unfastened the collar of his Sun Yatsen jacket to allow a slight breeze to cool him. Another staff member sauntered over.

Together they gawked, appalled. A group from Chile had returned to their hotel rooms, opened the windows wide, and taken off all their clothes. To make matters worse, the rural housekeeping staff, not knowing they should knock before entering, walked into the room and yelled when they saw the nude guests.

The next day An Wei discovered an even more mortifying fact. He had carefully assigned their unmarried men and women to separate rooms, but they had moved and now men and women were sharing rooms. Offended, the Foreign Affairs Office director reprimanded the Chilean leaders, who in turn were insulted. An Wei thought he knew Western customs from all the books he had read, but this was too much.

Even a Chinese American visitor embarrassed them by repeatedly asking how Chinese people had sex when peasant families all slept on the same kang. An Wei could not imagine why someone who was Chinese and knew their conservative cultural views about sex would ask such questions.

Then there were the American journalists and editors. Unlike others who had sympathy for the country's past, this large group viewed China as backward. An Wei answered questions that no one in China would even think of asking, and he was horrified yet fascinated by their comments.

"Why does everyone talk like they're reciting an editorial from *People's Daily*?" they asked. Such remarks caused An Wei and the other Chinese hosts an enormous loss of face, even though it was true that they all read the party newspaper before venturing to say anything about a topic.

As a way of testing one site guide's truthfulness at a location, a journalist asked why there were pieces of glass on top of the walls. Embarrassed, An Wei interpreted the guide's explanation.

"It is for catching the beautiful sunlight."

The Americans burst into laughter.

"She is treating us like ignorant children," one journalist told An Wei. "How can we trust anything she tells us?"

After he saw them off at the airport, An Wei breathed a sigh of relief. Later though, he read about the journalists' articles. In the worst one, the author wondered whether the dirt in the bathroom sinks and tubs was left over from the nineteenth century. When hotel staff members heard this, they were furious. From their point of view, those rooms were clean enough.

Although American bluntness bothered An Wei, as more groups visited, he realized that lies like the one about the glass shards fostered distrust. But what to do? China was poor, and the government wanted to hide that fact. Besides, the Cultural Revolution was still in full swing, and thousands of educated people were still being hounded to death. An Wei knew that if he or a guide told the truth, they would be in trouble. The official position was that there were no thieves in this great society, and glass on the walls was for beautification. Maybe some day it would be possible to tell the truth. But not now.

Beyond Yan'an, world alignments were shifting. In 1970, people throughout China were puzzled to see photos of Edgar Snow and Mao Zedong standing together atop Beijing's Tiananmen Gate to view the National Day parade. Why would a person from China's number one enemy, the United States,[5] be invited to stand beside the Great Helmsman? Meanwhile, in the West, rumors were circulating that both countries were making attempts at contact after twenty-two years of estrangement.

The very day An Qun was born, an American Ping-Pong team, its staff, and a collection of journalists arrived in Beijing. *Life* magazine photographers, anxious to capture all they were seeing, hung from bus windows taking thousands of photos. They wrote about "life-and-a-half-sized alabaster statues of the chairman" and of loudspeakers blaring Mao Zedong quotes. They reported that everyone wore similar clothes with Mao Zedong images pinned over their hearts. In the Guangzhou airport, journalists stared as a chorus line of airline stewardesses sang songs of Mao Zedong Thought, the little red book of his quotations clutched to their hearts. The adulation of Chairman Mao was jarring, but the journalists were also moved by the heartfelt interaction between the Chinese and US Ping-Pong teams.

Those journalists who had known China earlier in the twentieth century found the country now stunningly clean. Corpses of children and starving beggars no longer lined city streets each morning. People lived humbly, but poverty no longer dominated Beijing or Shanghai.[6]

An Wei and others who had privileged knowledge through the government paper *Limited Information* saw the Ping-Pong exchange as a move toward contact with the United States. At the final banquet for the players, Premier Zhou Enlai said that a new page was opening in relations between the Chinese and American people.[7]

A few months later, in July 1971, Henry Kissinger, President Richard M. Nixon's national security advisor, slipped away from a trip to Pakistan and flew secretly to Beijing to negotiate a visit by the US president.

The Shifting Relations of the US and China

In the fall of 1971, China's dream to move onto the world stage became a reality. The United Nations General Assembly passed a resolution that removed Chiang Kai-shek's Republic of China[8] from its seat on the Security Council and replaced it with the People's Republic of China.

Then on February 21, 1972, the entire world was stunned to see President Nixon stepping off the *Spirit of '76* at Beijing's Capital Airport and then shake hands with a waiting Premier Zhou Enlai. Long before the internet or Twitter feeds, this news ricocheted around the globe. The *People's Daily* printed photos of the meeting, telling the surprised Chinese population that Nixon was a friend of China. Though puzzled at the changed policy, the Chinese people were used to following Mao Zedong's dictates.

The US public was as surprised and bewildered at the photo of President Nixon and Chairman Mao smiling and clasping hands. Though some were adamantly opposed, among others there was quiet excitement.

Americans were even more surprised by the Shanghai Communiqué issued jointly by the two leaders on the last day of Nixon's visit. It not only affirmed that it was in the interest of all nations that the two countries work toward normalization of relations but also included a vague acknowledgment of a One-China policy, leaving the status of Taiwan in a state of what Henry Kissinger called "constructive ambiguity."[9]

For both leaders the meeting fulfilled a long-held hope. But they were cautious. Mao Zedong remarked to Nixon that despite the growing collaboration, "We will still have to curse each other a little in our newspapers."[10]

*   *   *

As the due date for An Wei's second child neared, his work was too demanding to allow him to spend time in Xi'an with Niu Jianhua. Instead, they got permission for her to fly to Yan'an for the birth. Arriving early August, she stayed in his little bedroom office, and they waited. She exercised, they walked up Pagoda Mountain, now brightly lit for foreign visitors, and still they waited. Finally, on August 27, 1972, their son, An Xiang, was born in the Yan'an hospital, and An Wei found a room for mother and son in one of the historic sites, Wangjiaping.

An Xiang was an easy baby. An Wei bicycled back and forth to work, and when he was not traveling with a visiting group, he and Niu Jianhua enjoyed the wonderful shade trees and open expanses of Wangjiaping, away from the city bustle.

At the end of the month, however, his heart sank as mother and baby boarded the plane for Xi'an. They had named him An Xiang—"peaceful flight." As the plane taxied down the runway, he wished for their safe travel.

Once again An Wei became frustrated by his scattered family. An Qun, now sixteen months old, still lived with her grandmother and grandfather. Niu Jianhua's aunt would care for An Xiang, and Niu Jianhua had to return to the aircraft factory. An Wei would not see them again until spring, almost a year away.

He buried himself in work. As the only competent English speaker in the Foreign Affairs Office, An Wei began to realize his value. His office mates seemed to treat him with great respect, and he realized that his English was becoming nuanced. He hoped his speech was now more like a native speaker.

At the historic sites, he became more self-assured and words came more easily: "After the outbreak of the Anti-Japanese War, young students, artists, and writers all flowed into Yan'an and formed a mighty army of art and literature workers . . ."

Although few Americans visited Yan'an, An Wei was fascinated by the backgrounds of those who did. There was the widow of a US airman who was shot down by the Japanese over northern China and rescued by the Communists. There were relatives of the revered Flying Tigers airmen, who risked their lives fighting the Japanese in Burma and prevented the conquest of western China. He found them to be straightforward and humorous, and he was impressed by how much he was learning from them.

Despite the exhilaration of meeting so many foreign visitors, each month without his family seemed like forever. An Qun and An Xiang were growing and learning to walk and talk, but they hardly knew their father.

An Qun, about two years old.
Source: An Wei.

2008

An Wei and I went to Yan'an dressed for autumn and woke up to snow. It was freezing. The hot water in the showers was not even warm, and I reverted to my habit of decades earlier: wearing everything that was in my suitcase. I noticed that An Wei was using a lapel pin to fasten his suit jacket closed.

When we were not preparing and giving lectures to hundreds of students at Yan'an University, we toured revolutionary sites, with An Wei describing to me each building and each room—who lived there, what important meetings were held there, and what policies were created.

I struggled to get An Wei to talk about what Yan'an was like in the 1970s when he lived there. Were there any shops? Cars? Were there a lot of people? What did they wear? He pretty much ignored my questions. At each historic location, it was as if someone pushed a button and a well-practiced speech came out.

"Here is Chairman Mao's bathtub. He always had one because he came from southern China."

"Over there is where Chairman Mao had his own garden. It showed the people that he was a farmer and knew hard labor."

"This is the narrow valley Chiang Kai-shek's bombers flew up to attack the Communists."

On it went, more historic information than I could process. At one location, Yanyuan, where party leaders lived in a landlord's farm, we sauntered down a wide path strewn with yellow autumn leaves dappled in near-winter sunlight. I wanted to cover my ears and just sit for a few minutes to soak up the history that enveloped every path and building without his constant commentary. But on we went to the next building and the next.

Back in the United States several months later, I found an old book by Audrey Topping, who had been in the first journalists' group An Wei had hosted so long ago. In one section she quotes their guide:

> "From March 13, 1947, Chiang Kai-shek's airplanes bombed Yenan[11] day and night," the guide told us. "They dropped bombs into this courtyard and everyone went to the shelter except Chairman Mao.... On March 16 he met with his troops to explain their inferior position. He said, '... Now we must leave Yenan, but this action means we will liberate Nanking and the whole country.'"[12]

I sent a copy of the passage to An Wei and asked if this was the kind of thing he told visitors. Absolutely, he said. I went back to my recordings from Yan'an and realized that An Wei was giving me the same commentary he had delivered to visitors thirty-five years earlier.

· 7 ·

Building a Future

Summer 1973

An Wei pedaled along the dirt track leading out of Yan'an. The small city gave way to a broad, barren valley encircled by hills. The rhythm of his bicycle wheels against dry loess calmed his agitation over the separation from his wife and children. It seemed his family would never be united. A two-week visit each year was pitiful. The last time, two-year-old An Qun did not recognize him. In Yan'an, he tried to lose himself in work, but when he was idle, his longing grew.

Pedaling hard, he turned up a dirt path that rose into the barren hills where local people had lived in caves for centuries. The exertion felt good. As he rounded a bend, he startled an older man and wife wearing tattered clothes. The man had the local turban-like wrap on his head. Their sun-roughened skin, parched and creased from working the unforgiving soil, made them seem one with the earth.

The man stopped digging around the scraggly plants and straightened up.

"What are you working on?" An Wei asked.

"Our vegetables. But we don't have enough water for them," the woman said as she came over to greet him.

An Wei nodded, reaching down to pick up a dirt clod and watching dust fly away as he rubbed it between his fingers. "My parents and brothers are farmers too. They work from dawn to nighttime."

"Do you have enough food in your home?" They nodded, and the husband said they were doing all right for now, but that sometimes they went hungry.

They asked him how many brothers he had. Was he married? Did he have children? These northern farmers were always friendly, no matter their meager existence. Their warm-hearted conversation filled him with satisfaction.

An Wei soon got back on his bicycle and continued on, riding up the path until it was so steep he had to walk the rest of the way, up through eroded gullies to the top of the hill. He stopped to rest on a rock and gazed across the valley, his thoughts turning back to his family. If he shut his eyes, he could imagine An Qun's smile and eagerness to try the words she was learning. He could envision An Xiang's tiny feet and hands when he was first born.

If he ever talked about what he wanted for his families, An Wei would be accused of counterrevolutionary leanings. True revolutionaries, he was told, did not dwell on such trivial matters.

Refreshed by the breezes, he headed the bicycle back down the trail toward town.

An Wei didn't know that at that very moment his future was being reshaped by Lu Man, the director general of the Provincial Foreign Affairs Office in Xi'an, where he had worked after college. Lu Man often brought groups to Yan'an to view the historical sites.

Whenever possible he asked that An Wei interpret for them because of his detailed knowledge of the revolutionary period. An Wei gave them a much richer experience than other interpreters, connecting specific events to various sites. He knew where special meetings were held and important documents signed. He knew what tree Chairman Mao sat under when he lectured his son about learning from the farmers.

During his Yan'an visits, Lu Man sometimes chatted with An Wei. One day he discovered that An Wei had originally worked in the Xi'an Foreign Affairs Office. Although he did not mention it, Lu Man was desperate for qualified English interpreters. He needed An Wei in Xi'an. He had two staff members whose English studies had been halted by the Cultural Revolution. They could complete simple tasks but had no ability to interpret.

Because of the Cultural Revolution, however, even the director general had little clout. Nor did his other position as deputy secretary general of the Provincial Committee of the Communist Party do any good, even though it meant he managed all departments and worked on behalf of the governor. But Lu Man persisted.

October 1974

One fall day as An Wei sat down at his desk in Yan'an, his boss came in.

"We just got a notice. You are being transferred to Xi'an."

An Wei stopped breathing. "What office said that?"

"We have no idea," his boss told him. "We just have this message from the Provincial Committee. That's all we know. You need to go to Xi'an and register."

Shocked, An Wei thought it must be a transfer to the factory where his wife worked. His long-ago request was finally being granted. He called Niu Jianhua and then her parents. Everyone was ecstatic.

Over the next few days, An Wei finished remaining projects as quickly as possible and went to the local police station to transfer his household registration from Yan'an to Xi'an. In his room, he hummed as he fitted his belongings—mainly books and a few clothes—into a wooden suitcase made by a local carpenter. At a going-away gathering in the Yan'an office, he said a warm good-bye to the small staff. He would miss them. They had shared many good times together. But his excitement to leave was palpable. He had been separated from Niu Jianhua for nearly five years.

The next morning, as the autumn sun rose over the valley, An Wei boarded the southbound bus. His suitcase and quilt stowed, he settled into a seat, the official transfer notice safe in a jacket pocket. As the bus rumbled past the dry gullies and rugged hills, he wondered about the aircraft factory. What *would* his job be? Would it involve speaking English? Could he use any of the skills he had developed in Yan'an, especially interpreting? In truth, he didn't care what job they gave him as long as it was near his family. He even dared to wonder if they would be assigned a place to live together as a family, as improbable though that was.

The Danwei (Work Unit) and Living Arrangements

By 1960, Chinese society had been organized into *danweis* (work units) such as a factory, a government office, or a village. Each was run by a party branch office that followed the rules and procedures of the Chinese Communist Party. A danwei was usually a physically distinct living and work unit. A person's life revolved around that community. A large urban danwei often included a childcare center, all levels of schooling, housing, a healthcare facility, recreational facilities, and a factory or other work facilities. It was usually surrounded by a wall, and gatekeepers monitored the comings and goings of individuals. Danwei members were often born there, attended school there, worked there, met their spouse there, raised their children, and retired there. The danwei leadership assigned housing, provided wages, approved marriages, controlled when a couple could have a child, provided pensions, and oversaw political study sessions. In order to travel to another city, written permission was usually required in order to buy a ticket and to get food while away.[1]

Niu Jianhua, An Wei's wife, was assigned to a large aircraft factory danwei. She lived in a dormitory provided by the danwei, worked there, ate her meals there, received a small wage, and attended political meetings there. That danwei, and many others, did not provide childcare. When she flew to Yan'an to give birth to their second child, many levels of approval were required by her work unit and An Wei's. When An Wei worked for the Foreign Affairs Office, he was a member of its danwei. The one in Xi'an was overseen by Shaanxi Province and was much larger than the one in Yan'an. Unlike most, it was not surrounded by a wall, and housing, often very limited, was located in different parts of the city.

Villages were also considered danweis, but these agricultural organizations provided less to their residents. A party branch office oversaw land allocation, approved marriages, and gave permission to have a baby. But these danweis seldom had health facilities or provided pensions. They did give—or withhold—permission to receive food in other locations. This is why An Wei had very little food his first year of college. His village leader refused to provide him with written verification that he qualified for a food stipend.

Because China's economy has been liberalized since the 1990s, much of the danweis' power has eroded as they compete with private enterprise and changing social patterns.

*   *   *

When An Wei's bus pulled into the Xi'an station, the sun was sinking below the western horizon. He gathered his belongings and headed for Niu Jianhua's family home. Everyone was excited to see him. Shy An Qun peeked from behind Niu Jianhua's legs, but she recognized him. After a few minutes their three-year-old daughter was jumping up and down, her wispy black hair, pulled into two bunches, bouncing with her, and she had begun to talk a lot. But An Xiang, age two, was wary of this new visitor.

The next morning, An Wei reported to the Organization Department of the Provincial Committee of the Communist Party to register. It was in charge of placements for all jobs in the province. He handed his transfer notice to a clerk.

"Thank you for transferring me to the factory."

"What factory?" the clerk asked.

"Factory 172, Hong'an Gongsi, the aircraft factory," An Wei replied.

"You are assigned to the Foreign Affairs Office, not that factory."

Puzzled, An Wei said, "There must be a mistake. I requested Hong'an Gongsi."

"That's impossible. Lu Man wrote this request. He wants you at the Foreign Affairs Office here in Xi'an where he is the director."

Head spinning, An Wei took a bus to the Foreign Affairs Office and requested to see Lu Man, who he realized must have worked hard for the transfer. But An Wei could not stop himself from asking about the factory. The director's response left no doubt: "That factory job is impossible. We need you here. We need English interpreters."

Desperate, An Wei persisted, even though stating his personal needs was ill advised. His hands underscored every word as he spoke. "We have two young children and no one to care for them. We are separated in every direction. After all these years, we want to live together."

An Xiang, two years old; An Qun, three years old. *Source*: An Wei.

"It is impossible," Lu Man said. He added, however, that he would work on their housing.

That was it. He and Niu Jianhua would be separated by a two-hour bus ride. Her factory was well outside Xi'an.

Dejected, but glad at least to be back in Xi'an, An Wei registered for work at the Foreign Affairs Office. At least he might encounter interesting visitors coming to this important provincial office. Also, he knew Lu Man to be an honest man who, if he made a promise, would keep it if he could.

The next day An Wei said good-bye to his family and rode buses to the People's Hotel where the Foreign Affairs Office was now housed. He was assigned to share a basement room with another man. It was tiny, but nothing else was available.

Xi'an had changed little in five years. Few shops existed because everything was still run by the government. The only major difference was that there were no longer rallies to torture those accused of being Capitalist Roaders. The Cultural Revolution wasn't over, but such public demonstrations had given way to workplace study, with repeated readings about the evils of revisionism and the "four olds": old customs, old culture, old habits, and old ideas.

Food was still rationed, and everything was in short supply. Though he and Niu Jianhua now had two young children, their salaries were a meager forty-eight and a half yuan a month, the same as when they had left college. They would not get a raise until after Mao Zedong's death in 1976.

Pleased to have a qualified interpreter, Lu Man made extensive use of An Wei, who found himself much busier than in Yan'an. The protocols were similar, but the provincial office had many more administrative and bureaucratic layers.

An Wei was responsible for planning trips for foreign delegations and individual government guests who usually wanted to see ancient locales. The most popular was Banpo Neolithic Village, a remarkable site dating back about six thousand years. Other attractions included the Wild Goose Pagoda—not far from where An Wei had attended college—and the Forest of Steles with magnificent writing engraved in rock tablets that were housed in an old Confucian temple.

Winter soon closed in. Although Xi'an was not as cold as Yan'an, there would be few visitors until spring. The office staff members turned to studying every word of the *People's Daily* and discussing government documents, the routine An Wei had practiced for almost ten years. They wrote down what they had done during the week that was wrong or what was good, and what they would do next week, always referring to Mao Zedong's dictums.

An Wei began to notice that government directives seesawed back and forth as different factions gained control. What was absolutely important one year was declared trash the next. This year Confucianism and Lin Biao, who had once been Mao Zedong's heir apparent, were vilified.

Once spring sap finally pushed open new leaves and visiting groups began returning to China, An Wei's first assignment was to plan the visit of former British prime minister Edward Heath. Although it was a great honor, thirty-two-year-old An Wei found it a frightening responsibility.

Following detailed protocols, he studied Heath's requests and developed an hour-by-hour schedule, starting with arrival ceremonies and a banquet to be provided by the provincial governor. Once the Beijing Foreign Ministry approved his plan, An Wei pored over everything he could learn about policies and events affecting Britain and China. The United Kingdom had been quick to recognize the new country, but in 1967, massive riots had erupted in the British colony of Hong Kong, instigated by leftists supported by the Chinese government. The same year, a mob of Red Guards ransacked the British Legation in Beijing. Despite those tensions, the countries exchanged ambassadors, and diplomatic relations were normalized.

At the Xi'an airport, An Wei paced anxiously as he waited for the British delegation to arrive. Would he be able to understand Edward Heath's accent? Had he learned enough about current events to comprehend whatever was said? He fingered the buttons on his dark Sun Yatsen jacket to make sure it was buttoned properly. As the plane doors opened, An Wei stood erect and waited.

He was surprised at how tall and stocky Edward Heath was compared to the average Chinese man. Even though Heath was only in his late fifties, his hair was almost completely white, and like most Westerners, he seemed to bound as he walked, propelling his big frame forward. His face serious, Heath shook each official's hand and then An Wei's.

Once the delegation was settled at the Xi'an hotel, An Wei made sure banquet preparations were moving along. The beginning of any visit set the tone, especially the formal banquet toasts, and he wanted to make sure this one was perfect.

An Wei watched as the banquet hall filled with talkative guests and then took his seat at the head table. The governor of Shaanxi Province rose, raised his glass, and began to speak, and An Wei began interpreting. The Chinese governor welcomed the prime minister and highlighted the importance of friendship between the two nations. An Wei's words followed easily. But when Prime Minister Heath stood and raised his glass, An Wei could feel tension clenching his back and neck. English did not fit neatly into Chinese phrases. Much to his relief, however, his Chinese words came easily. When he delivered the last bit of interpretation, he took a deep breath and relaxed.

As the rest of the days passed, the prime minister's serious expression gave way to smiles. He seemed to love learning about ancient China. By the time An Wei wrote his final report, he was sure the trip had been a success. Heads of state were not so terrifying after all. That was good to know, since he would be interpreting for many more. Next would be the queen of the Netherlands.

Unlike Yan'an, Xi'an throbbed with activities. It had been China's capital during ancient dynasties. From here, long camel caravans laden with coveted spices, silks, tea, and salt had begun their journey across continents on what was known as the "Silk Road." The city continued to be a transportation hub in modern China. And its antiquities, which included one of China's few remaining intact city walls, drew foreign visitors, many of whom also wanted to see Yan'an. An Wei was put in charge of those excursions too because of his command of its history.

Often responsible for two or three groups a week, An Wei worked non-stop. Much to the annoyance of some fellow workers, his interpreting abilities, coupled with his careful planning skills, made him the most important staff member in the provincial office.

But An Wei grew increasingly frustrated with his housing situation. Niu Jianhua had been loaned to an aircraft engine company in Xi'an and lived in its guesthouse. An Wei remained holed up in the small basement room of the Foreign Affairs Office, and their children lived with different relatives. The family could only be together Saturday evenings and Sunday at the home of Niu Jianhua's parents.

In late summer 1975, however, Lu Man told An Wei that although housing throughout China remained extremely scarce, he had managed to rent two apartments. In the first apartment, the smaller room went to a French interpreter, Mr. Yu, and his wife; the larger room would go to An Wei and his family. Another family plus a couple moved into the second apartment. Everyone shared the public toilet in the hallway. There was nowhere to bathe, but each apartment had a tiny kitchen, a luxury for most people in China.

Because they needed An Wei's mother to stay with them to care for their infant son, they decided they should leave An Qun at her grandparents where she had been all her life. Although they sorely missed An Qun, the couple's worries and anxieties about family matters began to ease.

A double and a single bed filled most of their one-room dwelling with almost wall-to-wall bedding, but even this tiny space was a treasure. They kept a cooking pot under their bed, ate around a tiny low table on small wooden stools, and tucked the toilet pail, used mainly at night, into a corner. Niu Jian-hua cooked all their meals, preparing everything on a board stretched across their bed, then cooking on the coal stove in the little shared kitchen. After years of tolerating stomach pains, An Wei was finally eating healthy meals that helped him begin to heal from the damage caused by the Nanniwan diet.

Just as the family had settled into a satisfying routine, the Foreign Affairs Office announced in November that An Wei and four others must go to the countryside to help the farmers of Huxian County. For the next several months, he lived there, helping two Cultural Revolution factions resolve their disagreements.

Once again, Niu Jianhua, the children, and he endured separation.

	Apartment One			Apartment Two	
Stairs	Mr. Yu & wife	An-Wei & family	Big room (Another family)	Small room (A couple)
	Kitchen	Doorway			Kitchen
Stairs		Corridor			Public Toilet

The first Xi'an apartment where An Wei and Niu Jianhua lived with some of their family, from 1975 until 1978. *Source*: Drawn by An Wei on his computer, 2014.

* * *

Throughout the next year, events shook China. In January 1976, three months into his stay in Huxian County, An Wei was saddened to hear of Zhou Enlai's death on the radio. The ultimate diplomat, Zhou Enlai had served as China's premier and kept China connected to other countries despite the upheavals at home. In later life, however, he was persecuted as a traitor along with other survivors of the Long March. Still, the Chinese people cried as if they had lost a family member.[2] But Mao Zedong's wife, Jiang Qing, who controlled the government media and propaganda, delivered a final insult, prohibiting the public from mourning their beloved leader.[3]

Six months later, a massive earthquake struck Hebei Province, east of Beijing, that triggered an ancient and well-ingrained belief among the Chinese people that such natural calamities predicted the overthrow of dynasties.

Less than two months later, on September 9, 1976, a radio message blared the news across China: Mao Zedong was dead. Shocked citizens clasped their little red books of the Great Helmsman's words and mourned.

Since 1949, they had followed his directives. Despite the hardships caused by his errors and erratic policies, Chairman Mao was god to many, his words memorized by the vast population. Even those who criticized him, albeit secretly, knew he had dragged the country out of its decrepit state and that his thoughts had shaped the new China.

By 1978, Deng Xiaoping had consolidated enough influence to assume leadership of the country, and he began to promote a market economy. The Foreign Affairs staff became even busier, and An Wei felt proud to serve as a bridge between foreigners and China. Neither his ancestors nor his parents could have dreamed of such a possibility. But the bureaucracy of the big provincial office was wearing him down.

What would have taken two hours to accomplish in Yan'an took two weeks in Xi'an. He watched as a typical request, which had been faxed by an American professor who wanted to visit historic sites, moved from one staff member to another, taking four days to reach someone in authority who could act on it. But that person required several more days to have the request translated before he could pass it on to the director general for approval. Then the director, who worried about making the wrong decision, called a meeting of his associates. After lengthy discussion, they agreed to the professor's request, at which point it took several more days of writing, editing, and translating before a response was sent back to the professor.

Woven into this inefficient morass were people with no skills. Some were political appointees, but many were victims of the Cultural Revolution. Their education had come to an abrupt halt in 1966 when schools closed, leading to a ten-year gap of knowledge and skills throughout the country. Some staff members in the Foreign Affairs Office, including the two English translators who had only one year of college, did everything they could to be helpful and try to improve. But others spent their time playing cards, smoking, and fawning over leaders. They found An Wei irritating. Why didn't he socialize more or smoke? Why didn't he play cards or mah-jongg with them?

An Wei felt it was immoral to sit around doing nothing. He was the only member of his family to have had the privilege of an advanced education, and he believed he should use it. Besides, he had the habits of a farmer. To survive in the countryside, farmers had to act quickly before bad weather ruined their crops. "I'll harvest the corn next week" was not an option. Hunger always lurked in the background.

Shortly after becoming the country's leader, Deng Xiaoping launched a new government initiative that pushed An Wei to want to leave the Foreign Affairs Office. Called "Make It Clear" or "Say Clearly,"[4] it required people in every work unit or organization throughout China to spend two days a week or a few hours a day in meetings, telling others what they had done during the Cultural Revolution.

Did you participate in beatings, looting, or other violence?

Did you write or make public speeches against the revolutionary head-quarters of Chairman Mao?

Each person was required to make a confession. Staff members would then comment on what each person said. Similar in tone to the debilitating McCarthy-era anti-Communist sentiment in the United States, this new movement left many in An Wei's generation feeling trapped. If they had not followed Mao Zedong's orders during the Cultural Revolution, ruthless Red Guards would have attacked them. If they had participated, they would now be accused of wrongful actions, which could prevent them from future promotions. He and his peers were furious at those who kept trying to "find bones in the egg."

In order to collect information about what An Wei had done in those past years, the office sent staff members to track down people who had known him. Those who did not like him could say anything they wanted. Although he could never be certain, he was convinced he was tagged as suspicious in his records. Niu Jianhua was investigated too, but since she was not a party member, it was not as intense.

Fed up, An Wei began looking for another job. He was increasingly drawn to the university atmosphere and to his old high school dream of becoming a professional writer. That career path was still too dangerous, but An Wei's continued love of literature and writing tugged at him. If he moved to a university, perhaps he could get out from under the government bureaucracy.

While taking visiting groups to the Shaanxi Teachers University, An Wei became acquainted with the university's president and the chair of the English Department. Through the accepted means of dropping hints, he let them know he would like to work there. They were enthusiastic. His knowledge of English was strong, and transfers to a university were usually easy since many preferred government work. But Director General Lu Man refused. The workload was increasing, he said, making An Wei essential to the Foreign Affairs Office.

Another opportunity to improve his situation soon came his way. The government began a master's degree program, and in 1978, anybody in the country could apply. Without telling others, he registered. It was important to keep it confidential, because if he failed, it would mean a great loss of face. Moreover, if anyone in the Foreign Affairs Office reported it to the director general, that could be disastrous because Lu Man was still trying to find better housing for An Wei and his family.

An Wei passed the master's program exam and was admitted to the American literature program at prestigious Nanjing University. Acceptance in hand, he went to his immediate supervisor, the section chief. But both he and another section chief said that Lu Man would never agree to it and he should let it go. It was a time when changing jobs was very difficult in China, so An Wei set aside that dream.

By late summer 1978, Lu Man delivered on his promise. An Wei and Niu Jianhua were assigned their first apartment, just in time for An Qun to begin school. With two rooms of their own and a kitchen in the hallway, the whole family could finally live together and have an apartment to themselves. In one room they set up a big bed that took up most of the floor space. The other room became their living area where An Wei worked at night at a newly acquired writing desk. They still had to use the public baths, but it was a joy to be together.

Even better, Niu Jianhua was transferred to Xi'an Technical University, which was connected to the aircraft and space industry. There she taught English only three days a week, which gave her more time to spend with An Qun and An Xiang.

The ever-energetic An Qun was happy to be with her parents and she loved school, but she missed her grandparents, with whom she had lived her entire life. Her grandpa missed her so much that every Saturday afternoon he met her at the school gate and took her home for the rest of the weekend.

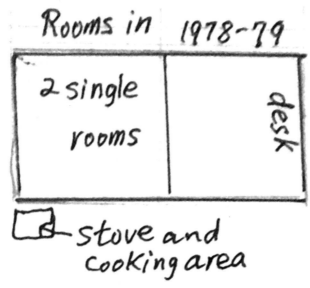

An Wei's first apartment with his whole family. *Source*: Drawn by An Wei, August 2016.

October 1978

When the director of the Xi'an Foreign Affairs Office asked him to plan a trip for a group that wanted to film in Xi'an and Yan'an, An Wei looked at the list of names and nearly leaped up from his desk. The group's leader was Helen Snow, whose book *Inside Red China* he had read enthusiastically at the Yan'an History Museum. He had been enthralled by her daring visit to interview Mao Zedong.

Detailed plans poured from his pen. He scheduled all the places her film crew had requested and added others he thought would be important to her. Best of all, he was to be the interpreter for her videographer and to make sure they got from one place to the next on time.

Looking out the plane window, Helen Snow scanned the list of requested locations her friend and videographer, Tim Considine, had sent ahead to the Xi'an Foreign Affairs Office, hoping the staff could squeeze their many requests into the schedule. She jotted down a few more. Shots of the railway station would be good as it was where she had arrived in 1937.

As the plane crossed the rugged Lü Liang Mountains, she recalled her time in Xi'an and Yan'an so long ago.

In 1936, she and her husband, Edgar, were tantalized by rumors that the Communists, after a horrendous six-thousand-mile trek to escape Chiang Kai-shek's troops, were holed up in northwest China and planning their next moves. Few in Beijing seemed to know much about the Communists, yet Chiang Kai-shek considered them a big-enough threat to spend enormous amounts of money and manpower trying to wipe them out. The couple decided that Edgar should try to make the dangerous trip to interview Mao Zedong. Accompanied by a sympathetic young interpreter, Huang Hua, Edgar Snow headed west by train.

Several months later, their dogs barked ferociously at the painfully thin but ecstatic Edgar as he stood before Helen. He had been amazed at what he found in the Communist area of Bao'an—discipline, intense writing and thinking about political and military theory, and plenty of hospitality. And he had been able to interview Mao Zedong himself several times. Miraculously, he had made it back with all his notebooks and a bag of films—material Chiang Kai-shek's minions would have killed him for had they known. He had information the world longed for.[5]

Edgar was soon consumed with writing what would become *Red Star Over China*. As he wrote, Helen had felt her own urgency to understand the revolutionary movements of China, as well as frustration at being in the shadow of a famous husband.

In 1937, the couple decided that she should attempt the dangerous journey to Yan'an. She made it to Xi'an even though the political and military situation had become more perilous. Chiang Kai-shek had intensified his campaign to destroy the Communists and to kill students or anyone else deemed a threat. When she checked into the Xi'an Guesthouse, where all foreigners had to stay, four armed guards met her. They had been assigned by Chiang Kai-shek's staff to make sure she did not reach the Red Army areas.

Precious days sped by while she tried to make contact with anyone who could help connect her with the Communists. As a subterfuge for her Xi'an presence, she visited historic sites and called on Western missionaries who were annoyed by her persistent attempts to find a way to the north. Finally she was befriended by the head of Standard Oil who, though disapproving of her mission, was willing to assist a lone woman's efforts.

Her escape night was set. At a signal she would climb over the guesthouse wall to meet the executive.

Well past midnight, as the four armed guards slept in the next room and soldiers patrolled beyond the walls, she put on all the clothes she could wear, arranged her blankets to look as though she was still in bed, and then jumped out the guesthouse window. Not finding her contact waiting at the wall, she hid in the darkness and then decided to bolt for the main gate. She managed to talk her way past guards, commandeer a rickshaw, and make it to the next meeting point. There she met an opium-saturated driver, who sped her in a car "borrowed" from one of Chiang's generals through the guarded city gates and along mud-thick roads to a rendezvous point with the Red Army liaison. From there it was a ten-day slog by car, horse, and foot to reach Yan'an.

For the next months, suffering from increasingly debilitating dysentery, she managed to interview Mao Zedong and the military leader, Zhu De. This gave Edgar valuable materials he was missing as well as photos he needed for his book. She also collected scores of biographies of young officers who would eventually become China's leaders, along with the stories of many influential women, including those who had survived the Long March.

Now, decades later, she was going to visit and shoot video at all the places that 1937 trip had taken her.

On a sunny October day, An Wei stood restlessly on the tarmac and watched the plane from Beijing land. He rocked toe to heel and back as the stairs were rolled forward and waited while passengers collected their belongings.

Soon a short, elderly woman appeared at the exit door, a red plaid tam o'shanter on her gray hair and a matching shawl thrown jauntily about her shoulders. Helen Snow looked around as if imagining her arrival forty years earlier and then slowly headed down the stairs to greet Lu Man, the director general of the Foreign Affairs Office. Her film crew followed, hauling video equipment to waiting cars. Lu Man gave a formal greeting, An Wei introduced himself to the videographer, and they all climbed into the cars for the trip to the hotel.

Once they had settled into their rooms, Helen Snow and her crew gathered around An Wei in the hotel's small conference room. He wanted to make sure they agreed with his plans and understood it would be a tight schedule. He greeted each of them and felt more excited to meet Helen Snow than he had at meeting Prime Minister Edward Heath.

While a hotel attendant poured hot water over the loose tea in each person's cup, An Wei went over the usual sites they would visit in Xi'an—the Drum Tower, Banpo Village, and the Wild Goose Pagoda. Next, he listed their requested locales, including the hot springs where Chiang Kai-shek had been kidnapped. Helen Snow asked question after question, her speech rapid like a fast-moving machine. An Wei listened intently to every word, hoping he understood her correctly.

He next led them through a list of places they would visit around Yan'an: Bao'an, where the Red Army had first ended its Long March and where Edgar Snow had interviewed Mao Zedong, and the various revolutionary sites,

Helen Snow (*center*) and An Wei (*second from the right*) during her trip to Xi'an and Yan'an, 1978. *Source*: An Wei.

starting with Phoenix Mountain. Finally, he said he had added a few others: the newly discovered terracotta army, which was not yet open to the public, and the guesthouse from which Helen Snow had escaped.

She stopped him.

"How do you know so much revolutionary history? About the sites and where Edgar Snow interviewed the chairman? And that I escaped from the guesthouse?"

An Wei briefly explained his work at the history museum and the Foreign Affairs Office in Yan'an. She was amazed that he knew their books and that he had spent years in the very places she had lived in 1937.

That night, at the opening banquet, Helen Snow made the expected formal toast. She praised her hosts for the plans they had made and for their generous hospitality and thoughtfulness. She just had one request. She said she had discovered that the young man from Lu Man's office not only spoke good English but also knew Chinese revolutionary history in the 1930s and was familiar with her own China experiences. She paused.

"Beginning from tomorrow, I want An Wei to sit in my car, and I hope you will agree with this."[6]

From then on he interpreted for Helen Snow many times during the trip and occasionally talked with her about her experiences.

A few months later, an envelope from the United States addressed to An Wei arrived at the Foreign Affairs Office. It was from Helen Snow. Pleased that she remembered him, but careful to follow the strict protocol, he did not respond. He read it and passed it on to his superiors. Interpreters should interpret; that was all. No secret communications were allowed between staff and foreign visitors.[7]

Later in the month, while An Wei was helping an American group check out of a Xi'an hotel room, he spotted books in their trash.

"Are you throwing those out?" he asked.

A silver-haired woman nodded. "Can you use them?"

She picked up the two children's books, *Charlie and the Chocolate Factory* and *Mr. Popper's Penguins*, and handed them to him.

Later, when he read An Qun and An Xiang the beginning pages of *Charlie and the Chocolate Factory*, they were thrilled and pleaded for more.

When An Wei had a chance, he translated more sections for them. In the process, he realized that the two books could help solve a serious problem. He was desperate to improve his English-to-Chinese interpreting because he still had trouble understanding casual conversations in English. Each day he interpreted for someone different: an agricultural official from a Western government, next a group of medical professionals, and then a writer. Before meeting with each group, he studied its members' backgrounds and interests, but that was not enough. Translating *Charlie and the Chocolate Factory* would improve his idiomatic English while delighting An Qun and An Xiang. Because foreign groups stopped visiting in cold weather, he looked forward to spending winter nights at home translating the books from English into Chinese.

In mid-November, however, An Wei was told he must spend several months in the countryside again.

How could they do this to him? Not only were they sending him away from his family again, but also they were taking him away from his nights of translating.

Filled with anger, he did the unthinkable. He refused to go.

Told he must obey, he argued with his bosses. His words poured out. He had grown up a farmer and had been sent to Nanniwan for a year and a half, to Huxian for four months the year before, and to yet another rural area for several months. That was enough. What about the office staff members that had *never* been sent to the countryside? They should have the experience, rather than this farmer, he told them.

"When everyone in this office has gone at least once, I will go for the fifth time, but not until then."

His boss backed off. In later years, An Wei said this was the first and only time he successfully refused an order. But it left him with the conviction that as long as you speak the truth publicly, and so long as the leaders have made a wrong decision, they have no way to force you to do anything.

December 1978

Wrapped in the warmest clothes he could pile on, An Wei stamped his icy-cold feet and placed them carefully back on the hot water bottle he had refilled. The apartment was freezing when he got up at 3:00 a.m. to translate *Charlie and the Chocolate Factory*, and it seemed to get colder as dawn neared. But he loved the task he had set himself. It was so much better than the boring daytime meetings to endure at the Foreign Affairs Office.

He sucked in a swallow of tea, letting the hot liquid spread across his tongue and then warm his throat. With pen in hand, he pushed a stack of books to one side and moved his pages of Chinese translation to a convenient place on the desk. An Xiang coughed in his sleep, still tucked under the heavy cotton quilts with Niu Jianhua and An Qun in the other room. At his request, his wife and children were now going to bed at 7:00 or 8:00 p.m. so he could get some sleep and then wake up to translate in the main room of their apartment the rest of the night.

A truck rumbled by in the street below as An Wei concentrated on a passage, pondering how to put the English into Chinese. They were so different. He read the sentences again: "Only once a year, on his birthday, did Charlie Bucket ever get to taste a bit of chocolate. The whole family saved up their money for that special occasion, and when the great day arrived, Charlie was always presented with one small chocolate bar to eat by himself."[8] An Wei skipped ahead to see what might be a challenge to translate on the next page; then he began making notes of words he needed to look up in the Chinese/ English dictionary. It was difficult—and sometimes tedious—work, but the story delighted him. When he finished this chapter, he knew that he would have enough to read some more to the children. He could already imagine An Qun running off to tell her friends about Charlie's adventures.

Spring 1979

Along with the new leaves on trees lining the ancient city wall, spring brought a stream of new visitors to Xi'an. Even before US president Jimmy Carter formally opened diplomatic relations with China on January 1, 1979, its leader, Deng Xiaoping, had been encouraging connections with other countries. As more and more foreign groups came to Xi'an, An Wei's mastery of English grew.

Standing straight in his dark Sun Yatsen jacket and trousers, his body finally recovered from years of deprivation, a handsome, relaxed An Wei greeted visiting dignitaries with ease and confidence. He shared his vast knowledge of the city and the history of modern China with one group after another. In late April US secretary of state Henry Kissinger arrived in Xi'an, where he was heralded for negotiating the meeting between US president Richard M. Nixon and Mao Zedong several years earlier. Interpreting Kissinger's German-accented English was a challenge for An Wei, but he enjoyed their brief time together. Next came the US vice president Walter Mondale.

The spontaneity of Americans, especially politicians, never ceased to surprise him. In August 1979, while traveling in an entourage of thirty cars, Mondale noticed a line of singing children on their way home from school. He asked his driver to stop and sprang from the car. An Wei jumped out after him. Curious, the children pressed around this foreigner. The vice president, with An Wei's help, started asking questions.

"How old are you?"

"What school do you attend?"

"What do you study in school?"

As they answered, the vice president chatted on.

An Wei interpreting for Henry Kissinger, 1979. *Source*: An Wei.

But behind them, a huge traffic jam had formed. All the cars in the entourage had screeched to a halt, along with numerous trucks and buses. Panic-stricken security guards rushed to see what was wrong.

The vice president explained that he just wanted to say hello to the children. But seeing the commotion he had created, he quickly headed back to his car.

An Wei planned, prepared, led, and interpreted for one group after another that spring and summer. Amid the whirlwind, he received a second letter from Helen Snow. She enclosed an article she had written about the visit she and her video crew had made to the small town of Bao'an the year before.

He read the letter and her article carefully. Though receiving it was still awkward, he was overwhelmed that this famous woman had written him twice. He dutifully passed the letter on to his bosses but decided to keep and translate the article. When he finished, An Wei sent it off to the Yan River literary magazine whose editors made it the centerpiece of their edition celebrating the thirtieth year of the People's Republic of China. This time he wrote back to Helen Snow and had the Foreign Affairs Office messenger mail her a copy of the magazine.

· 8 ·

American Connections

Early 1979, Connecticut

Thousands of miles away, events were happening that would affect An Wei's life.

In Madison, Connecticut, Helen Snow sat in her carton-filled living room carefully combing through the files and memorabilia she had shipped from China decades before. She smiled when she finally found the message from Mao Zedong to Deng Xiaoping, now vice premier of China. Deng was in the United States to formalize the normalization of relations between the United States and China. Helen had been invited to attend a banquet for him in Washington, DC, and Tim Considine, her videographer and long-time friend, had persuaded her to attend, suggesting this was her chance to deliver that old note.[1]

In 1937, the Chinese Communists and Nationalists and the Japanese were at war when Helen had tried to leave Yan'an after spending five months there interviewing people committed to the Communist Party. She asked Mao Zedong for help. She thought that if she carried war correspondent credentials, she could get back to Beijing. Though dubious that this dysentery-ridden, hundred-pound woman would succeed at such a task, Mao Zedong wrote a note to Deng Xiaoping, then head of the Red Army, asking him to aid Helen if he could. By the time she reached the front, however, Deng and his troops had already left to fight the Japanese. She tucked the note carefully inside her coat and hunted for other means of safe passage.

At the glittering reception in the nation's capital, Helen Snow, dressed in her exquisite Chinese silk jacket, approached the reception line where Deng Xiaoping stood flanked by other Chinese officials. She politely held out Mao Zedong's note to Vice Premier Deng with both her hands, a broad grin spreading across her face. The other Chinese, recognizing Chairman Mao's handwriting, gathered closer.

Deng Xiaoping took the note.

"You are a very difficult person to catch up with," she said.

They all had a good laugh. Tim Considine, who had escorted her, snapped a photo, and a few days later a *New York Times* article appeared.[2]

At her beach house in Madison, Connecticut, Sharon Crain put down that *New York Times* article and picked up the phone book. An attractive middle-aged woman with wavy brown shoulder-length hair, she had been an activist determined to improve relations between the United States and China since her college days and was well read on everything about Chinese affairs. Over the last few days, she had immersed herself in the myriad articles chronicling Deng Xiaoping's US visit. But it was the last paragraph in the *Times'* article that excited her. Helen Snow also lived in Madison, Connecticut, only a few miles away.

Sharon had long been enthralled by Edgar Snow's *Red Star Over China* and Helen Snow's *Inside Red China.* Why hadn't she known that this important woman lived nearby?

She found the number and dialed.

"Hello?" Helen Snow's voice was unexpectedly high pitched, though reserved.

Sharon's eyes sparkled as she gripped her phone tightly, nervous at making this call. She told Helen she had studied China for years, had traveled to China and read her book.

"I would be honored to meet you," Sharon continued. "Would it be possible to come visit you?"

"Well, I don't know. I will have to think about it," came the response. Sharon could feel resistance in the terseness that wrapped around Helen's every word.

Several phone calls later, having convinced Helen of her genuine interest, Sharon pulled up to a white clapboard house on Mungertown Road. It was like so many of the town's colonial homes, but it looked tired and was overgrown with trees and low-hanging limbs. The front door, partially hidden by uncut bushes, was obviously not the normal entrance. Sharon followed a well-worn path around to the side of the home, crossed the deck strewn with remnants of food for animals in bent aluminum tins, and knocked on the side door. A voice called, "Come in."

Helen Snow sat at her cluttered desk. Vines climbed to the ceiling and across windows. Knickknacks, mainly Chinese and some probably quite valuable, crowded bookshelves. A heavy cardigan hung over her comfortably loose shirt and pants. Sharon estimated Helen to be about seventy years old. She looked tired, yet her eyes had an alertness that Sharon could not ignore.

Helen pushed herself up—followed by her old, scraggly cat named Mao—and led Sharon into the front room stacked with paper-filled grocery boxes. Sharon gazed around the room as she sat down in an old chair. Cartons were stacked nearly to the ceiling. Above the unused fireplace hung an oil painting of Helen stunningly beautiful in her youth.

Sharon told Helen Snow a little bit about her own background and explained how valuable she had found her book and Edgar Snow's. Helen talked of her time in China, sharing a lot of historic detail, especially about her months in Yan'an.

Helen mentioned a trip to New York for a reception for the country's foreign minister, Huang Hua, who had been a good friend of the Snows in Beijing. But Sharon realized that the New York and Washington trips were probably her only excursions in recent years. After an amazingly active life in China, she had become a hermit—and from the looks of her house, she was poor.

Concerned not to overstay her welcome, Sharon got up to leave, telling Helen how much she admired her.

"If I can help you in any way, just call me if you need something."

Helen responded, "I'm too important to give you a call." But she added that Sharon could call her.

Since Helen did not drive, she agreed to let Sharon run frequent errands and especially to making six copies of everything she wrote. Since her divorce from Edgar Snow, when he left her for another woman, she wrote constantly, primarily about China.

Sharon took advantage of every opportunity to listen to tales of the Snows' involvement in tumultuous 1930s China. She was eager to learn and willing to help Helen, even though "thank you" seemed an unknown expression. Helen was an unpolished diamond hidden from public view. Her knowledge of a critical period of modern China was enormous, and somehow she could find whatever document she wanted in her myriad cartons.

Helen spoke almost solely about her own interests and had opinions about everything. When Chinese officials, who had known Helen and Edgar well during their student days, visited her, she told Sharon to buy them meals from McDonald's.

Reacting to Sharon's surprised look, Helen said, "The Chinese spend far too much time cooking. They should just get down to talking instead. They need to learn about fast food."

One evening, Helen told Sharon to hide in the bushes near her deck and gave her detailed instructions on how to photograph a three-legged raccoon Helen had befriended. Trying to ignore the mosquitoes, Sharon waited for the raccoon, named Twasi, to get used to her scent. After an impossibly long time,

Twasi loped gingerly onto the porch with her uneven gait and reached for some food morsels. Her camera flash went off, perfectly timed. Helen loved the photo. But that was only one small bond Sharon made on the long road to gaining Helen Snow's trust.

As months passed, Helen began giving Sharon copies of her manuscripts to send to publishers. She also asked her to help Madame Sun Yatsen's adopted daughter, who was attending college in New England.

Wanting to help this unique woman who had been face-to-face with Mao Zedong, Sharon rose to the challenge.

Eventually she persuaded Helen, who was leery of strangers and public outings, to come to her beach home for her favorite lunch—tuna salad and a Coke. Helen adored the beach, and Sharon began taking her there regularly to spend hours swimming and reading. Gradually Helen began to trust that Sharon loved China and wanted to learn from her.

One day as the women relaxed on the deck watching the water lap the pebbled beach, Sharon mentioned that she would be leading a group of Americans on a trip to China.

"Are there places I should show them in China, or people I should introduce them to?" Sharon asked.

Helen sat upright quickly.

"You have got to meet An Wei! It's worth a trip to Xi'an. He is one of the best and the brightest in China."

Sharon leaned forward to hear better.

An Wei, Helen said enthusiastically, was different from others. He knew how to get things done, and he was very organized. "You have to get to know him!"

The next day, unbeknownst to Sharon, Helen wrote An Wei to tell him of all that Sharon had done for her and that he must meet her.[3]

Soon afterward, An Wei began to correspond with Sharon, and they eventually met in Xi'an in spring 1981. Each was thrilled to find another person dedicated to helping Helen Snow, for they both understood the value of her work.

In the summer of 1980, Helen received the Yan River literary magazine with the article of her Bao'an trip with An Wei. Pleased he had translated it into Chinese, she called a Yale University professor of Chinese. She wanted to assess An Wei's translating abilities. Was his work accurate? Did it read well? Once the professor reassured her that it was good, she shifted into high gear, sending An Wei more articles, plus long letters about her ideas. Her letters were too frequent, though, to receive at a government office without drawing unwanted attention, so he had her send everything to Niu Jianhua at her university.

Although it was not always easy reading, Helen's writing was full of information: capsule biographies of key players in China's revolutionary times, in-depth interviews of women who had survived the Long March, and important dates and places. Her attention to detail and accuracy was remarkable. An Wei asked her to send more. She was delighted. Never at a loss for ideas, she suggested new projects with every mailing. He should write a book about the Xi'an Guesthouse she had escaped from so long ago, along with short biographies of all the foreigners who had stayed there on their way to visit the Communists. Another time, in capital letters, she told him he should write an opera about the guesthouse.

An Wei was amazed, not just by her energy, but also by her intellect. Not only had she written volumes about China and her experiences in the middle of the chaotic 1930s, but also she was writing histories of New England towns, a book of fables about minerals and vegetables, and a history of her ancestors in Europe.

She sent him a full book manuscript of "My Yan'an Notebooks." It was huge. How could he find time to translate it? Though he felt it important to get Helen Snow's work into the hands of Chinese historians, his heavy workload at the Foreign Affairs Office—planning and interpreting for one group after another—meant that he could only translate at night or during brief vacations. But she was impatient.

She then had a heart attack, and her pressure on An Wei intensified. She wanted all thirty-two of her unpublished books to be available in China because she was sure her point of view and experiences were important for the Chinese people to read and understand. She urged him to translate as many of her books as he could.

Fall 1980, Xi'an

An Wei looked around the director general's large office as he took a seat. Lu Man seemed unusually stern.

"A very serious accusation has been made against you."

An Wei sat respectfully on the chair facing him. Lu Man said someone had reported that An Wei was pursuing fame by translating books and shirking his responsibilities. This was shameful behavior for a party member.

Pleased with his translation of *Charlie and the Chocolate Factory*, a book his children and their friends loved, An Wei had sent it to Guizhou People's Publishing House. They were enthusiastic, and within the year An Wei had received a copy of the published book, which went on sale at the government bookstore near the Foreign Affairs Office. *Mr. Popper's Penguins* soon followed. How could this be a scandal? The translating had improved his facility with English.

Lu Man was a fair director, but a jealous troublemaker had obviously been busy. An Wei was sure it was Zhu Da'an. Images flashed through his mind of Zhu chatting with the bosses and doing everything he could to please them. Although he had no real skills to be working at the Foreign Affairs Office, Zhu Da'an had managed to rise to vice section chief. And he and Lu Man were from the same province, which by Chinese tradition meant they would be willing to help each other.

Quanxi. Connections. Zhu had a lot; An Wei had none.

Lu Man needed the facts about how hard he worked at the Foreign Affairs Office.

An Wei leaned forward in his chair.

"I take care of more visitors than anyone else in the office." An Wei was careful to control his anger.

The office gave him all the important English interpreting jobs and asked him to plan detailed schedules for the delegations, interpret for them, and meet all their needs. He named several groups.

He described how he prepared for each delegation by learning the special words they might use and their history in relation to China. After they left, he submitted the required reports, thoroughly written.

He followed office protocol with care.

He interpreted for other staff members when they asked.

He attended all the office meetings and discussions.

He also explained to Lu Man that he needed to gain more flexibility in interpreting. He understood what visitors said but had a hard time putting that into Chinese. Translating books from English to Chinese gave him a more comprehensive understanding of the language subtleties. Moreover, he did that on his *own* time, at night and on weekends—*never* on office time.

"I had these two books published so children have something to read now that China is opening up."

The accusation was eventually dropped. He suspected, however, that it was noted in his file.

August 1981, Xi'an

Former US president Jimmy Carter pointed to a photo in an album that the governor of Shaanxi Province had given him.

Jimmy Carter and An Wei examining a gift book given to the former president, Xi'an airport, 1981. *Source*: An Wei.

"That's the Wild Goose Pagoda," An Wei said as he leaned toward President Carter to get a better look. They were sitting on a sofa in the Xi'an airport VIP lounge waiting for Carter's plane.

It had been a hectic, but unusually enjoyable visit. An Wei had interpreted and planned for a large number of foreign officials, but he knew of none who would have been so at home in Fenghoe, where the former president talked as an equal with villagers. Although Carter was very presidential at formal banquets and gatherings, in the village he was different. He was curious about everything. Who in the village built your table? What type of fertilizer do you use? Have you ever tried to grow peanuts? He was just like an old friend.

April 2014

An hour and a half out of Xi'an, a representative of Farmer Wang, waiting in a dust-covered black car, signaled us to follow him down what had once been a country lane. Along with a colleague and a driver, An Wei and I were on our way to the same village Jimmy Carter and his family had visited in 1981. Fenghoe's leader, Wang Baojing, was looking forward to telling us about the president's time there.

Heavy construction trucks sped past. Dust from the loess plateau swirled everywhere, the dry soil working its way around the edges of our closed windows and into the car.

We turned left and headed down a road lined with newly planted saplings. The road curved down into a broad valley, hugging a hill filled with tiers of caves that had been dug into the loess. We rounded the last bend and entered the village, stopping in the middle of a tree-shaded street.

Eighty-year-old Wang Baojing pushed through plastic strips hung over his doorway to keep out insects and dust. There was no doubt who was in charge. Though slightly stooped, he moved with agility, an old cadre hat pushed back on his head. Dark blue pants and shirt with sleeves rolled to his elbows were topped with a bright red sweater vest that hung on his thin frame.

Wang Baojing shepherded us into a small, parlor-like room dominated by a large fish tank and urged us to wash our hands in a flowered enamel basin of hot water. Then he took my arm and led me to a 1981 photo hanging on a wall above the tank. It showed him and Jimmy Carter in animated conversation, with An Wei seated between them, interpreting and obviously enjoying it as much as they were.

As family members came and went, bringing glasses of scalding tea, apples, and candies, Mr. Wang guided me to the preferred seat beside him, anxious to provide the closest possible repeat of President Carter's visit—beginning with their conversation in this very parlor. Reminiscences of the Carter visit poured from him and other villagers. As the conversation gained momentum, I noticed An Wei and his colleague slip their mobile phones onto the table, recorders turned on to capture every word.

When Wang Baojing was Fenghoe's village head in the 1970s, at the height of the Cultural Revolution, he and other leaders had been honored because they had the villagers build identical houses to erase class differences. The rows of connected homes, with arched entranceways, reminiscent of the caves many of them had lived in, stood two stories high. No longer would there be hovels or affluent homes; they would all be the same—quite comfortable, especially for the poorer villagers.

Carter had requested to see a farm during his two days in Xi'an, but why his farm? Wang Baojing wondered aloud. Another village leader broke in.

"Mr. Wang will not tell you this, but it was no surprise to others. He was known as an effective village head, and he had found a way to double corn output. Mr. Carter had been a farmer and would understand this."

At lunch, I again replaced Carter in the seating arrangement, for the same meal served to the Carters. Crowded around a small table in the Wang home with family members, a few village leaders, and An Wei, we had a traditional, though sumptuous meal for a country village. Family members first brought cold dishes of fried peanuts, sliced duck, and steamed and salted soybeans. We waited for Mr. Wang to select a morsel, and then we followed suit.

Main dishes began to arrive. Everyone pushed aside plates to make room. Wang Baojing dipped into a sautéed spinach-like vegetable with bits of pork. Two more arrived—sautéed tofu with pieces of red chili and sliced sausage-like meat. Conversation stopped as everyone focused on selecting a piece from one dish, then another. More dishes followed: sliced red peppers, bean sprouts in a pungent sauce, dark fungus with onions, and grated potatoes in chili sauce so hot it brought tears to my eyes. I noticed that when a villager stopped talking to take a few pieces of fungus, An Wei sneaked a bite, and then quickly returned to interpreting. The dishes kept coming.

A bottle of good Maotai and small glasses appeared, and toasts began. Thanks to President Carter for his visit and then Mr. Wang's appreciation for my visit. I shared my appreciation for my hosts. We all thanked the cooks for the delicious meal. The slight malt aroma of the strong liquor hung over the table.

An Wei (*center*) translating for Jimmy Carter and Farmer Wang Baojing, Fenghoe village, 1981. *Source*: An Wei.

Memories rippled through the conversation. Wang Baojing talked more than once of their surprise and pleasure at spending so much time with the friendly president. Although the people in the United States did not like the former president enough to reelect him, everyone in China—villagers, city dwellers, and officials— respected him for successfully negotiating the normalization of relations between China and the United States. In Fenghoe, they loved his unassuming nature. He talked with them as one farmer to another and asked how they grew their crops. His daughter loved their chili sauce and took a bottle home. His wife admired how they heated the kang they slept on. They took him to their workshop, and when he fingered some of the tools, a villager stood aside and invited the president to saw some planks for a bookcase.

Wang Baojing led us up rickety stairs to the attic where a museum collection awaited transfer to a vacant village building and then out to the fields surrounding the village.

Worried about tiring Mr. Wang, we viewed a few other village homes and headed for the car. At the car door, Wang Baojing put his hand on my shoulder, his eyes locked on mine. "Please send an email to the Carter Center when you get back home. Tell them the Wang family sends its greetings and wishes of good health to former president Carter, and his wife and daughter."

Fall 1981

Not long after Carter's visit to Xi'an, An Wei put an English textbook on his desk by the open window of their bedroom and pulled a chair next to his children, who were fidgeting on their stools.

"Good morning, An Qun."

"Good morning, An Xiang."

He noticed them moving their lips to mimic his English pronunciation in a silent whisper. He repeated the phrases. Then, in Chinese, he explained what he had said and how they should answer him. He repeated the greetings again.

"What should you say to me?" he asked.

Ten-year-old An Qun brushed her wispy bangs to one side and tried. "Good morning, *Baba*."

"Not *baba*. It is 'father.' 'Good morning, Father.'"

She tried again. "Good morning, Fa . . . ba."

"Not fa ba. It is 'father.'"

She straightened up, pushed her bangs aside again, and said, "Good morning, Fa . . . ther." He had her say it two more times to help her remember.

An Wei knew how he wanted to teach English to An Qun and eight-year-old An Xiang. Not to memorize the language word by word, that was for sure. He knew parents who had done that, and their kids ended up knowing nothing. An Xiang and An Qun were going to learn to *speak* English.

An Wei had tape recorded the lessons from an English textbook for children that was published in Hong Kong. He wanted An Qun and An Xiang to listen to them every day and repeat the sentences. He and Niu Jianhua found their own English valuable and believed it was critical for the children to learn it while they were young. Being able to speak it naturally would benefit them throughout their lives.

An Wei turned to An Xiang, who sat on his hands rocking back and forth on the stool. "Good morning, An Xiang."

Slowly, getting a feel for the new tones on his tongue, he said it. "Good . . . morning, Fa . . . ther."

"Try it faster."

"Good . . . morning, Fa . . . ther."

That was enough for today. He said they must practice those phrases every morning before they went to school. Then the next Sunday morning, he would teach them the second lesson.

The children settled into the daily routine: get dressed, practice English, eat breakfast, and then go to school. "My name is _____." "I am in grade _____." "This is a chair." "This shoe is black."

One day, An Xiang said he didn't want to learn English anymore.

An Wei told him that if he skipped the ten minutes of English study, he could not have breakfast.

"I don't want breakfast."

"That's okay. You can go without breakfast," An Wei said, "but you can't go to school either." If he did not study English for ten minutes every day, nothing else could follow.

Tears ran down An Xiang's cheeks. "I have to go. Or the teacher will criticize me." An Wei was well aware that the students obeyed their teachers 100 percent. An Xiang needed to leave for school in five minutes.

An Wei persisted, "You can skip breakfast, but not your English practice." He turned on the recorder. An Xiang, wiping his eyes, repeated the sentences. An Wei pressed on. "A little louder."

"My name An Xiang. I in secum grade."

"Say it again. My name is An Xiang. I am in second grade."

An Xiang tried again and repeated one more sentence. Two minutes later, An Wei turned off the recorder and told him he could go. An Xiang grabbed his schoolbag and flew through the door.

September 1982

An Wei looked out as the plane's engines lifted him skyward from Xi'an. Over the last year, he had been working with high-profile American visitors and translating Helen's writing. Now he could barely believe that he was going to see the United States.

He glanced sideways at the two officials for whom he would interpret— Mr. He, a division chief in the Foreign Affairs Office, and Mrs. Sun, wife of the governor of Shaanxi Province. She expected to be treated as royalty at all times and often found fault with people's work.

Their plane shuddered as it climbed steadily and headed eastward. Xi'an with its ancient tombs and modern factories slipped away, replaced by mountain ranges and valleys where farmers and workers toiled endlessly, unaware of what was happening in the outside world.

An Wei took out their schedule and went over every detail once more: a brief visit to New York City and then a week in Minnesota so that Mr. He and Mrs. Sun could begin preparations for a meeting between the governors of Minnesota and Shaanxi Province to create an ongoing relationship.

Thank goodness Sharon Crain was exuberant about hosting them during their time in New York, for each of them carried only twelve dollars, not even enough to take advantage of the Chinese consulate travel service. He hoped they would also be able to visit Helen Snow. A well-known Chinese author, Ding Ling, had asked An Wei to deliver a note to her. But with only two days in New York, the officials might not want to spend one of them traveling to Connecticut.

At La Guardia Airport, Sharon greeted them enthusiastically and maneuvered her car into New York City traffic, heading for the Chinese consulate near the United Nations in midtown Manhattan.

Despite their exhaustion after the long trip, An Wei and the two officials gawked at the city's streets. They were jammed with cars, some polished to a high shine, others dented and covered with dirt. It was a year for long, boxy Cadillacs and small, practical VW Rabbits. Not a bicycle could be seen. The nearly empty sidewalks were a shock, but the few pedestrians they saw wore a palette of vibrant colors, so different from the dark blue and gray clothing worn back home. People walked as if late for an appointment, some of them women who pounded along on skinny high heels. Everyone had different skin and hair colors. Almost no one had black hair like the people in China.

The next morning, long before the travelers were up, Sharon was at the Chinese consulate guesthouse ready to go. She whisked them to breakfast in Chinatown and then on a tour of the city. An Wei was brimming with excitement. He guessed that Mr. He and Mrs. Sun were in shock. Neither he nor they could have imagined a country so different from China.

An Wei wanted to see everything. But as interpreter, he was tied to the officials' questions and needs. At the Statue of Liberty, though, Sharon urged them all to go to the top. Slowly and methodically, An Wei climbed the 354 stairs to the crown and pondered what this statue meant to Americans and to the French citizens who had given it to them in 1886. What a gift of friendship. Winded, he stepped onto the enclosed platform at the top and peered out a window. On the walkways below, visitors looked like black specks in motion.

An Wei gazed at the New York harbor, where the East River and the Hudson River met. Lower Manhattan seemed nestled between them, its buildings clustered together with the World Trade Center towering above them. A ship plied the water heading toward the Atlantic, destination unknown. He could see Ellis Island nearby, the nation's historic port of entry for legions of immigrants.

Back at the bottom of the monument, Sharon insisted that they examine an immigration exhibit. For the first time An Wei realized that America was an open land that welcomed everybody—"Give me your tired, your poor, Your huddled masses yearning to breathe free . . ."

As soon as they stepped off the boat that had ferried them from the statue, Sharon took them to the World Trade Center, built during the years An Wei was in Yan'an. As the September sun glinted off the glass, they squinted up at the twin towers. The three Chinese visitors had never seen such tall buildings. They were terrified as they rode the elevator to the top, where the view of miles of city and even woodlands was breathtaking. Then they drove through Manhattan traffic to the United Nations complex at Forty-Second Street.

The immensity and warmth of the wood-paneled United Nations General Assembly hall made An Wei stop to think. Sitting in the visitors' chairs at the back of the great hall, he took a few minutes to absorb its purpose. All the countries of the world met here, under the golden seal of the United Nations. China had been represented since 1971, when his country replaced the awful regime of Chiang Kai-shek and Taiwan. He envisioned the room filled with delegates, all voicing their viewpoints. Along the sides of the hall he saw the interpreters' booths and imagined how stressful their jobs must be.

One reason for the whirlwind tour was that he and Sharon had made a plan for the second day to see Helen Snow in Connecticut. Mr. He and Mrs. Sun wanted to spend the day window-shopping, but Sharon, persistent and diplomatic, convinced them to go to Connecticut. She was sure the drive through the countryside of autumn colors and the visit with this friend of many Chinese leaders would make the trip worthwhile.

An Wei was eager to greet Helen Snow in her own home. To truly understand someone well, he believed, one had to know as much as possible about that person. His own lifestyle and background told a lot about him, he reasoned; that would be true of her as well.

Her house looked sumptuous to them. It was the first private home they had ever seen. Though Helen had described it as small, to An Wei the white clapboard building was huge and surrounded by unimaginably generous lawns and bushes. Sharon led them to the side door where Helen stood waiting, a broad smile on her face.

She gave An Wei a big hug. Enclosed in her arms, he grew increasingly embarrassed. She should have greeted the important officials first. Chinese did not hug in public, and he knew the other two were horrified by her familiarity. To his relief, she finally welcomed the division chief and first lady and took them to her overstuffed office that had no room for chairs. From there she led them into her small bedroom, where everyone seated themselves gingerly on an old sofa and chair.

Helen sat on her bed and asked the Chinese where they were from, soon focusing on the home area of the division chief that interested her. When she discovered that An Wei's village was near Baoji, she launched into a detailed description of the industrial cooperative that she and a few others had begun there in the 1930s, trying to overcome Japanese destruction of China's industries. Sharon fetched a chair for herself from another room and brought along water for all of them. Helen Snow had no interest in serving tea. She wanted to talk.

She began a monologue about her years in China, the people she had met, and the movements she had been involved with. On and on she went, her speech so rapid that her small voice sounded to An Wei like a machine—ta, ta, ta, ta. Though taxed by the quick pace of interpreting, he could sense Mrs. Sun's mounting anger. This American woman was ignoring her.

Tactfully, Sharon steered their encounter to a conclusion, and An Wei delivered the note from the Chinese author, which delighted Helen.

The next day, the Chinese trio was welcomed at the Minneapolis airport by ten people carrying large banners. It was a better start than their arrival in New York, where Mrs. Sun had been annoyed that the president of their Minnesota host organization had not met them there. In China, she was treated as a queen, and she expected no less from her American hosts. In New York, she had been displeased with several situations, but the city was so exciting that she made no major demands. Now she and Mr. He were in Minneapolis to arrange a trip for her husband, the governor, and the Americans should show deference and respect.

On their first full day, they met the Chinese Friendship Association president, Mr. Patachni, who had personally made all their arrangements. First they would visit the famed Walker Museum. Embarrassed, An Wei had to interpret Mrs. Sun's response. "I do not want to visit that." Mr. Patachni, a little surprised, said he would see what he could do for her.

He told them that the next morning, they would visit the Breck School, where Chinese was taught. They would be welcomed at the school, and children would give a Chinese language demonstration.

"No, we do not want to visit the school. We want to see a company."

An Wei could see that Mr. Patachni, easily in his seventies, was beside himself. He had spent hours arranging the schedule, but he knew this woman was important, so he would have to change everything. What would he tell the students and teachers who had practiced so long?

The following evening they visited the home of a host committee member. Ushered into a sitting room, they settled themselves into the comfortable chairs for tea and conversation. Within minutes, Mrs. Sun began behaving like a policeman on a search, investigating all the rooms in the house. If a door was closed, she opened it, walked in, and looked around. If she was curious about something, she picked it up. She inspected bedrooms and objects on bureaus. Their host was obviously uncomfortable but said nothing. The governor's wife came back to the sitting room looking satisfied, sat down uninvited at the piano, and began to play anti-Japanese songs. An Wei was mortified at her cultural insensitivity. He did not know whether to laugh or cry, nor did he know how to stop her.

Back in the hotel, he knew he had to say something because they still had several days ahead of them in Minnesota. He tried to address her as politely and quietly as possible.

"American customs are different from ours. When we get to somebody's home, we can ask permission. We can say something like, 'May I have a look at your house?' Then we just follow the host to see what they show us. If you want to try out their piano, also ask permission. You can say, 'Oh, this is a very nice piano. Can I try it?' Just ask their permission for the sake of politeness. This is their custom." He knew he had said too much.

She glared at him and yelled, "It seems to me everything you said was right, and everything I did was wrong."

Distraught and embarrassed, An Wei stuck strictly to interpreting for the rest of the trip. In San Francisco, while they waited for their plane to China, Mrs. Sun, who no longer needed him to interpret, ripped into him. Why did he keep teaching her all the time? He needed to be modest, to not criticize. He should do everything she wanted him to. On she went.

He said nothing, but Mao Zedong's expression kept running through his mind. Talking to people like her was like "playing the piano for a cow."

Since their first meeting, Sharon and An Wei collaborated easily. They both valued Helen's detailed knowledge of Chinese events and her keen mind. They also understood that her contributions to China had been eclipsed by Edgar Snow. Sharon and An Wei dedicated themselves to reestablishing her reputation in China, and they knew it would be hard work.

They decided the best way to accomplish this was for An Wei to spend several months in Connecticut hearing Helen talk about the details of her life in China, what she had been trying to accomplish, whom she had helped, and what she and Edgar worked on together, while also sorting through her voluminous writings and notebooks. He needed firsthand information from her. Only then would he be able to convince others of her accomplishments and her dedication to China.

For An Wei to become a visiting scholar was the most obvious strategy, and Sharon worked assiduously to make that happen, including writing a powerful letter to a senior Shaanxi Province official extolling An Wei's talents. Making the arrangements took almost two years. An Wei mentioned their plans to Helen briefly in a few letters, but he focused mainly on her primary interest of having him translate her articles and manuscripts. He and Sharon decided not to trouble her about all the details so that she could recover completely from the heart attack.

In the end, Trinity College, not far from Madison, offered An Wei a position, and Sharon managed to cobble together funding from educational organizations in New York and from the college. The Xi'an Foreign Affairs Office granted him a full year in Connecticut.

In November 1984, he sat down at his desk after his family had gone to bed, and with almost childlike eagerness, he began a letter to Helen. He explained that he had been granted an entire year's leave to spend at Trinity College in Hartford, Connecticut, starting the following September. He could help her in whatever way would be most useful, and he would be able to collect the information he needed to restore her reputation in China. He expressed amazement that it had all worked out.

Helen's response came quickly. Niu Jianhua collected it from her mailbox at the college where she taught and tucked it into her bag. She gave it to An Wei as soon as he got home from the Foreign Affairs Office. Fingering the lightweight airmail stationery and looking at Helen's handwriting, he sat down at his desk and slid an opener under the edge of the envelope. He unfolded the paper and flattened it out on his desk, anticipating her pleasure. He read it once, then again, hardly believing what she said. Why would he do such a thing as spend a valuable year in Connecticut? she asked. "It's a waste of your time. You need to stay in China and translate my writing."

· 9 ·

Setting the Record Straight

Summer 1985, Hohhot, Inner Mongolia

No matter what Helen thought, An Wei planned to spend the year in Connecticut, and he knew he needed to prepare thoroughly. A conference to be held in Hohhot, Inner Mongolia, by the Three S Society provided his first opportunity. Helen Snow had long been a taboo subject in China, and he wanted to know how the historians gathering at the conference about Edgar Snow and others who had reported on the Communist revolution would react to information he was going to present.

An Wei watched the Beijing and Shanghai experts as they arrived and greeted each other at a hotel in Hohhot. They would all make formal presentations, but he would have to deliver his material surreptitiously. Edgar had remarried after he and Helen divorced, and his widowed second wife was attending the conference. Chinese etiquette demanded that no one speak of a first wife, who traditionally was blamed for a divorce. Not even Helen's good friends from her years in China could speak publicly about her. An Wei knew it would be difficult to have Helen recognized for what she had accomplished.

Furthermore, An Wei was, in Chinese terms, a small potato—an unknown from the hinterlands of China, lacking prestige, while those confident and polished experts from Beijing were academically respected.

He watched with apprehension as the registrar's assistant inserted copies of his paper into participants' bags. It consisted of selected letters he was translating for Helen. She and Edgar Snow had written them to each other when Edgar was in Beijing drafting *Red Star Over China*, his seminal book about the revolution, while Helen was in Yan'an interviewing and photographing Mao Zedong and other Communist Party leaders.

139

An Wei knew that she had an enormous amount of knowledge about a crucial time in China's history that could be lost. He was determined to right this wrong, and he was not alone. Both Sharon Crain and Tim Considine also believed that Helen was a genius with extensive and invaluable knowledge about China's revolutionary history. An Wei increasingly dedicated himself to preserving her work for the young people of China—and to reestablishing her reputation. The Hohhot conference would help him gauge how difficult this would be.

As more participants arrived, An Wei sat in the hotel foyer envisioning thin, dysentery-ridden Helen Snow sitting beside Mao Zedong in a Yan'an cave house, taking quick notes with her prized fountain pen. She described him as unusually tall and well built for a Chinese person, with "a shock of plentiful hair" that flopped down to his ears. Clothed in the steel-blue Red Army uniform she wore to protect her from looking like a foreigner, she probed the chairman on his evolving political theories. He was the brains and theorist of the party, she wrote later, "made of steel, of hard resistance and of tough tissue."

An Wei believed that the letters he was distributing made it clear how much Helen had contributed to *Red Star Over China*, even though only Edgar was named as author. Their correspondence documented that Edgar asked her many times to interview and photograph the revolutionary leaders he had missed when he was in Bao'an. She wrote him about her in-depth interviews with Chairman Mao and the Communist Party's policies, including the fact that they were forming a united front with the Nationalist army to fight the Japanese invaders. An Wei hoped that by sharing their correspondence, the conference participants would realize that Helen and Edgar Snow worked as a team on *Red Star Over China*.

Toward the end of the first day, An Wei listened to a scholar describe the important connections Edgar Snow had made at Yenching University in Beijing, never once mentioning Helen. In fact, none of the speakers even suggested that there had been a valuable partner in Edgar's life. It made An Wei more determined than ever to gather enough material during his year in Connecticut so that Helen's role could not be ignored.

As the formal sessions ended, An Wei could not tell if participants had read his translations. He thought he saw a few people paging through them, but they remained silent—a typical Chinese way to oppose something.

His assigned roommate, however, had plenty to say. He was a scholar from a premier academic research center and an expert on a female American Communist whom many viewed as unstable.

"Why are you starting lies about Helen Snow?" he asked. "She is a terrible person who opposed our revolution."

*   *   *

On the third day, the conference organizers took participants to the nearby small town of Salachi, where Edgar Snow had stayed during the 1920s famine. Open grasslands spread before them in all directions as An Wei maneuvered to walk beside Huang Hua, who knew Helen and stayed in touch with her. Although An Wei had interpreted for heads of state, he felt timid in the presence of Huang Hua, vice chair of the Standing Committee of the National People's Congress and China's former foreign minister. As a young student, Huang Hua had worked closely with the Snows. In 1935, they had opened their home to him and other students who were planning the December 9th Movement to oppose the Japanese, providing censored information and hiding some of them from the police. He had also been Edgar Snow's interpreter on the dangerous trip to Bao'an where the Communists first lived at the end of the Long March.[1]

An Wei took a deep breath and began to speak.

"Good morning, Vice Chairman. I am An Wei from Xi'an. I will be spending a year with Helen Snow in Connecticut."

"You are An Wei!" The vice chair beamed a toothy smile. "I have heard a lot about you from Helen Snow. She says you have many talents."

Floored, An Wei demurred. "I hope I will be able to help her."

Huang Hua, who had been to Helen's Connecticut home while he was posted at the United Nations, knew how much help she needed. After a short conversation, he asked An Wei to meet him in Beijing before he left for Connecticut.

A couple of months later, An Wei arrived in Beijing with Huang Hua's home address tucked carefully in his belongings. He arrived at Xi Songshu Lane ten minutes early to be sure he was not late. A guard at the gate stopped him, but Huang Hua's secretary soon appeared to lead him across the traditional Beijing courtyard to a sitting room where the vice chair waited.

He greeted An Wei with a smile and offered him tea, which they sipped as they talked about An Wei's trip. Among other things, he asked An Wei to visit Helen Snow's doctor and find out if her physical condition permitted her to travel to China.

"If you can, ask Helen if she would be willing to stay in China." The Chinese government would find her a quiet place and provide her with a secretary, cook, driver, and doctor. Huang Hua continued with hope in his voice: "She could have a comfortable and carefree life without a single worry here."

Another task, he said, might be more difficult. He wanted An Wei to help promote the establishment of a sister city relationship between Xi'an and Kansas City, Edgar Snow's birthplace. But Xi'an city administrators were not enthusiastic. Huang Hua asked An Wei to visit Kansas City and collect all the information he could about its possibilities for the Xi'an municipality.

As the conversation wound down, An Wei described Helen's serendipitous 1978 visit to Xi'an that he had organized. He also told Huang Hua how some at the Hohhot conference had spoken unfairly about Helen. Somewhat reserved until then, the vice chair launched into animated conversation. He talked of Helen's heroic actions and support of the 1930s student movement as well as her dangerous escape in Xi'an on her way to Yan'an. The more he talked, the more emotional he became. Finally, in anger, he burst out, "Where were those Hohhot people when Helen shared 'weal and woe' with the Chinese people? They are unimaginably ignorant."

An hour after their meeting was scheduled to end, An Wei departed with a hearty farewell from Huang Hua.

As he left Huang Hua's courtyard and threaded his way through crowded streets, An Wei pondered the year ahead. Helen Snow had been shunned, not just by the conference scholars but also by most people in China. To convince others of her importance, he must become a recognized authority on her work, collecting a wealth of irrefutable facts in Connecticut and proving how she and Edgar had worked together.

He quickened his pace. In two days he would leave Beijing for his year in Connecticut.

Fall 1985, Connecticut

As soon as Sharon Crain picked up An Wei at the New York City airport, they began to strategize. Both had been shocked at Helen's hostile reaction to his planned year in Connecticut. They had to figure out how to overcome her resistance and make it a productive time for An Wei.

The Hohhot conference had made it abundantly clear that if her work was to be recognized in China, An Wei must arm himself with facts that no one else had. He needed details about how she started the Gung Ho cooperative movement and her involvement with students during their protests about the Japanese invasion. Whom did the Snows hide in their house and for how long? What was in the journal about democracy that she had edited? Helen still believed that once her books were translated and published, the Chinese people would want them. An Wei needed to persuade her that he and others would first have to generate public interest about her deep involvement in important historical events and that media attention would be essential.

Because Helen had been ill, Sharon and he decided they should wait a couple of weeks until her birthday for An Wei to greet her face-to-face. For now, as he settled into a routine as a visiting scholar at Trinity College, he would simply call her to say hello and update her on projects he had been pursuing.

An Wei's sponsor, Michael Lestz, walked quickly across the campus lawn, hand outstretched in greeting. They headed across the quad, dominated by an iconic 1920s brownstone building with tiers of white-trimmed windows, to Michael's office, which he invited An Wei to use and urged him to try out the computer.

By evening An Wei was settled into the rooms the college had rented for him in a young lawyer's two-story white clapboard house. He took stock: a bedroom, a bathroom, and a huge living room just for him, with a porch where he could read. He sat down at the typewriter they had provided and began a letter home, the click of the keys hitting paper a reassuring sound. He looked around the living room as he wrote. It was larger than the two-room apartment he and Niu Jianhua shared in Xi'an with their two growing children.

Over the next several days An Wei began making notes on the aspects of Helen Snow's background and projects that would probably yield the most important information. He also listed areas of her personal life that might help him understand her better—her work habits and how she had sustained her own interests while supporting her husband's writing. Who were their friends in Beijing and Shanghai? With a bit of trepidation, he picked up the phone and called her. She sounded ill, but not angry. He kept the conversation simple. He looked forward to seeing her on her birthday, he hoped she was getting better, and if she had any notes or correspondence to be translated, he would be glad to do it.

September 21, 1985

An Wei thought about the year ahead as Sharon drove him to Helen's place in Madison. When they pulled into her dirt driveway off Mungertown Road, he admired the old house once again, even though this time he noticed the peeling paint.

At the side porch, they stepped around the collection of food scraps left for raccoons and knocked. Helen opened the door slowly, still weak and not fully recovered from the flu, a bag of magazines near her feet.

She was dressed in loose pants and a jacket. A smile lit up her expression when she saw An Wei. She took his hand in a half shake, holding it for a time. He smiled broadly. It was good to see her, even though she looked wan. She handed him a folder containing a few items she wanted translated—copies of an inscription, a 1941 letter written by someone in northwest China to a friend, and an ad from *People's Daily*. She then gave him a large bag filled with magazines, including several issues of *Parade*. Curious, An Wei poked through them.[2]

"To learn about the United States," she said.

Later, on the deck of Sharon's beach house listening to the sea lap on the nearby rocks and talking with Helen, An Wei could not have been happier. She put a crumpled sun hat on her head and chatted. Sharon brought out lunch, an extra jacket to keep Helen warm, and a birthday cake. As she cut it into pieces to serve them, a neighbor's dog bounded onto the low deck and ran off with a piece before anyone could react. Helen laughed, tickled by his swiftness.

A few days later, An Wei finished his exercises and then sat down to write Helen. He laid his finished translations on top of his desk. He would include a letter along with them telling her how he valued her 1930s work and

The Gung Ho Industrial Co-ops

Soon after devastating Shanghai in 1937, the Japanese invaded vast areas of China, destroying industrial capacity. The Snows and Rewi Alley, a New Zealander, spent weeks in Shanghai brainstorming ways to help China regain some industrial footing.

They decided that industrial cooperatives, led and owned by the Chinese people, could create pockets of production in villages and cities throughout the country. They enlisted a set of engineers who designed the details. High-level Chinese and Westerners connected to China founded an international committee to support the cooperatives and raise funds in many countries.

The cooperatives organized workers and refugees displaced by the Japanese invasion into manufacturing cooperatives to aid China's resistance effort. *Gung Ho*, which means "working together" in Chinese, became its working motto. Led by the Chinese Industrial Cooperative Association, sometimes referred to as Indusco, the small-scale, self-supporting cooperatives, located primarily in rural areas, were owned by the workers, who produced materials for the war effort, including blankets, uniforms, and other military supplies. By 1941, it had become a nationwide movement with more than 1,800 cooperatives that included nearly thirty thousand members. Later the idea spread to other countries such as India.

Rewi Alley became the driving force—both in China, where he worked in villages to set up the cooperatives, and internationally—spreading information about the desperate need and what the cooperatives were accomplishing. Helen Snow turned her energy to writing articles, followed by her book *China Builds for Democracy*, focusing on the power and importance of the cooperatives.[3]

offering a few suggestions of how he could help her. For instance, he said, he could translate materials about topics important to her current writing. That should be a good setup for his next visit with her.

The next week, An Wei climbed into Sharon's car for the hour drive from the college in Hartford to Madison, on the Connecticut coast. He enjoyed the trees beginning to turn wonderful colors as he and Sharon discussed how he should proceed. He planned to spend the entire day with Helen unless she tired early.

When Sharon pulled into Helen's driveway, he looked at the overgrown bushes and nodded to Sharon. On the deck, he knocked, listened for Helen's greeting, and walked in. She was sitting at her desk, the keys of her old IBM electric typewriter clicking fast as she poured ideas onto a white paper curled around the roller. The rest of her desk was covered with haphazard heaps of papers that spilled into each other. A carton lid full of papers, balanced on the edge of the desk, threatened to hit the floor at any moment. She looked up and smiled.

As he greeted her, An Wei's peripheral vision took in the jungle of plants in large and small pots that crowded around. She called it her "Nature Connection Corner." Although he respected her love of plants, he wondered how she could organize her thoughts amid all this clutter. Vines wandered along strings, past a bare light bulb in the ceiling, and climbed across the two large

Helen Foster Snow at her desk in Madison, Connecticut, 1986. *Source*: An Wei.

windows. As she got up—a bit stiffly he noticed—he followed her down the narrow hallway crowded with stacks of papers to her bedroom. It was the only place where two people could sit. She pointed him to a small sofa, and she propped herself against the bed.

One job he thought he could do would be to help her organize the cartons filling her house. What was in all of them? He knew she wrote continuously, but was it all about China?

He asked her how the idea of industrial cooperatives got started, a topic he needed to understand in detail if he wanted others in China to respect her accomplishments. Although they had been her idea, Helen's name was never mentioned in relation to them after the birth of the People's Republic of China in 1949.

Helen pushed herself onto the bed, leaned on her elbow, and began talking rapidly. She started with the co-op history, but one topic led to another and soon she was describing her genealogy projects in Madison. She stopped suddenly.

"Do you have a tape recorder?"

An Wei nodded.

"You'd better turn it on. This is important, and you should remember it."

Though frustrated that she had strayed from the co-ops, he turned on the recorder and listened for almost an hour, while she described the genealogy work she had developed to help support herself after she, Edgar, and many other innocent people had been attacked by Senator Joseph McCarthy and his House Un-American Activities Committee.

As the afternoon wound down, An Wei offered to help her identify historical data that might be in her files. Perhaps he could translate notes or clippings from China that would be helpful to her. Her response was quick.

"My files are highly valuable. I shipped forty cartons of them from Shanghai in 1941; I know what's in them, and no one else should touch them. They are too valuable."

He would have to be very patient if he wanted to help Helen.

An Wei dialed the phone, making one of his frequent calls to Helen while he was at Trinity.

"Hello." Helen's small voice still surprised him because he regarded her as such a powerful woman.

After inquiring about her health, they discussed several items. He also wanted to ask some questions about the Gung Ho co-ops but thought better of it. He realized it would be best to send her a questionnaire that would keep her focused. If he wanted to reestablish the fact that she had initiated the co-op idea, he would need in-depth information about her involvement.

He hung up, rolled paper into the typewriter, and started the questionnaire. He hoped if she stayed on topic, she might pull relevant materials from some of those cartons. At least that way he could find out what was in them.

When Saturday came, he rode a bicycle for the first time from Sharon's beach house in Madison to Helen's, pedaling hard up Mungertown Road to avoid being late.

Catching his breath, he pushed his bicycle to Helen's side porch and gazed around at her ample land. An Wei knew she enjoyed its wildness and the raccoons and squirrels that lived there.

He waited until his watch read nine and knocked gently.

"Come in. It's open," Helen called out.

She was in her sunny office typing, with her much loved cat, Marilyn Monroe, curled on a cushion nearby. She looked up, nodded, and then turned to stroke the cat while An Wei pulled out his tape recorder.

"There's nothing in this whole world that is as beautiful as the face of a cat. Those little whiskers twitching, little eyebrows—and always the eyes have a wonderful expression," she said.[4]

Helen petted her cat once more and then slowly rose from her chair.

"Let's get started on the Gung Ho movement," she said.

She headed into the bedroom.

He was relieved. Had she actually read his questionnaire? He had tried to keep it short, asking only about critical parts of the movement, and especially her involvement with it. An Wei made sure his tape recorder was running and asked her to start from the beginning. How had she gotten the idea of cooperatives? Why were they important to China, given the Japanese destruction? And how were they received? As she dug into her memories, he listened intently, amazed at the depth and detail of her comments. Her recall was incredible. It seemed as though she were reading from a paper as she reeled off dates and names.

As the Meals on Wheels delivery person arrived with her lunch, she suggested they look at some papers she had mentioned. He got up eagerly and followed her into the living room filled with cartons.

Was he finally going to see inside these boxes? An Wei guessed she had probably written more on the movement than he knew about. That meant he might uncover material unknown to Chinese experts. Without hesitation, she headed for a particular set of cartons. He watched with anticipation as she leafed through documents. While it looked like cluttered confusion to him, she knew her way around those thousands of papers.

Helen dug through several files and pulled out a large manuscript, "The Gung Ho Papers." One reason she had so many cartons was that she had made several copies of each of her myriad manuscripts. She put the original back in the carton and handed An Wei a copy.

"Take this home and read it," she said. "It will tell you a lot of history."

He was elated. If he gathered enough new information about the movement, he could publish a series of articles in China and perhaps an academic paper setting the record straight.

One day toward the end of October, An Wei received two letters from Helen. The first one contained her usual lecture—this time about the importance of Harrison Salisbury's book on the Long March, when the Communists fled from the Nationalist army, and how the Chinese should learn to review books and point out errors that foreigners made. "You need classes to study book reviews." She knew a lot about them, she pointed out, because she reviewed books for the *Saturday Review of Literature*.

The second envelope was a different shape, and he opened it carefully. It contained a handmade card with yellow clover blossoms from her garden. He smiled as he read her enclosed note. "It's a winter garden for your desk."[5]

Another letter arrived two weeks later, with bits of information about her relatives who were traveling in China and her usual comments about her work, this time on one of her many eclectic books, *Ethics and Enertism*.

"You should study this and translate it if possible, now. Love, HFS."

Maybe, he hoped, she was beginning to trust him.

November 20, 1985

As An Wei wrote Helen about some money that had come from China, he smiled. He had finally succeeded in solving a problem that had troubled the former foreign minister, Huang Hua, and other prominent Chinese leaders, who as rebelling students in the 1930s had been helped by Helen and Edgar Snow.

In past years, they had visited Helen, seen her rundown house, and wanted to help. But she had already turned down Huang Hua's offer for an apartment in Beijing. She appreciated his generosity, she said, "but there is not a quiet place in China." Knowing that her days were numbered, she wanted to stay in her old farmhouse to continue writing. When the Chinese offered her a stipend to help her in the United States, she refused that too. She would not allow money to taint her ability to report objectively about China.

An Wei came up with a different plan. When her book *My China Years* was translated and sold by the Chinese government publisher, he suggested to Huang Hua that the government pay Helen what they could call "royalties." Although the book did not bring in much money, they sent her $5,000. Helen was enormously happy to receive the proceeds and to learn that the Chinese were finally promoting her book.

December 4, 1985

An Wei put Helen's photo beside his typewriter. If she liked it, he would have prints made for her.

Outside his windows, winter grayness had closed in. But in the warm living room his fingers slid easily along the typewriter keys, describing his impression of her when he had taken the picture.

> Looking much younger and more beautiful as if still in your 50s, you were deep in thought, in LONG THOUGHTS, recalling your prime days and your unique experience in China. The brilliant rays of the sun came into your house through the windows, shining on your hair and your valuable manuscripts as if it were the first days when McCarthyism had finally come to the end and you, full of confidence, were looking ahead and planning to start doing your OWN WORK which had been interfered with and delayed for many years!

He enclosed the photo with the letter, pulled on his winter coat, and walked a few blocks to a mailbox.

The next day he mailed her a second photo. This one was for her to sign so he could send it to the editor of a Beijing weekly that had published segments of her book. He wrote, "Recently I have been thinking what should be done to honor you in Xi'an, and how to get as many of your manuscripts published as possible when you are still alive. I hate the Chinese idea of *Gai Guan Lu Ding* (Only when a person is dead can he finally be judged and assessed) and only publishing one's works after his death. I want to race against time."[6]

Helen, sounding agitated, was on the line.

"Why did you take my letter from Gao Xiaoyuan?" she demanded. She wanted it back immediately.

An Wei said he was fairly sure he did not have it, but he would search his apartment and get back to her.

He hung up and looked through all his papers. All he had was Mr. Gao's address, not the letter. It had been a hectic visit. Helen wanted An Wei to translate some items, while he was trying to get specific information about the Gung Ho movement. If he called back, she would just become more agitated. She could become impossibly angry.

He sat down at his desk, selecting his words carefully. He wrote that he had searched all his papers but did not have the one she was looking for. He had read it at her house, copied Mr. Gao's address, then put it on her tea table. He was sorry if he had not pointed out that it was there.

He could picture that tea table with papers hanging off the edges. Only her prodigious memory kept her from losing more.

The weather in Connecticut turned cold, much colder than in Xi'an. An Wei and Sharon made just a few trips to see Helen during the winter months. Fog, rain, and snow made the drive between Hartford and coastal Madison hazardous. Also, Helen had hurt her back while moving cartons, and she needed to recover. An Wei spent most of his time reading, studying, translating, and trying out Michael Lestz's computer. He and Helen phoned each other with questions, and he wrote lengthy letters to her about material he was studying and about her connections to China. He also encouraged her to rest and reenergize during these winter months so they could accomplish useful projects in the spring and summer when he would travel to Madison more frequently.

An Wei's responsibilities at Trinity College were minimal. He helped out in Michael's class and gave occasional public lectures about China. When not engaged directly with Helen's translations and requests or the classes, he spent hours in the library digging for material he could photocopy related to the 1930s, plus special books such as Pearl Buck's *The Good Earth*, which was still banned in China. But his curiosity also led him in other directions. One of his favorite walks was to a local cemetery that was as beautiful as a garden. Reading inscriptions on the tombstones added to his knowledge of American history. He even discovered the grave of Yung Wing, the first-known Chinese student to attend Yale.

An Wei asked a policeman who attended his lectures at Trinity College if he could ride along in his car one night to see how policing worked in the United States. What kinds of problems and crimes did police handle, and how did they get to know people in the community? He learned a lot but was a little disappointed when it turned out to be an unexciting routine patrol. He attended services at the Memorial Baptist Church down the street from his house to see what they were about. They invited him to give a talk about China where they asked him a lot about Communism and he asked them about Christianity.

Abhorring the nearly nude photos of women he saw in US ads, he wrote an article for the campus *Forum* about the Chinese view of pornography. It was republished in a Hartford newspaper, and he was grateful to learn that some Americans agreed with him.

And he observed everything going on around him. On Christmas Eve he wrote Helen:

People are still rushing here and there, doing their last desperate shopping and preparing their sumptuous family party. It seems to me that Christmas, just like the Spring Festival in old China, is a contest of wealth and social influence. Walking on the deserted pavement in the Southern end of Hartford, I am like the only audience member in a gigantic theater, watching a Christmas performance of American society. The festival atmosphere is overwhelming, but it means very little to me.

Finally the winter weather broke, and he resumed weekend visits to Helen. One day at lunch, he probed for details of her life in 1930s China.

Did she go to Shanghai as a reporter for tourism in 1931? Yes. She even bought a trench coat and hat to wear cocked to one side because all newspaper reporters were supposed to wear them. She laughed. She and Edgar had even had a photo taken in their reporter outfits.

Did she report on tourism opportunities? Well, her job as a tourism correspondent for a US paper was short lived. The first photo she sent was of monsoon-inundated Shanghai. The second was of thousands of refugees pouring into the city to escape rampaging waters, cholera, and dysentery. She wrote about the corpses in the streets every day. Then she and Edgar witnessed the horrors of the Japanese attack on the Chinese part of Shanghai. Segregated in the foreigners' section of the city, they watched the bombs fall and the straw Chinese houses burn as thousands ran for their lives. Her dispatches did not do much for the tourist trade.

What of their life in Beijing, living in a house with servants while Edgar wrote and taught at Yenching University and she studied Chinese literature and philosophy? She had difficulty with the Chinese traditions of using servants. But she and Edgar both loved the dedicated students, who were so distraught they cried when the Chinese government ceded northern China to Japan.

And once they returned to the United States, what about the McCarthy period? How often did the FBI interrogate her? How did she support herself, An Wei asked, after all her work had been attacked? She and Edgar were both interrogated and accused of being Communist sympathizers. Because she was sick when she received a call from Senator Joseph McCarthy's witch hunt, she did not need to go to Washington, DC.[7] Instead, she was sent a questionnaire to complete for the FBI. Although she was not forbidden to write about China, publishers would not touch her writing, or Edgar's. They could not find jobs.

In the midst of this trying period, she and Edgar divorced. She began to live on her wits and Social Security. She knew how to scrimp, save, and find bargains. She also made a little money researching genealogies for local families. Edgar, meanwhile, remarried. Disgusted with McCarthyism, he and his new wife moved to Switzerland permanently.

*   *   *

In late spring, An Wei showed Helen a letter he had brought with him from a Beijing scholar who was seeking information about the Snows' contact with Lu Xun, a well-known author. One of his most powerful works was *The True Story of Ah Q*, a novella in which Ah Q convinces himself that he is superior to his persecutors even as they destroy him. Lu Xun saw it as a metaphor of the Chinese national character of the 1920s and 1930s.

An Wei had not wanted to trouble Helen with this request in the fall because she had not been well. Now seemed the right time.

Helen read the inquiry and led An Wei into the living room to several cartons containing information about their friend, Lu Xun, and about the literary movements in China during the 1930s. She said she and Edgar had worked assiduously to make the Chinese writers accessible to the West. They began by having Lu Xun's stories, and then the works of other writers, translated into English. Eventually, these translations were included in a book edited by Edgar, titled *Living China*.[8]

"You can go through these while I type my essay," she said, resting her hand on top of the files. An Wei assured her with his deepest sincerity that he understood her manuscripts and files were part of her life, and that he would be extremely careful.

Thrilled to the core of his being, he settled onto a stool and leafed through the fifty-year-old papers about authors and literature of early twentieth-century China. He took great care not to rip the edges and to keep the papers in perfect order—one letter, one article, and one set of notes after another. He inspected them and read some completely, taking thorough notes. Then he hit gold: a long questionnaire Edgar Snow had used to interview Lu Xun that included all the author's responses. Spellbound, An Wei read it from beginning to end. He discovered that Helen had developed the questionnaire.

"In what way did Russian literature produce positive effects on Chinese writers?"

"Of the youngest writers, who writes the best stories?"

Lu Xun had answered more than thirty questions, and they were all there. What better proof could there be that Edgar and Helen had worked hand in hand? And what a topic to write about, for no one knew of Lu Xun's views about other writers, even though he was greatly respected throughout China.

An Wei was so excited he could hardly contain himself as he reread the questions. At the Hohhot conference, he had presented the letters that showed Helen had contributed significantly to *Red Star Over China*. Now here was more proof that they worked as a team.

*   *   *

"We need significant items, like the fountain pen you used when you interviewed Mao Zedong." An Wei had begun pestering Helen for artifacts.

She looked at him steadily. "You can have it."

An Wei was laying out plans for his return to China. To celebrate the fiftieth anniversary of her trip to Yan'an and her eightieth birthday, dates Chinese valued, he planned to open an exhibition in Xi'an. He would call it *Helen Snow in China*. He needed mementoes and other significant items. By now she was beginning to believe his commitment.

"The Red Army uniform you wore in Yan'an."

"All right." She pulled open another carton in the basement.

"The blanket the first industrial cooperative in Baoji gave you as a thank-you for your help."

She pulled it from a box and fingered it thoughtfully. "Take a photo of me with it first," she said.

Excited to be able to start a new era of appreciation for Helen, An Wei packed the larger artifacts in cartons, a smile creeping across his face as he taped the last one shut. These items sat in cartons on a Shanghai dock forty-five years earlier while Helen and Edgar argued about how much she was shipping to the United States. Now they were headed back to China.

October 1986, Xi'an

Back in Xi'an, An Wei found himself depressed by the size of their tiny apartment. But he was more struck by how much older An Qun and An Xiang looked and acted. Now fourteen and fifteen, he wondered if his one-year absence had given them opportunities to become more independent. They were taking on more responsibilities and had continued to improve their English. An Xiang's love for computers had intensified. But An Qun had changed the most. In fact, she had changed her name.

She had always been strong willed. A year earlier some boys had teased her by mispronouncing her name as "An Chun," which means "quail, a bird with nutritious eggs." They made it even worse by emphasizing her family name, saying "AN ... Chun," like a sneeze, and An Qun had insisted on changing her name to An Lin.

An Wei wanted to spend more time with Niu Jianhua and the children, but he knew he had to move quickly to prepare his first project about Helen and begin to rebuild her reputation. Timing was critical. He began to plan a short December conference to celebrate the Xi'an incident, an important event in the Chinese revolution when Chiang Kai-shek was captured. Helen had reported about it long before anyone else.

In every free moment that he was not working at the Foreign Affairs Office, An Wei and a friend at the Shaanxi Translators Association set to work inviting all the historians, museum experts, college professors, and reporters they could think of. They also managed to get permission to use the prestigious Shaanxi Province Communist Party auditorium. If this symposium was to be a success, An Wei had to stir up interest and support from every imaginable quarter. The well-known auditorium would be a drawing card. He also spent hours honing his keynote talk and making sure that all the facts he gleaned from Helen's materials and their long hours of talk were correct.

When the conference day arrived, An Wei looked out over the audience. Given the number of experts and reporters in attendance, it looked as though they had succeeded in developing significant interest. The next week, his speech was published in a Xi'an newspaper and reprinted by many others. He hoped these results would make Helen believe he was going to work to reestablish her reputation in China.

A few weeks later, An Wei approached the curator of a Xi'an museum about hosting a Helen Snow exhibition. The curator, who had heard An Wei's talk and been impressed, immediately agreed.

December 1986

An Wei and his journalist friend Ma Ke sat at the small table in the Shaanxi Translators Association office to relax for a few minutes, the honking of truck horns and bicycle bells from the street below intruding on their conversation. As they drank tea, An Wei mentioned his discovery of Edgar Snow's comprehensive notes from his interview of the famous author Lu Xun and the questionnaire.

Ma Ke suddenly straightened. "What did they say?"

As An Wei described the interview, Ma Ke got more agitated, asking one question after another.

"An Wei, this is big news."

Within hours, Ma Ke had told a friend in the large Xi'an office of the Xinhua News Agency, who immediately asked An Wei to draft a short article about the find. That night An Wei wrote about the interview contents and the questionnaire Helen had created, plus a few details about where they were found, and then sent it to the reporter.

The next day, his phone rang. A journalist from the Beijing headquarters of Xinhua News wanted to talk with him. This was vital news, she said. They wanted more information. He hung up, and the phone rang again, and again, from *China Journalists*, from the Lu Xun Museum, and from the People's Literature Press in Beijing. They kept calling.

The reporter from *China Journalists* was the first to fly to Xi'an and interview An Wei at length. She wrote a detailed report that intrigued the editors of the highly regarded journal *Historical Data of New Literature.*

An Wei knew he had unearthed important information, but he hadn't expected such a dramatic response. The well-known publisher asked him to translate into Chinese the questionnaire Helen had developed, as well as Lu Xun's answers. As soon as they received his translations, they asked him to write an article about his discovery and give more background about Edgar Snow's interview. The editor-in-chief decided to publish all three pieces in *Historical Data of New Literature.* Suddenly all of China was discovering the positive comments Lu Xun had made about young writers of the New Culture Movement, which had emerged during the 1910s and 1920s when China had just overthrown its last dynasty and intellectuals were discussing intensely how the new country should develop. Many of them had been criticized unmercifully and labeled as bourgeois thinkers with counterrevolutionary ideas under Mao Zedong's leadership. Some of them, such as Lao She, Ding Ling, Zhou Zuoren, Lin Yutang, and Hu Shi, had been sent to labor camps, committed suicide, or escaped to other countries.

Any new material about Lu Xun would have made news, but An Wei's discovery was spectacular.

News outlets throughout China, including *Xinhua Digest*, the most prestigious magazine in the country, reprinted and reported the story.

March 1987, Shanghai

An Wei gathered his courage and walked to the lectern to address the same academic society that held the Hohhot conference. Before him sat Edgar Snow's widow, Lois Wheeler, along with Chinese officials who had been intimately connected with the massive Gung Ho Industrial Cooperatives project. He straightened the pages of his talk.

Buoyed by the clear successes of the Xi'an symposium and the Lu Xun interview discovery, he felt confident about what he was going to say. Yet it was risky. No one had mentioned Helen Snow in relation to Gung Ho for decades.

Determined to speak the truth, he had chosen a bold title: "The Beginning of Indusco: The Hitherto Untold Story of Helen Snow in the Chinese Industrial Cooperative Movement." Although her name may have been omitted from any material since 1949, this paper was going to prove that Helen had initiated the movement and had worked hard to convince others of the idea.

"As everybody knows," An Wei began, "the Chinese cooperatives came into being when the Chinese nation was in peril." China needed ways to survive Japan's brutal bombing of all its factories, and the co-ops proved one valuable means.

An Wei relished the next paragraph as he read it.

Edgar Snow himself had written that the self-supporting co-ops throughout China were the brainchild of Helen Snow. She prodded him and others to develop a detailed plan and to seek support anywhere they could. "It was the soundness of her original concept," Edgar wrote, "and the genius of her faith and enthusiasm" that created the movement.[9]

An Wei scanned the audience. Its members were obviously drawn to what he was saying.

Summer 1987, Xi'an

An Wei lugged cartons of Helen's artifacts into the museum whose curator had agreed to exhibit *Helen Snow in China*. The red and yellow plaid wool blanket from the Baoji Gung Ho cooperative, the Waterman fountain pen she had used while interviewing Mao Zedong night after night, the army uniform the women in Yan'an had made for her, and her photos—they were all there. The enthusiastic curator had assigned a work group to develop the exhibit, but an enormous amount of sorting and mounting lay ahead, and the July 10 opening loomed. After working all day at the Foreign Affairs Office, An Wei wrote the introduction and organized information for the displays, photo captions, and the English versions.

Since no plywood was available, they had to make the exhibit with logs. They had no computer or printer, so everything had to be written by hand. An Wei began recruiting. A former college classmate agreed to write the English headings and captions; a good calligrapher who worked with him years earlier in the Yan'an Museum agreed to do the Chinese.

June was scorching in Xi'an. There was no room in the museum to lay out large materials, so they worked at night in the courtyard with a fan running. Toward the end of June, enough had been finished for An Wei to feel confident about sending a letter to a Beijing friend, asking him to contact Huang Hua to see if he would send an official telegram of congratulations. Then he held his breath. The Chinese people took notice of who supported events such as this one. If Huang Hua, vice chair of the Standing Committee of the National People's Congress and former foreign minister, sent a message, it would draw the media.

July came too fast. They worked every night, all night. An Wei kept checking for a telegram. He needed to contact the newspapers soon. Five days before the opening, Huang Hua's telegram arrived. An Wei read the full-page message from beginning to end, and then over again. "Helen Snow is a devoted and longtime friend of the Chinese people," it began. He was so excited, he felt like dancing.

With the arrival of that telegram, An Wei finally believed that the exhibit would have far-reaching influence.

Then came another telegram. He could not believe what he saw. Madame Zhou Enlai, chair of the Chinese People's Political Consultative Conference and widow of China's beloved leader, had heard the news of the exhibit and sent her own message of congratulations. She, too, had been a friend of Helen's in the 1930s.

An Wei flew into action. He invited a famous scholar, who had translated Edgar Snow's *Red Star Over China*, to speak at the opening. He and his colleagues sent out invitations to all the news media. With Huang Hua's message in hand, An Wei told his boss at the Foreign Affairs Office about the exhibit. Then the vice governor of Shaanxi Province heard about the event and instructed the director of the Foreign Affairs Office to give full support to this "great celebration" and have other leaders accompany him to the opening and symposium.

On July 10, exhausted but exhilarated, An Wei inspected the last sign and photo, took one more look around, and headed for the opening events.

· *10* ·

Gathering Storm Clouds

2016, Xi'an

"Sharon told me that 'red-eye disease' is one of the really difficult problems in China. Can you tell me something about that?"

I had already been interviewing An Wei for two hours in his home office. He sat on his preferred four-legged stool, trouser legs pulled up to his knees, absent-mindedly scratching his shins in the unseasonable heat.

"Yeah." Energized, he leaned forward. "She is right. It is the worst element of Chinese culture. Whenever someone sees a person better than himself, his eyes get red with jealousy." Mouth turned down, An Wei opened his eyes wide as if showing me eyes filled with jealousy. He laughed.

"Then the person hunts for a way to destroy the other's reputation or work."

He described a university dean who held back promising young faculty members by awarding state scholarships for overseas study to only those with limited ability. That way he could keep the most capable faculty from advancing past him.

"In my life, Mr. Zhu Da'an, who accused me of translating during work hours, was consumed with red-eye disease. People like that spend most of their energy trying to destroy you."

Spring 1987, Xi'an

His face taut with anger, An Wei looked at the leader. "Deputy Director Hu, why did you give me an apartment with only two bedrooms?"

His boss replied that he was only a staff person. The larger apartments were for section chiefs or higher.

When An Wei returned from Connecticut, the Foreign Affairs Office was building new housing. He was sure he would be offered a larger place, given that he had been with the office longer than most staff and had inter-

Niu Jianhua and An Wei in their small Xi'an apartment. *Source*: An Wei.

preted for more dignitaries than anyone else. Besides, for almost ten years he and Niu Jianhua had lived in a tiny two-room apartment with their daughter, now sixteen, and their son, now fourteen, sharing a room. Long ago, Director Lu Man had promised them better housing.

"Am I qualified to be a section chief?"

Director Hu agreed that he was.

"Then please give me that position right now. Assign me my apartment, and I will give the position back to you." Mr. Hu said it was too late. He needed to accept the two-bedroom apartment.

An Wei's fury broke loose. He looked straight at the director. "Again and again you leaders promised to give me a bigger apartment. Whenever we have a key assignment, you want *me* to do it, but you have not kept your promise. You treat me like a slave."

Shortly afterward, an unusual event occurred. The Famen Temple, where An Wei had gone to study during high school, collapsed from an earthquake. When the provincial government tore down the remaining structure, the excavation uncovered a trove of beautifully preserved Tang Dynasty artifacts, among them an ornate silver tea set and silver plates. Most remarkable was a contrivance made of a series of eight boxes, each fitting inside the next larger, all closed with silver locks. The innermost one contained a small, yellowish cylindrical relic reputed to be a finger bone of Buddha that matched a description written by a Tang Dynasty monk.

Excited to tell the world, the government scheduled a press conference that required a skilled interpreter. Both Chinese journalists and foreign correspondents would be there. Mr. Hu, who was in charge, did not dare ask An Wei to fill the slot.

He sent a video of the excavation to the Foreign Languages Institute requesting an interpreter. But the archeological terms were in classical Chinese, and the topic was unknown to anyone. They said no.

In desperation, Mr. Hu turned to An Wei, who responded, "I will never do that kind of thing for you again. You remember me now. Why didn't you remember me for the apartment assignment?"

Mr. Hu apologized but told An Wei he had to do the interpreting. "The radio program is already scheduled, and the reporters are about to arrive."

An Wei knew he was putting Mr. Hu in an awkward position, but he refused again.

"Just go ask a section chief with a three-bedroom apartment to do the interpreting. I will not do it. You have been mean and unfair to me."

The next day one of An Wei's best friends arrived at his apartment. He squeezed by the sofa in the tiny living room. An Wei knew his friend thought he had been treated badly.

He pulled up a small stool. "An Wei, you have to stop this refusal. It's useless." An Wei looked at him intently.

"If you keep refusing, everyone will be mad at you." They could bully him in subtle ways for a long time, he knew.

His friend continued. The press release would announce to the world this amazing discovery found in a temple close to An Shang village. Being the interpreter of such difficult material would enhance An Wei's reputation as a local person and an accomplished interpreter.

An Wei ran his fingers along the edge of his wooden desk. "All right, I will do it to honor your persuasiveness, but for no other reason."

The archeologists sent him a videotape of the excavation process and written material that included the ancient Chinese vocabulary. He bent to the difficult task of understanding the words and then wrote an English press release that foreigners would understand, working to meet the tense deadline.

At the press conference the Chinese presentation came first, but the Chinese journalists looked blank. They understood almost nothing because so much was left in classical Chinese. When it was An Wei's turn, the foreign correspondents listened to every word he said and wrote furiously.

September 1987, Beijing

On September 25, An Wei pulled open the heavy front door of the publishing house. Two well-known writers followed him.[1]

Most people thought Edgar Snow's notes that An Wei had found accurately reflected Lu Xun's responses. However, some questioned whether Snow had quoted the famous author's answers or merely summarized them. As a result, the editorial department of *Historical Data of New Literature* had decided to hold a symposium in Beijing, including well-known writers and poets, to discuss the material's authenticity and its potential contribution to future scholarly work. An Wei was to be the honored guest.

The writers and An Wei introduced themselves while they walked to the small meeting room. Large windows cast warm autumn light across a long oval table. An Wei glanced at the seating arrangement. He was not sure whether to sit in the armchairs around the table or to sit at a set of smaller chairs behind them. One of the hosts showed him to an armchair at the center of the table, the place of honor.

A buzz of conversation rose as old acquaintances met and took their seats. Although the excitement from the first news of An Wei's discovery had worn off, attendees were still amazed that such substantive new material had surfaced. The editor in chief of *Historical Data*, a well-known author himself, called the gathering to order.

An Wei began with a description of his work and why Helen had asked Edgar to interview Lu Xun in the first place. As he talked, he could see in his mind the cartons that had contained these prized documents, and he could hear Helen explaining how she and Edgar had felt compelled to inform Westerners of the new writing emerging from China. A dozen experts followed with detailed talks addressing the accuracy of Edgar Snow's interview summaries, the importance of his notes, and Lu Xun's evaluation of the so-called controversial writers of the 1930s. They also had many good words for An Wei and his work on the translations.

Helen Snow wrote An Wei continuously, often suggesting startling projects and ideas.[2]

> January 3, 1988.
>
> Dear An-Wei . . . I hope that you and Liu Liqun and the few others of that kind realize that you are the New China with modern minds as well as neckties. You must all help each other to survive. I also hope you are not overworking, for if you ruin your health, you cannot function at all. You must eat red meat now and then, since it has amino acids. . . . Amino acids are necessary for brain cells to grow and even without one or two of them the human brain cannot develop in thinking and reasoning.

Between letters there were phone calls and faxes. An Wei could imagine Helen hammering out one long missive after another on the secondhand IBM typewriter, surrounded by her plants and with Marilyn Monroe, her favorite cat, sleeping comfortably nearby.

July 13, 1988, "BASTILLE DAY MINUS ONE." Helen suggested creating a Museum of Travels to the Northwest of China. Two of her friends could write a book about it, which An Wei should publish. Then he should "have a nice T-shirt made for tourists and also Chinese, with the name of the Museum on it." He could have T-shirts made for all important occasions. "You should only run the department, where books are published, and not do the leg work at all, or just do the mechanics."

Although Helen was aware An Wei had a full-time job and only worked on her materials at night and on weekends, she asked him to do more and more.

October 3, 1988. "I hope you will try to get a Disney cartoon series done in China on my raccoons. I have about six articles about them. . . . Maybe Huang Hua could find a film place."

March 15, 1989. After telling him the different ways Gung Ho Industrial Cooperatives should be restarted, she added, "I know that you are much too busy to take care of all these things. I think you should have a committee of three or more to handle this. You should be the supervisor and my 'agent.'"

1988, An Shang Village

Over the years, An Wei had grown close to his inquisitive Brother Number Five, who was a farmer in their village, An Shang. Unlike many in the countryside, his brother was open to new ideas and often talked with An Wei about future possibilities for the village. When An Wei visited An Shang, he stayed with him.

Number Five also cared for their mother. An Wei sent money, but that wasn't the same as attending to her daily needs. He often felt guilty he did not have the time to visit.

When Brother Number Five decided to build a better home to accommodate his family and their mother, An Wei jumped in. His brother had received permission to build on the small parcel left from the dismantled commune cattle shed. He told An Wei he planned to construct a traditional set of rooms around a tiny courtyard, but An Wei, who had seen different types of housing in the city, urged him to make it two or three stories. That way, they would have a larger courtyard. Although An Shang had no such homes, his brother eventually agreed. His family and their mother would live on the first floor where they would build a Western-style bathroom; the second floor would be for his sons and An Wei when they visited, and the third floor would be for grain storage. Number Five, terrified another famine would strike, had saved almost ten years' worth of grain.

The explosion of firecrackers filled the village air to drive away evil spirits as family and friends gathered for the groundbreaking ceremony. Materials began to arrive—bricks from a village near An Shang, steel and cement from a town by the railway, and sand from the Wei River. Under Number Five's supervision, village workers started the construction while curious villagers came by to investigate. New buildings always created excitement, but as word spread that this would be three stories high, curiosity increased. Who would live on the second and third floors? And what was that small room on the first floor for?

When the framework arched above the third story, friends, family, and construction workers gathered for a second celebration. A red flag on a tall pole attached to the top marked the accomplishment, and a quick-footed young man lit the firecracker fuses and ran.

Neighbors milled around. "You mean you're going to put a toilet inside the house? That's a terrible plan," said one. The information buzzed around the village. The farmers were horrified.

A few weeks later, An Wei arrived in the village to see how construction was going and discovered that Number Five had given up on the Western-style toilet. Instead, he would build an outdoor toilet by the pigsty and court-yard entrance. That night, An Wei talked long and hard with his brother.

"Don't change it. If more villagers comment about having the toilet inside, just tell them you were teasing." He suggested that they say the room was for storing farm tools that would not fit in his sons' rooms. Number Five finally agreed they could construct the Western toilet later. Meanwhile, An Wei convinced him to have water pipes installed in the house because he was optimistic that, in a year or two, water would be brought to village homes.

The final celebration marked the building's completion, and it, too, came with plenty of firecrackers. Because it was the Year of the Dragon, a large plaque was mounted on the wall with 龙, the character for dragon, designating power and strength for all.

For the time being, they put tools in the room for the Western toilet to satisfy the villagers. Let them get used to the height of the house first.

Spring 1988, Xi'an

An Wei felt cautious optimism as he listened to the new director general of the Foreign Affairs Office talk at a staff meeting. Zhang Jingwen and his deputy director began to introduce better policies. He told department chiefs

Brother Number Five's new home in An Shang village.

that, within weeks, they needed to know much more about foreign affairs. Those who worked directly with visitors from other countries needed a good command of at least one foreign language. An Wei was delighted to have such far-sighted bosses.

He continued his high-quality interpreting, and from time to time the director called him in to discuss visiting groups. By April he had promoted An Wei to deputy secretary general of the Friendship Association, the part of the Foreign Affairs Office that worked with nongovernmental visitors. He was the obvious choice with twenty years in foreign affairs work, overseas contacts, and English fluency. However, another man, Mr. Li, who through connections had transferred to Xi'an from far western China, thought he deserved the position, even though he had no skills. An Wei knew he would have to watch out for him.

From the first day in the new position, he immersed himself in his expanded responsibilities. An Wei cut a handsome professional figure, greeting guests at the airport, his slightly receding black hair swept back neatly and wearing a Western business suit and tie that were becoming the fashion for men in China.

He loved the work much more than his former duties, which required adhering to the inhibiting protocol of the rest of the Foreign Affairs Office that hosted foreign government dignitaries.

An Wei stepped forward as Margaret Stanley and another former nurse walked across the tarmac at the small Yan'an airport. He was pleased the military had finally given permission for the women to visit the areas where they had worked in the early 1940s, near China's border with the Soviet Union. He would accompany them and a US public television crew to retrace the nurses' experiences during the civil war between the Nationalists and the Communists.[3]

Part of a Quaker medical team devoted to "work for peace in the midst of war," they had been sent to Yan'an. However, when the Nationalist troops drew close, with plans to obliterate the Communists, Mao Zedong evacuated the area, moving north into mountainous terrain. Under bombardment, the small medical team walked out of Yan'an with the hospital staff, carrying patients on stretchers with donkeys hauling their supplies. For the next year they traveled on footpaths, setting up a makeshift hospital for brief stays in one village after another. They often performed operations in caves. The women had now returned to visit some of the villages and learn what the local people remembered of those times.

For the next few weeks, An Wei enjoyed trekking the small dirt roads to assist the women in hunting down locations they recognized and in connecting with the poor, but spirited, farmers. Wearing a tan sports jacket zipped up to his chin and orange-brown aviator sunglasses, he often found himself in the midst of villagers, nurses, and television crew members, enthusiastically interpreting back and forth as the villagers and Americans remembered incidents from the past. An Wei loved this type of work.

*   *   *

Back in Xi'an a month later, a large, heavy carton from Margaret Wong in Minnesota arrived at the Friendship Association office marked "Attention, An Wei." She had said she was going to send a computer.

He knew Margaret from his visit to Minneapolis and through the high school students she taught and took to China.

An Wei felt his energy quicken as he carefully sliced open the carton. He slowly pulled back the top, removed the plastic and paper packing material, and stepped back so other staff members could peer in. What a gift.

An Wei cleared his desk, lifted the light gray desktop computer from the box, and set it down gently. He ran his hands over it. The office staff just stared. They had seen photos of computers, but no one had touched one.

Thank goodness for his experience learning to use a computer in Michael Lestz's office at Trinity College, he thought.

He rummaged through the carton until he found the instruction manual. Then he unwound the power cord and hunted for the plug adapter he had brought from the United States.

After the staff members had satisfied their curiosity, An Wei sat down with the manual. He flipped through it quickly. He was confident he would be able to get the computer running, but he must go slowly. He needed to make sure he was following the instructions correctly since he was the only one in the office who had any experience with one. His fingers began to find the right keys. In a few weeks he became proficient, while some staff members were in awe—and others were envious.

June 1988, Beijing

As he packed for a week in Beijing, An Wei hoped his presentation would succeed. The society that studied Edgar Snow and two other Americans who had made it to Yan'an during the war-torn 1930s was holding a symposium titled *"Red Star Over China* and Me." It was to focus on Edgar's life in relation to the book. An Wei planned to challenge that. His paper was called "A Great Woman Unsung: *Red Star Over China* and Helen Foster Snow."

He spent months preparing. He knew Edgar's widow would again be there, as would others who continued to ignore Helen's contributions. But attitudes had changed since the Hohhot conference when he had not dared to present a paper and instead had merely suggested her significant role by distributing letters exchanged between Helen and Edgar.

An Wei submitted his paper with the rest, but he decided to break tradition. Instead of reading it during his time slot, he would give an impromptu talk to entice attendees to read it themselves.

When the first afternoon speaker finished, An Wei walked to the podium. He described Helen's role in *Red Star Over China*, emphasizing that she collected significant sections of the source materials. He also told about his year in Connecticut, getting to know her work and developing respect and affection for her.

At the tea break, Harrison Salisbury, a Pulitzer Prize–winning American journalist, sought him out. An Wei had interpreted for him in Xi'an years ago. He took hold of An Wei's hand and told him that he had seen the title of his paper the night before and read it immediately, finding the information invaluable. Then, a well-known scholar, who had produced an authentic Chinese translation of *Red Star Over China*, approached An Wei and said he had been startled to learn that the material for two of Edgar's chapters had all been collected by Helen. He sat An Wei down and had him point out every photo in the book that had been taken by Helen, not Edgar.

As the conference wound down, An Wei could sense that both old and young scholars now recognized that he had collaborated directly with Helen for a year and, in the process, had discovered a considerable amount of valuable material.

Spring 1989

From the time An Wei was promoted to deputy secretary general until early 1989, he talked occasionally by phone with Helen but was too busy to write her. At the end of February, however, he finally sat down to report briefly on several projects and suggest that in his new position he would be able to ensure the publication of her book, *China Builds for Democracy*, as well as publicize more easily the work she had done in China.

A month later, in March 1989, he was promoted to secretary general of the Friendship Association. It was an inauspicious time. Student unrest was increasing. College graduates were discovering they lacked the proper skills to find a job in the emerging economy that had been introduced by Deng Xiaoping. Demonstrations grew, and although most were in Beijing, cities the size of Xi'an were affected as well.

In the United States, images of the Chinese demonstrators flooded the news media. Americans rooted for the students and applauded the workers of Shanghai and other cities for their stance against the government. I can remember being captivated by the images of crowds of common people standing up to an authoritarian government. But I also feared the outcome. I knew there had been awful crackdowns in China before. Although the government had begun to liberalize policies under Deng Xiaoping, I wondered how much rebellion it would tolerate. Newspaper photos

Lead Up to May–June 1989 Demonstrations and Massacre

After Mao Zedong died in 1976, Deng Xiaoping began moving China toward a market economy. By 1988, the country was beginning to reap both its benefits and its problems. The danwei—the "iron rice bowl" arrangements of guaranteed jobs, health care, housing, and other necessities—began to fade away as private enterprise competed with cumbersome government-run industries. Increasing inflation worried people, and students exited college without employment skills. Getting a job required personal connections, not skills. Corruption grew.[4]

By the mid-1980s student protests had increased, but the government vacillated about how to handle them. Hu Yaobang, general secretary of the Communist Party from 1982 to 1987, supported reform-minded students, while conservatives thought reforms had gone too far. By 1988, many threads of frustration fed student discontent, and in April 1989, when Hu Yaobang died unexpectedly of a heart attack, students gathered by the thousands to mourn his death and praise his ideas.

Within days, the demonstrations in Beijing's Tiananmen Square and in other cities such as Xi'an morphed into demands for ending corruption and gaining more democracy. Although the government ordered Tiananmen Square cleared for Hu's funeral, more than one hundred thousand students breached police lines and marched in with huge banners. Dissatisfaction with government was palpable. In Xi'an, demonstrations led to burning cars and looting shops. Government leaders were alarmed.

Shortly afterward—while the new, reform-minded Communist Party general secretary, Zhao Ziyang, was out of the country—*People's Daily*, the official party newspaper, ran a front-page editorial that enraged the students and became a sticking point for months. It declared the demonstrations an unpatriotic revolt against the government.

When Zhao Ziyang returned, he arranged a dialogue between student leaders and government officials. Many students, feeling this arrangement satisfied their demands, returned to their campuses, and most university students ended their boycott of classes.

But a significant number remained dissatisfied and decided to use the historic visit of the Soviet leader, Mikhail Gorbachev, as leverage for insisting on change. Gorbachev's state visit would mark the end of thirty years of hostility between China and the Soviet Union.

The protesters launched a hunger strike in Tiananmen Square that drew thousands of students back to the huge public space and galvanized widespread public sympathy. Protests spread to other cities.

As the Gorbachev date drew near and the Chinese government was focused on that critical event, it relaxed press restrictions. Foreign correspondents arrived, and state media began to broadcast images of protesters, including the hunger strikers. Students continued to ask the government to retract the April editorial, but the premier, Li Peng, refused.

Friction grew among factions of the student movement and within opposing elements of the government, while the hunger strike continued to draw increasing public sympathy. By mid-May about one million Beijing residents demonstrated on behalf of the students and launched their own complaints against the government. Young and old from all walks of life took to the streets: army personnel, police officers, doctors and nurses, members of government-sponsored labor unions, and even junior party officials. They asked for redress for their own grievances. Students from elsewhere in China arrived in Beijing, and demonstrations spread to four hundred cities.

A meeting between student leaders and party officials resulted in deadlock. Afterward Zhao Ziyang, tears in his eyes, went to the square to apologize for not succeeding in conciliation. Soon after, he was stripped of all his posts and forbidden to appear in public.

Deng Xiaoping and other party officials declared martial law on May 20 and began to mobilize the army.

showed workers surrounding and stopping army trucks filled with soldiers and of a huge, improvised sculpture made by the students that resembled the Statue of Liberty. Along with large numbers of Americans, I hoped for reconciliation, but it seemed less and less likely.

Only later, from news reports and from An Wei and other Chinese, did I learn of the long string of failed talks and of the struggle inside the government between those who wanted to negotiate with and listen to the students' grievances and those who wanted to take a hard and brutal stand. Although the students tried to communicate that they wanted to improve the country, not bring down the government, Deng Xiaoping refused to believe them.

June 1989

While Beijing was the center of protests, students in large cities across China erupted into passionate demonstrations of discontent. At universities they painted huge silk banners of red and gold and roared their demands through makeshift loudspeaker systems and rallies. They called for the ouster of Deng Xiaoping. In Nanjing they lay down on railway tracks and bridges in protest.

By mid-May Xi'an students had rioted. An Wei was enormously preoccupied with overseeing groups from Australia and the United States at the time. But even though he was staying in a hotel on the outskirts, south of the city wall, he could feel tensions rising in the city.

Truckloads of People's Liberation Army soldiers, mobilized by the government from rural areas and often unaware of what was happening, entered Beijing, but thousands of residents surrounded them. The situation turned into hours of street seminars with citizens lecturing the soldiers. They appealed to the puzzled young recruits, asking them to join the people and reminding them that the People's Liberation Army's main task was to protect Chinese citizens. Eventually, with no other choice, the army turned around and left as thousands applauded.

While the public and the students heralded this a victory, the government, determined to end the demonstrations, was making other plans. Rumors flew. The roar of protests enveloped cities across China. Confrontations increased, and state television warned residents to stay inside. Reports spread that thousands of troops, backed by tanks, were infiltrating Beijing from every direction, all dressed in civilian clothing. When they neared the edge of the city, citizens barricaded intersections with anything they could find, from buses, trucks, and earthmoving machines to piles of bricks. To the shock of everyone, soldiers fired live ammunition at demonstrators and onlookers alike, and raked nearby apartment buildings with semiautomatic rifles, killing citizens standing on their balconies.

Infuriated by the killing, city residents hurled rocks and abuse at the soldiers. Troops fired randomly, while strangers threw wounded citizens onto bicycle lorries and rushed them to overwhelmed hospitals. Doctors were seen on their knees giving mouth-to-mouth resuscitation, while people screamed at Western journalists, "Take pictures. Tell the world what's going on."

When army personnel carriers rammed through burning buses and debris at one intersection, citizens barricaded the next. The army pressed on toward Tiananmen Square, which by this time was occupied primarily by students from outlying areas of China. Many Beijing students had left. Mayhem ensued as the soldiers and tanks advanced across the huge square with orders to clear it by 6:00 a.m. As students fled, others at the back of the crowd were crushed. Some chose to remain, clustered in the center of the square. Although they expected to be killed, the army stopped and told them to leave or be cleared forcefully. They took a vote, and although many believe the majority said they wanted to stay, their leader said the "goes" had won. They marched south out of the square, banners displayed, singing the Internationale, the anthem of the Communist Revolution, to show their patriotism.

By morning, Beijing and the cities across China were silent.

It is unclear to this day how many were killed. Some say hundreds, others thousands.

* * *

In Beijing the next day, adults, primarily parents of students who had been in the square, walked down huge Chang-an Boulevard toward Tiananmen Square. As they drew nearer, a military spokesman ordered them to disperse. Then, within seconds, a line of soldiers fired. The citizens turned and fled, but scores were shot in the back. When an ambulance arrived to help the fallen, the driver and medical workers were also shot and killed.

Within weeks, thousands were arrested, public executions were held on television, and handwritten notice boards appeared in streets listing those from the neighborhoods who had been arrested.

The international response was immediate. China was labeled a pariah.

Summer 1989, Xi'an

Two weeks after the Tiananmen Square crackdown, An Wei sat down at his desk to write Helen. The situation was tense. He kept his everyday conversations to mundane topics and was meticulously careful about what he wrote. Helen had already written him twice about the demonstrations and massacre, and she had included articles from the US newspapers. She was concerned for the Chinese people and asked him for his impression of the situation.

As he began to type, he knew he could not be direct. She must know that. He decided to begin with an update on the movie being made about her 1930s trip to Xi'an. He had been working with the television crew and was very pleased with the actress who was playing Helen as a young woman. Having spent several paragraphs on that, he turned to the current situation: "What happened in Peking[5] was indeed something unexpected. It has been covered, discussed and talked about by the whole world. You are an Old China Hand and I'm sure you can make a correct judgment yourself."

He decided to use roundabout language to tell Helen everything was starting to settle down but was still tense. When he was in Connecticut, they had often referred to the peacefulness of her quiet Madison farmhouse, its grounds full of butterflies. He was sure she would understand his reticence to say more. He paused a minute and then continued typing: "Xi'an, called Chang'an in ancient times, is worthy of the name—quiet, peaceful and beautiful. Everything has now returned to normal. The ripple is gone and 'all was quiet / and the butterflies came again.' You know everything, including 'the old Chinese manner!'"[6]

The months following the Tiananmen massacre were filled with upheaval, as the government hunted down organizers. Universities that had worked since the Cultural Revolution to establish connections with Western professors saw their foreign collaborators flee the country. When students returned in the fall, those who had participated in any way had to attend political sessions and write confessions.

The government also struggled. The world had turned its back on China. No one wanted *any* contact with Chinese officials. Government offices, as was their tradition, invited other nations to visit during the October national holiday. Almost none accepted their invitations.

With government encouragement, citizens with international links began inviting friends of China to return. Nanjing University invited a California professor with a concurrent position to return with two graduate students, their housing paid for. An Wei, in his new position as secretary general of the Friendship Association, convinced a few of his contacts in the United States to visit. After many tries, he finally persuaded Tim Considine, Helen's 1978 videographer, and his family to visit with all their expenses paid by the government.

Sharon Crain came to support An Wei and those Chinese who had worked so hard for more democratic ways and for connections with the out-side world. One night, Sharon and An Wei were visiting a friend in Beijing. They stayed long into the evening, talking about their lives, the changes that had happened, and how difficult the times now were. When they left the seventh-floor apartment, the stairwell lights were out as was often the case. It was pitch black. They felt their way down, hanging onto the railing and sliding their feet along the edge of each step.

Behind Sharon, An Wei commented, "We're just groping in the dark like China is right now." She was amazed that An Wei was able to look at immediate events and see the big picture. Even in that awful time he real-ized that China was hunting in the unknown for a solution to the horrible situation it had created. No matter what, he could sense future possibilities through the gloom.

Spring 1990

Despite China's terrible relationship with foreign governments, the director general and his deputy continued to enhance the professionalism of the For-eign Affairs Office staff. They were well aware of An Wei's abilities, his work ethic, and the effort he made on his own time to reintroduce Helen Snow's valuable work into the archives of Chinese history.

When new housing opened up at the beginning of the year, An Wei and his family were listed for a three-bedroom apartment. What a relief. They had lived in their tiny two-bedroom place for twelve years while An Lin and An Xiang had become teenagers.

Their new apartment, which was a good walk east of the city wall and very close to the ancient Baxian Temple, had a balcony, a kitchen, a bathroom, a nice-sized living room, and three bedrooms, and the family bought their first computer.

The Foreign Affairs Office leaders, including An Wei, met constantly to find ways to repair the international damage that had resulted from the Tiananmen Square massacre. People-to-people exchanges through the Friendship Association seemed one of the few ways to assure old friends that they were still welcome in China.

The provincial leaders decided to send An Wei to the United States to connect with old friends and make new acquaintances. He made a three-month plan, pointing out to the director general that this trip would require more time than most. He would begin in Minnesota, where he had many connections, and then move on to Kansas City, New York City, Connecticut, and Florida, winding up in Los Angeles. He needed to have informal meetings and chats to encourage friends and acquaintances to resume their associations and exchange programs. He would attend their activities and speak to groups who were still interested in China. The officials agreed and told him that those who were interested in visiting would be the guests of China.

Amid the planning, staff transfers brought unexpected change. Zhang Jingwen, the forward-looking director general, was promoted to another agency and replaced by Zhang Kairou, who was transferred from an aircraft engine factory and had little knowledge of foreign affairs.

2009, Altadena, California

At my home in the hills above Los Angeles, An Wei and I made tea and walked along the deck to my office for some interview time. He was at the end of a trip to work on Helen Snow material. As we settled into a conversation, he mentioned that when he was in the United States or another country, he could see Chinese events more clearly. He had been retired now for seven years, and he said China was showing interest in developing democracy in rural villages, a direct result of the government's efforts to recover their world status after the Tiananmen Square massacre. As he reflected on that awful time, he said,

> When I have talked about trying to swim in the dangerous ocean and save myself, I have been talking about critical times. I had my own ideas about the big issues involved in the student movement and demonstrations. But government employees like me had to be extremely cautious in regard to the party's political lines.
>
> I supported the students ideologically and politically; that is true, not only now, but then. But those who wanted to attack me could not get the facts to show that's what I was thinking. I was sympathetic with the students and also very

angry when the army suppressed the young people. But I did not openly say anything. I did not participate in the demonstrations. Those of us who participated in the Cultural Revolution learned a great lesson on how to be careful.

An Wei sat in my desk chair watching the olive tree branches dip in the breezes. He then leaned forward, making emphatic chops with his left hand, his loose watchband sliding up and down with the motion. "You have to believe in yourself. You have to believe you can make things happen."

Summer 1990

In June, An Wei began his trip to the United States with a month at the Concordia Language Villages in Minnesota, where several thousand high school students gathered to learn languages. While An Wei was enjoying the intense program and helping participants understand Chinese culture, jolting news arrived from his office manager in Xi'an. He had been removed from his position as secretary general at the Friendship Association. It had something to do with his support for the student demonstrations.

When he told Margaret Wong, his Chinese American friend in Minneapolis, she reacted instantly. She knew China's political scene.

"An Wei, you will be in trouble if you return. You can stay in the United States. Your friends here can help you get a visa extension and a green card."

Stubborn to the core, An Wei refused her help. "It's not serious. I know I did not make any mistakes, so I don't need to stay here or seek political asylum." He told her he was not afraid.

"I will complete my visit according to my original plan and go back."

He went on with his work. In addition to his teaching, he reestablished relationships with those who had previously hosted Chinese visitors and began to seek out retired teachers who might be interested in volunteering to teach English in Chinese schools. He knew that if China was going to reconnect with the world and have trade relationships with other countries, the young people needed to know English. Foreigners were certainly not likely to become fluent in Chinese.

Then a letter arrived from Niu Jianhua confirming that he had been removed from his position as secretary general. She wrote that people in the Foreign Affairs Office accused him of showing sympathy to the student demonstrators. This time his anger surfaced. It was illegal to remove officials or punish staff members while they were out of the country. If they did that, the person might flee. The new director general of the office, Zhang Kairou, obviously did not know the law.

An Wei flew to Kansas City where he and Sharon had arranged for Chinese farmers, skilled in painting rural scenes, to demonstrate their techniques and talents. It was a magnificent success. But a friend from the Xi'an office, who had accompanied the farmers, reconfirmed that he had been stripped of his position. He was accused of standing on the sidewalk outside the Foreign Affairs Office applauding the student marchers.

Undaunted, An Wei went on to Connecticut, Florida, Nevada, and then Sacramento, San Francisco, and Los Angeles. He gave talks, participated in meetings and conferences, and visited old friends and acquaintances. He was sure a number of them would travel to China for this year's national holiday celebrations.

Tim Considine's Los Angeles home was his final destination. Margaret Wong in Minneapolis continued to offer help and warn him to be careful, but An Wei was adamant. Political struggles were common in the government. At any time someone could send a "black letter" to a higher-up accusing you of something, and it could be anonymous.

Was he frightened? Yes, he told Tim.

Was it dangerous? No. He was guilty of nothing. He was going back to clear his record. Whoever accused him was lying.

Before he left, though, he agreed to this request from Tim: If things became bad for him, he would write Tim that the weather was great. If things were okay, he would say the weather was bad.

· *11* ·

Working in Limbo

Fall 1990, Xi'an

"Good morning, Director General Zhang, I am back," An Wei greeted his boss as he sat down in a chair facing Zhang Kairou's desk. The husky director, who had unusually fleshy cheeks and double chin, was cordial but not enthusiastic. He still had not informed An Wei that he had been stripped of his job.

An Wei plunged in as if nothing had changed and began regaling Zhang with all of the successful events in Kansas City and all the Americans who agreed to visit China during the National Day celebrations.

It was essential that Zhang Kairou, who did not know him well, understand how much he had accomplished during these post–Tiananmen Square times when countries were condemning China. An Wei went on to describe the useful contacts he had made for China and the importance of the conferences he attended.

The director general said he was glad it had been a fruitful time and then added, "You must be very tired. You can have a week vacation." Zhang obviously wanted no further discussion.

If the director was not going to raise the topic, An Wei would. He took a deep breath and edged forward on his chair.

"Director General Zhang, when I was in the United States I was told, though never officially notified, that I had been removed from my position as secretary general of the Friendship Association. Why? If I made any mistakes, I am ready to receive punishment, but you have to tell me what I did wrong."

Zhang waved a dismissive hand at An Wei. "I will talk with you another time."

*   *   *

A week later, having heard nothing, An Wei called the director general. When they finally met, An Wei asked why he had been removed, and Zhang Kairou told him it was the organization's decision.

"We received a report that you made serious mistakes," Zhang said, but he refused to say what.

An Wei would not be put off. "Let me tell you what the accusations are and see if I am correct." He told the director general that an unsigned letter had been sent to the disciplinary committee saying he had stood on Jiefang Road by the Foreign Affairs Office just before June 4, 1989, clapping for the student demonstrators as they passed.

Zhang's face remained impassive.

An Wei continued. His accuser also claimed that at a party meeting An Wei had said he would be lying if he had to agree with the Party Central Committee's policies toward the demonstrators.

"Are these the reasons you removed me? Without an investigation and without allowing me the right to speak?"

The director general remained silent, but An Wei could see the redness creeping across his fleshy cheeks, a sure sign of anger.

What could Zhang be thinking? Why didn't he follow party procedure? An Wei had trouble disguising his frustration, but he chose his words carefully.

"Mr. Zhang, you may not have read an important document from the Party Central Committee from several years ago," purposely omitting Zhang's title when he addressed him this time. That document, he reminded Zhang, said that no matter what kind of mistake a cadre had committed, he should never be accused while visiting abroad because he might flee to another country. Though tense, An Wei continued.

"I heard of your decision to remove me while I was in the United States." He pointed out that if he were not patriotic, he could have stayed there. There were several American friends who offered to help him get a green card.

"If I had stayed in the United States, you would be in a lot of trouble."

Zhang Kairou shifted in his chair, his jaws clenched tight.

Met by silence, An Wei left the office.

Several weeks later, in a calmer meeting, An Wei offered proof to Zhang Kairou that he had been nowhere near Jiefang Road during the demonstrations. He was in charge of large visiting groups from the United States and Australia from May 25 to June 10, 1989, and was staying with them in the Oriental Hotel in the southern suburbs, a long way from Jiefang Road. During those days, he explained, he had worked nonstop for the groups, often long into the night.

"You can check the records to verify that," he said.

After a month of silence, An Wei requested another meeting. Zhang was cordial. His broad cheeks relaxed; he said the investigation into the charges had been completed. It verified that An Wei was with large groups at the Oriental Hotel during the time of the demonstrations. In addition, when party members were queried about whether he refused to follow party policy, all except one said An Wei had never made such remarks.

Protocol prohibited An Wei from asking that person's name, so he proceeded in a roundabout way.

"Director General Zhang, I won't ask you who said this, for I am sure who he is." Only one person in the organization would tell such lies: Mr. Li, the man who had come from an assignment in western China and wanted An Wei's job. Most people in the office knew that Li had tried different ways to secure it under the previous director general, and he was now trying with Zhang.

Zhang Kairou made no response.

An Wei, although furious, felt a sense of relief as he left the director general's office. The investigation effectively cleared him since party policy required three people to independently concur with an accusation. Now he just needed to wait to be reinstated to his job.

But he also realized that Zhang himself was now in a difficult position. He had removed An Wei from his job without proof, and he would have to find a way to reinstate him without losing face. Still, An Wei was hopeful.

Every day at 8:00 a.m. sharp, An Wei arrived at the Foreign Affairs Office. Trying to remain upbeat, he greeted other employees and climbed the stairs to his office, hoping this would be the day he would get his job back. He had made a lot of contacts on this trip and wanted to follow up with them, but without an official position, he could not.

He put on water for tea and dusted the accumulated coal soot off his desk and the windowsill. Once the water boiled, he made tea, planning the work he would do at home that night. He sat down at his desk, swirled his tea jar, and watched the leaves settle. Except for attending occasional meetings, he read newspapers until noon. *People's Daily* was filled with government edicts. He preferred the local papers, where he often zeroed in on ads and lost-and-found lists, including the stolen bicycles held at the police station. He especially looked for ads for translator jobs. A travel service in Shenzhen looked promising, though far from their home. Even more interesting were translator positions for a pharmaceutical company in Xi'an that was a joint venture enterprise with Belgium. Maybe he should consider applying there.

Periodic calls to Zhang only resulted in more stalling.

An Wei began to take Helen Snow's manuscripts to the office to read. But he dared not translate them there since someone might accuse him of doing self-serving work. At least he had his old office, where it was convenient to read and work on his computer. He still shared the space with his trusted longtime assistant. They got along well, although he was no longer An Wei's assistant and had to keep his distance because An Wei was considered tainted.

One day he reached for an envelope to mail a letter to Helen and then decided to try faxing it as he had when he was secretary general. He walked down to the typing and printing room. Had the young woman in charge of faxing been instructed not to do anything for him? He tried to act normally.

"Good morning, can you send this fax as soon as possible?" He handed her the letter and the fax number.

She took it, saying she would send it soon. Relieved, he thanked her and returned to his office, pleased with the result. He needed to be judicious about how many he sent, though. It was innocuous material, but if troublemakers found out, they might create problems. Everyone knew he had been removed from his job.

The next week, An Wei decided to try an international call. He dialed the woman who ran the switchboard, a neighbor who had played with An Lin and An Xiang when they were young and who had taken English courses he taught.

"Good morning, Xiaoyuan; please switch on the distance line," he said and then waited for the tone, dialed Helen's number, and hoped for the best. Within minutes, the call connected and he heard Helen's familiar voice. He asked her questions about a manuscript he was translating at night, keeping the call short.

Now he knew he could also make international calls—just not too often or too long.

Weeks with no job passed into months. He felt his talents and knowledge being strangled. He also felt awful that he was unable to develop the connections he had made during his US trip.

He attended required meetings, sitting in the back row where he could doze and save up energy for nighttime when he gave talks at schools, taught English lessons, and translated Helen's work. An Wei also spearheaded the development of an Edgar and Helen Snow Studies Center and kept Helen abreast of its progress, and he worked with scholars to plan two symposiums about Helen's involvement with the industrial co-op movement.

His frustration built as his job situation remained unresolved. He had the same rank as before and was still receiving the same salary, but he needed to *do* something. The government was paying him; he should be working for the people. Lunchtime brought relief when he retreated to his apartment to eat and have a nap, a standard Chinese habit. At 2:00 p.m., heavy hearted, he would return to the office for another four hours, hoping to hear from Zhang and being careful to follow office regulations so no one could attack him.

He returned to Zhang again and again, increasingly outspoken.

"If I made mistakes, you can expel me," he said one day. "If I did something against government laws, you can punish me. But you need to make everything fair. In the early days you wanted me to make everything clear. Now, I want *you* to make everything clear."

After three years of jobless agony, An Wei began to boil over with anger. His friends counseled that he should speak nicely to Zhang Kairou. He should beg him for a response or give him an expensive gift, but An Wei refused to consider that. At yet another meeting with Zhang, he said, "During the Cultural Revolution old cadres were put aside for one or two years, but you have put me aside for three years now. *I cannot live with this.*"

Zhang Kairou looked at him.

"I don't need to be secretary general of the Friendship Association," An Wei added. "Use me as an interpreter." He could translate faxes to save others time. But An Wei knew they would not assign him those jobs because they were afraid he might insult them. If they did not trust him to do anything else, he could be the reading room librarian or greet people at the front gate. He wanted some type of job. Although he was finding productive projects to do at night, he felt he might go mad. Maybe that is what Zhang Kairou wanted.

In another meeting with Zhang Kairou, he lost his temper.

"I come to the Foreign Affairs Office every day. Everyone is busy with visiting groups, with specific work assigned by the office while I just sit drinking tea and reading the newspaper. I do not want to be a professional newspaper reader."

Zhang Kairou slammed his hand on the desk, his face red with fury, but he said nothing.

Coiled like a spring, An Wei leaned forward and pounded his hand on Zhang's desk. Greeted with more silence, he stood up and stalked out.

1994

In spring 1994, An Wei found himself surrounded by constant family activity. In preparation for a year of teaching at a Kansas City community college, Niu Jianhua was collecting books and organizing the household for her absence. An Wei, who had joined a small Xi'an group to use email, outfitted his son's bedroom with a phone, a computer, and a fax machine. He used it for his weeknight office but had to vacate it each weekend when An Xiang, a student at China's Northwest Polytechnic University, returned home.

An Lin was more complicated. After middle school she side-stepped high school and the college entrance exam by attending a four-year vocational school, which was somewhat like a US community college. After that, much to An Wei and Niu Jianhua's disapproval, she took a job at a cigarette company. They hated smoking.

But neither he nor Niu Jianhua realized that An Lin had been seeing a young man for several years. When they finally met Zhou Jing, they did not approve of him for their daughter but eventually gave in to strong-willed An Lin, who was deeply in love. Just before Niu Jianhua left for a year in Kansas, An Lin, wearing a lovely red Chinese wedding dress, and Zhou Jing, in a dark Western-style suit and tie, were married in a traditional two-day ceremony.

Soon after, An Lin quit her job and entered a program to study English. She had become interested in her parents' work of building bridges between the Chinese people and Americans.

Spring 1995

An Wei slit open the airmail envelope from Concordia College and skimmed the letter, which took him by surprise. He read the details again, but more carefully. Could he serve for at least a month this summer as a senior Chinese consultant for their language learning villages? And would he recruit a young person to teach Chinese all summer? They would pay their round-trip fares to Minnesota.

An Wei sat back in his comfortable wooden desk chair and came close to smiling. He needed this. Not only would it alleviate his stalemate with the director general, but also it would allow him to continue the work he had started during his 1990 trip. His mind began churning. He also could continue his search for retired American teachers or others who might be interested in teaching English in China.

Moreover, he would be able to pay Helen a much-overdue visit. Niu Jianhua, in Kansas for the year, was planning to meet her in May, but Helen's health was waning and he longed to see his mentor again after five years. Although they communicated by letter, fax, and occasional phone calls, he wanted to be in the same room with her, to assure her that as her life drew to an end, he would continue carrying on her work and making her writing available in China.

First he had to get permission from Zhang Kairou. Their relationship had become more cordial in recent months, even though the director wouldn't give An Wei any work or discuss his case. The trip would cost the office nothing. But he still needed to convince the director general to let him leave.

Before he could even broach the subject, Zhang Kairou approached him as An Wei finished giving an evening talk to a college group. The director's expression and even his posture seemed to suggest uncertainty. He told An Wei the senior provincial leader in charge of the courts and police stations had requested that the Foreign Affairs Office arrange a US visit for a delegation, but the office had no way to organize such a project. Zhang said he had heard that An Wei had connections with the US government. Would he be able to help?

An Wei smiled inwardly. Here was his chance. Director General Zhang needed to impress the provincial leader, and he needed An Wei's help to do it.

"Well, let me try," An Wei said, knowing full well he had enough contacts in Minnesota to make the arrangements.

A few weeks later, with his tentative summer schedule organized, An Wei approached the director general for a three-month leave of absence. He showed Zhang the invitation from Concordia College and added that in order to pave the way for the legal delegation's trip, he needed to talk with his contacts in person. He also dangled another benefit for Zhang. Would the Foreign Affairs Office be interested in selecting a young person to teach Chinese all summer in Minnesota?

"Can it be a student?" Zhang Kairou asked.

"Of course, as long as he or she can speak English well," An Wei said.

Zhang quickly granted An Wei his summer trip to the United States.

The Foreign Affairs Office arranged for people who spoke English to apply for the summer position at Concordia. All six applicants showed up for interviews. The student Zhang had recommended could speak no English except "My name is _____." He was eliminated immediately, and a fluent high school English teacher was selected.

Zhang Kairou was angry that his candidate hadn't been chosen. He had helped An Wei go on this trip and felt he should have returned the favor by accepting the unqualified student. But it was too late for Zhang to forbid An Wei to go. Besides, he was desperate for him to make arrangements for the legal delegation.

*   *   *

An Wei pulled up Niu Jianhua's email address at Maple Woods Community College in Kansas and told her the good news. They would meet in Minnesota after her classes ended and after she visited Helen.

To ensure that his wife made the most of her few days in Connecticut, An Wei emailed her a list of critical topics to address. Could Helen give them, in writing, authorization to translate and publish her books in China after her death? Could she provide a list of her books that still needed publishing in Chinese and indicate which were the most important? Finally, he asked Niu Jianhua to persuade Helen that the manuscript of her family history he had found in her cartons several years earlier was vitally important to include in her biography. (She had refused to let An Wei have a copy.) "As a woman," he wrote, "perhaps you will be able to get these materials from her."[1]

June 1995, Madison, Connecticut

Niu Jianhua set the aluminum tins of leftovers from Helen's Meals on Wheels lunch out on the deck for the raccoons to scavenge and returned to Helen's living room, where her bed had been moved. Seated beside Helen, she admired an oil painting of a young, beautiful Helen Snow that hung on the dark paneled wall. Helen smiled a little. She had long been regarded as a ravishing beauty during her time in China.

They carried on long conversations, with Helen doing most of the talking. Niu Jianhua listened attentively, often gently holding Helen's hand. She already knew much of Helen's life story from An Wei's work, but she was eager to learn more.

Though Helen trusted few people, she felt an immediate connection with Niu Jianhua. At one point in their few days together, Helen told her of the precious fabrics she had brought from China. "I've never wanted to give them to anyone," she said. "But now I know they are all for you."[2] Helen also gave Niu Jianhua photos and documents for the museum in Xi'an, along with many of her clothes—all accompanied by a detailed list that Helen had typed:

> Three hats of Helen Snow's—one Navy velvet with a rose, one leopard skin that went with her leopard skin coat which she wore in China, one green knit winter cap . . .
> One multicolored plaid long skirt, which she wore at Christmas time . . .
> One mustard colored robe from India
> One black velvet jacket and short pants . . .

Two white collar pieces and two white cuffs
Two fur collar pieces to button on
One pair of felt suspenders yellow with flowers . . .
Two colorful handkerchiefs
One hairpiece braided[3]

But her family history never materialized.

Summer 1995, Minnesota

An Wei was ecstatic to be back in Minneapolis, where he and Niu Jianhua were staying with Margaret Wong, their good friend who had given the Friendship Association the computer and in 1990 urged An Wei to remain in the United States.

At a party hosted by Margaret Wong's relatives, they met Sarah, a young woman who wanted to know more about China. During the conversation, she mentioned her job with a nongovernmental organization, Global Volunteers.

An Wei straightened up, intrigued.

"It sends volunteers all over the world," she added. "They spend their own money to serve others." Was this the answer to his search for retired teachers who might want to teach English in China?

Sarah's descriptions sounded too good to be true, but maybe, just maybe, this was the right organization. He and Niu Jianhua listened carefully.

Sarah told them about Global Volunteers programs in various countries—from staffing health clinics to helping install water pumps in villages and teaching English. They pulled some chairs closer together. An Wei's leg jiggled with excitement as his questions poured out. He also told Sarah why their program would be good in China.

An Wei described his extensive background with foreign affairs dignitaries, his connections with US government officials such as former president Jimmy Carter and former vice president Walter Mondale, his experience planning for visiting groups, and his ability to connect volunteers with schools. His fingers tightened on the chair arms when he explained that he was looking for retired teachers who would want to visit China and teach English. He inched forward in his chair and added that China was a nation rising in the world and Xi'an itself was a historic center that volunteers would enjoy visiting.

Was he saying too much? He hoped not, but he had to sell this young woman on the value of Global Volunteers coming to China.

"Can you arrange for us to meet your president?" he asked.

She agreed.

*   *   *

In the low-slung building that housed the Global Volunteers' modest office, An Wei and Niu Jianhua shook hands with Bud Philbrook, a tall, blond American who headed the organization. From his comments, it was obvious Sarah had told him everything.

Being as aggressive as he dared, An Wei said he hoped that Global Volunteers would set up a service program in China. "The best city would be Xi'an."

Philbrook knew little about China, so An Wei offered every detail about Xi'an he thought might impress him. It had been the ancient capital of China, the seat of many dynasties, and the site where the ancient terracotta warriors from China's first emperor had been unearthed. The Silk Road began in Xi'an, and the first woman empress ruled from there. It had a remarkable intact city wall and a very old mosque. Furthermore, its schools welcomed foreigners, and An Wei knew many of them well. He handed the CEO his résumé and proposed a few ideas for possible programs.

As the meeting drew to a close, Philbrook asked lots of questions and then said their proposal was very sound. "However, we will need to discuss it at our next board meeting in two weeks. I will contact you after that."

Exhausted yet hopeful, An Wei and Niu Jianhua returned to Margaret Wong's and packed their bags for the long ride to the Concordia Language Villages in northern Minnesota to begin their assignments.

The next month just before going to teach a Chinese class, An Wei's heart pounded as he answered a call from Global Volunteers. The caller told him that the board had approved the proposal to investigate a program in China.

That evening at his small desk, he smoothed out a sheet of paper damp from Minnesota's humidity and wrote to the Friendship Association in Xi'an. He quickly faxed the letter in which he noted that while he was no longer a real staff person, this was a marvelous opportunity the group should sponsor. He explained the Global Volunteers program and how it would benefit Chinese teachers and schools. He included his summer contact phone and fax numbers and asked them to respond at their earliest convenience.

At a meeting with Bud Philbrook two weeks later, An Wei presented a proposed schedule. Bud would need ten days—a week in Xi'an and a few days in Baoji, a city two hours away. An Wei had added Baoji because he had learned of the organization's desire to consult about business practices and of Bud's special interest in cooperatives. The Gung Ho Industrial Cooperatives had begun in Baoji, making it a good place to explore a short-term project. They would also try to visit all the Xi'an schools where volunteers would work. An Wei proposed that he arrive in early October, and Bud agreed.

During the next weeks, An Wei checked eagerly for a response from the Xi'an Foreign Affairs Office or the Friendship Association to express interest in the Global Volunteers program, but no one replied. Not having a Chinese sponsor could cause him serious problems, but he plunged ahead with the plans anyway.

August 1995, Madison, Connecticut

An Wei thought he was prepared to see an elderly Helen, whom he had not visited for five years. But seeing her so ill made him sad. She was gaunt, a shadow of her former self, yet her greeting conveyed her usual assertiveness.

He and Sharon Crain had arranged to have a friend from New York join them to film an interview. For two afternoons, An Wei, Sharon, and her son interviewed Helen as she lay in bed, talking nonstop. Occasionally they had to force her to rest. But she was eager to talk about her unpublished manuscripts and her regrets about what she hadn't accomplished, about her desire for An Wei to continue translating and promoting her work, and about what should be done with her files after her death. Peppered throughout the conversations were her reminiscences of the Chinese leaders she had known so well. An Wei decided not to mention the biographical information he wanted.

When he said good-bye at the end of the second day, he reminded himself that she wrote for future generations and did not fear death. In fact, she had taken him to her graveyard plot years earlier and told him that when he visited her there he could bring her yellow roses and good news from China.

Fall 1995, Xi'an

Returning to the Foreign Affairs Office, still with no job, An Wei had two items to report to Zhang Kairou, the director general. First, he had succeeded in making substantial arrangements for the provincial legal delegation to visit experts in the US and state of Minnesota judicial systems. Impressed that An Wei could set up such important meetings, Zhang was pleased and approved him as the group's interpreter for its November trip to the United States.

More important, An Wei needed approval for the Global Volunteers project. But Zhang Kairou was not interested unless it produced financial profits. Nor were the other leaders of the Foreign Affairs Office. They refused to let An Wei describe the program at a staff meeting. He tried to explain anyway. It was not a profitable program but rather a volunteer service. "If we sponsored it, our students and teachers would benefit a lot, not only by learning a language, but from the spirit of volunteering. It is a wonderful concept."

They still were not interested.

What could he do? He had already invited Global Volunteers to China, and the law required a sponsor. Bud Philbrook was arriving for his inspection tour in a few weeks. If An Wei went back on his word, these Americans would think Chinese could not be trusted. Besides it was a wonderful opportunity for Xi'an students. He had to find a willing organization.

Did a possibility lie with the Shaanxi Translators Association, the nongovernmental group he helped form in 1980? He had been the unpaid secretary general for a decade and was now the executive vice president. Journalist Ma Ke, whom he had met during Helen Snow's exhibition, was the unpaid secretary general. They called it the "Three Withouts Organization." They had no money, no official backing, and almost no office space. More problematic, they had no government authority to host foreigners. He hoped its members could produce an idea.

At the next meeting of the association's executive committee, An Wei explained the need. Despite the roadblocks, the organization decided to host the Global Volunteers inspection team.

Relieved by the support, but concerned by its nongovernmental status, An Wei turned to a former schoolmate, Yuan Xu, who headed the International Cultural Exchange Center of Shaanxi Province. After hearing An Wei out, he expressed enthusiasm for the program and said he would be glad to welcome Bud Philbrook in the name of his organization.

An Wei breathed a large sigh of relief. The Cultural Exchange Center was very prestigious and had more clout than the Friendship Association of Shaanxi Province. His friend gave An Wei a warning, though. The center might be a good umbrella, but it had a very small staff, which meant that the Translators Association would need to do all the day-to-day work.

The autumn sun cast a warm glow over Xi'an on Bud's October arrival day. The American's face shone with enthusiasm as An Wei whisked him and a colleague through a ten-day schedule of nonstop banquets, school visits, and meetings. Impressed by what he saw, Bud approved Xi'an as a new Global Volunteers site before he left.

Once he returned to Minneapolis, Bud began a frenetic email and fax exchange with An Wei to hammer out details. An Wei was exhilarated. His work for Helen was going well, and Global Volunteers gave him a new purpose. The first team would arrive in April, to be followed by several more. He was doing work he loved, despite Zhang Kairou's refusal to give him a job.

Spring 1996

Ma Ke and An Wei worked side by side, determined to make this first Global Volunteers experience a major success. When they had met, An Wei was impressed by Ma Ke's English fluency and the long article he wrote about Helen that appeared on the front page of *Shaanxi Daily*, the top newspaper of the province. When Ma Ke later confided his frustration about the corrupt bureaucracy in which he worked, An Wei persuaded him to volunteer with the Translators Association. "You won't get any money, but you will get satisfaction that you are doing something good for people."

Ma Ke, whose congenial face was dominated by thick eyebrows, helped formalize arrangements with several Xi'an schools, making sure each one would have the staff to welcome and help the volunteers. An Wei handled the rest. If he could make successful arrangements for a US president, surely he could do it for these volunteers. He arranged housing at the Oriental Hotel, checked on permits and visa applications, and organized the welcoming program. He loved thinking through all the small pieces and coordinating tasks.

An Wei and Ma Ke worked long hours the week before the Global Volunteers team arrived in April, making sure every detail was in place, including laying a red carpet for the welcoming ceremony. In the small courtyard of the Oriental Hotel, the sixteen US volunteers and their group leaders were escorted up the steps on the carpet and greeted by provincial and local leaders. Li Lianbi, the former Chinese ambassador to the European Economic Community and an important figure in Shaanxi Province, made a brief, heartfelt speech on behalf of the government and the Shaanxi people. Unlike Zhang Kairou, he praised volunteering as a noble service and called people-to-people diplomacy the foundation of governmental relations. He lauded the Global Volunteers as American Lei Fengs, referring to the young soldier who sacrificed himself to help others and inspired selfless volunteering during An Wei's college years.

Children from Xi'an schools sang, danced, and presented the Americans with their red Young Pioneer scarves. That evening Ambassador Li hosted a sumptuous banquet, and the next day the local newspaper published an article with the headline "Lei Feng Is Back from America." Soon everyone in Xi'an seemed to know about the American volunteers.

By the time the second team arrived, the Translators Association had formed a new organization within its structure—the Sino-American Society, an English-speaking subset of members acquainted with US culture, devoted exclusively to the Global Volunteers programs and their needs. The staff was the same as the Translators Association, though. Ma Ke remained its unpaid secretary general overseeing all the day-to-day work, and An Wei was the unpaid executive vice president.

2014, Xi'an

After a short break in my interviews, I found An Wei sitting on the usual small stool in his office, gazing out the second-story window of their new condominium into the dense, light-green foliage of the Chinese scholar trees. He and Niu Jian-hua had moved here a few years before, escaping the noise and pollution of their apartment in the middle of Xi'an. An Wei turned toward me and continued the topic we had interrupted.

> I sat in that Friendship Association office with no job for over five years. I had figured out how to keep myself sane and to continue my study and research, translation, and the publishing of Helen Snow's work. I did a little in the office and a lot at night and on weekends. I also spent a lot of time promoting translation work in the provinces and working for the Translators Association. That was all volunteer work. Zhang's punishment was backfiring. The Foreign Affairs Office was paying me a full salary, and I was working as an unpaid volunteer outside.

An Wei gave himself over to laughter, his eyes closed and a big grin creasing his cheeks.

> From the time the Global Volunteers program started, I worked for it almost full time in my Friendship Association office, preparing for the teams. I loved giving them the best experiences we could think of, and the schools were so grateful to have native-speaking English teachers. It made me realize that I wanted to spend all my time on down-to-earth programs, ones that were good for society. No diplomacy, no government bureaucracy. I just wanted to work for all the people.

June 1996

An Wei paused to review the letter he was writing to his superiors: "Nearly six years have passed since I was dismissed from my post of secretary general of the Friendship Association without any tenable reasons. . . ."

He wondered what the leaders of the Foreign Affairs Office would do when they read his request.

He glanced at papers stacked on his desk. He wanted the leaders to remember the impossible situation they had put him in. He adjusted his fingers on his pen and continued writing. He reminded them that he had asked many times for a job, any job. He had even offered to work as the office librarian or the gatekeeper. He told them he felt guilty sitting in the office doing nothing while receiving his full salary.

An Wei's chair creaked as he leaned back to read his letter a final time. He thought about all the work needed to prepare for the next Global

Volunteers team that was arriving soon. With a firm hand, he brought the letter to a close. "I am applying to retire early. Beginning tomorrow, I will stay at home and await your notification telling me to complete the retirement formalities."

Good, he thought. Even though he knew Zhang Kairou wouldn't know what to do with his retirement application, he was freeing both of them. Zhang was like a man riding on a tiger's back; he could not get down from the running beast. He had refused to give An Wei a job and would also have trouble granting him retirement at the young age of fifty-three. Well, that was Zhang's problem. An Wei smiled. Beginning tomorrow, he would be free to work full time on his own projects.

He pushed back his chair, walked to the personnel division, and asked to see the chief, whom he disliked intensely. The man was oily tongued, and he fawned on leaders. Long ago, he had changed An Wei's office work start date to a year later, which had reduced An Wei's wages.

An Wei held out the one-page letter to him.

"This is my retirement application. Please submit it to the group of five leaders." Zhang Kairou was the head of that group. The chief took the letter but said nothing.

Back in his government office, An Wei straightened a few papers and looked at his books and other documents. He would leave them here until he was officially retired. He had never felt comfortable with the bureaucracy, but over these last years he had grown to loathe it. The sign at the entrance gate said, "Serve the People." It was their mantra, but he knew the leaders never thought about the broad masses of people.

As 6:00 p.m. neared, he got up slowly from his familiar desk, fished for the office key, and closed the door behind him. The click of the lock brought a feeling of accomplishment. In the hallway, he nodded to a few staff and walked down the steps to the front entrance. As he mounted his bicycle to head home, he looked back. Serve the people, ha. They were giants with words and dwarfs of action.

Summer 1996

An Wei and Sharon kept in touch about Helen Snow's health, even though phone calls were expensive and e-mail connections were erratic. Although she was still opinionated, Helen was growing weaker. An Wei was saddened to learn that she had been moved to a nursing home. He knew that her relatives in Utah were much too far away to be able to give the kind of personal care his Brother Number Five was providing for their mother, who lived in a large room in their village homestead where family members could sit on the kang and visit with her.

Guilford, Connecticut

"These are going to be my last written messages," Helen told Sharon.

"I am eighty-eight years old but weigh less than eighty-eight pounds." It was difficult, she said, for her to find a comfortable position in bed.

She wore a tattered purple sweater fastened with a large safety pin. It had been given to her by her old friend Lu Cui, who as a young student had been small enough and brave enough to wiggle under a huge Beijing gate and open it to let students demonstrating against Japanese occupation into the city. It would become known as the December 9th Movement.

Sharon tried to keep up with Helen as she dictated letters to her closest Chinese friends. Even in her failing condition she spoke quickly and insisted that her exact words be used. As Sharon scribbled fast, she was amazed at Helen's words of praise. She had never praised anyone.

Xi'an

An Wei opened the airmail envelope from Sharon and read Helen's letter. He was moved that she was using her limited energy to dictate so much. He read it slowly once, and then again, thinking of the years he had spent developing her trust and learning her ways.

He was touched that she remembered details of her 1978 trip, such as the visit he arranged to the newly discovered terracotta warriors site, which had not been made public. And she was impressed that he was able, on the spur of the moment, to have the Banpo Neolithic Village Museum opened so she and her video crew could see it. Why would she remember such trivial events?

He slowly reread the letter. She wrote that he was capable and good with words and actions, and that his marriage to Niu Jianhua doubled each other's effectiveness, just as she and Edgar had added to each other's strengths.

Tears rolled down his cheeks as he reread the last sentence: "You are one of the most promising young men I have ever met."

Still holding the letter, he rededicated himself to translating more of her books. He resolved that he would also contribute as much as he could to world peace.

December 1996, Guilford, Connecticut

Sharon pushed Helen's wheelchair into a quiet section of the nursing home. She was very ill, but she sat as tall as she could, her sparse grey hair neatly combed. She wore a hand-embroidered red silk jacket she had brought back from China so many years ago.

Helen's face lit up at the sight of so many Chinese and American journalists crammed into the nursing home's low-ceilinged room. Nobody would have guessed that minutes before she had resisted going because she didn't want to be seen in failing health. After all, she had been so strong and beautiful in those days in China.

Smiling Ambassador Mei Ping, the consul general in New York for the People's Republic of China, greeted her, as did Deputy Consul General Gu and Consul Li. They had come to present Helen with the Friendship Ambassador Award, one of the highest honors China offered to foreign citizens, for her "outstanding contribution to Sino-US People's Friendship."

Ambassador Mei, a large man with a strong voice, explained that the award had been given to very few people and that Helen was the only American to receive it. Though she was having difficulty hearing, Helen was keenly aware of the honor being presented to her. In a soft voice, she challenged young Americans and Chinese to do at least as much toward mutual understanding as she and Edgar had done long ago.

Ambassador Mei Ping leaned over and gently slipped the gold-and-red-striped ribbon that held the large award medallion over Helen's head. He then handed her a bouquet of yellow roses. Helen was deeply touched. As soon as everyone left, she told Sharon, "This award makes me feel that my life and struggles in China have been appreciated. My life was worthwhile."[4]

Helen Snow died six months later, on January 11, 1997.

An Wei rustled through papers on his desk for a poem of Helen's that he had always loved. He read it aloud:

> I'd like a little rosemary
> A-growing on my grave
> I want to face the east because
> The sun comes up that way.[5]

· *12* ·

Stately Maples

January 2000, Xi'an

Niu Jianhua's father straightened the cover on a nearby chair as An Wei sat down. Her mother poured tea into ceramic cups, and her face lit up with pride and expectation.

"Is An Lin eating well?"

"Yes," An Wei said. "She's getting used to American food."

"Where is she living?"

"She lives near the university with her cousin." The words nearly stuck in his throat.

One question followed another.

He and Niu Jianhua had planned what to say to An Lin's grandparents.

"What is she studying?"

"She is taking English courses and studying hard," he said as his voice quavered at the lies. "She is doing fine."

He paused a moment, and the image of her grandfather showing An Lin how to hold her chopsticks flashed through his mind. He could hear her repeatedly saying the word *rice* after her grandmother taught it to her. When An Wei had finally been assigned an apartment large enough for An Lin to move in with them, her loving grandparents arranged for her to spend Saturday nights with them.

As An Wei and Niu Jianhua later walked to the bus stop, each realized they would have to keep up this fiction until An Lin's grandparents died. The thought of making up stories about the life she should have lived was horrible. But the truth would kill Niu Jianhua's frail mother and father. An Lin had died during her first semester in the United States.

195

*   *   *

Two years before her tragic death, An Lin had been a vibrant and cheerful young woman with shoulder-length black hair, loved by the American volunteers. As she chatted with them and studied conscientiously, her spoken English had become much more fluent. At the same time, the Global Volunteers programs had expanded, and arrangements had become increasingly complex. An Wei and Ma Ke had added a summer English program in the city of Baoji, and still more schools wanted volunteers to help their students. An Wei's heavy, self-imposed workload tripled.

He noticed An Lin's improved English and her growing ability to handle complicated planning. She seemed anxious to help, so they asked her to make the Baoji housing arrangements. It was a difficult assignment that required tact and attention to detail, but she knew her way around Baoji because of her cigarette factory job. By the end of the new program's first week, it was obvious she had succeeded in handling everything.

As An Wei's confidence in his daughter's abilities grew, the Global Volunteers leaders turned over increasing amounts of responsibility to her in Xi'an. An Wei wondered whether some day An Lin would be able to take on major portions of the program, even becoming the Global Volunteers' leader in China.

Relieved by An Lin's help, An Wei turned his energy to the myriad projects related to honoring Helen Snow's life: translating a massive bilingual book about her life that Helen's niece was writing, updating the Xi'an exhibit, writing a commemorative book, and organizing a trip for visiting Snow scholars. The opening of the new and expanded exhibit, *A Great Woman*, celebrated Helen's life magnificently. It was crowded and vibrant; Huang Hua and his wife traveled from Beijing to honor their dear friend, and the press coverage was significant.

A few days later, An Wei checked the final arrangements for the twenty Americans and Chinese who had signed up for a Yan'an tour to learn more about Helen's achievements, and then climbed into the bus with them. As the driver pulled onto the roadway heading north, An Wei leaned back. Exhausted from working day and night for months, he relaxed into the seat as he realized that, with the help of many, including An Lin, he had managed to draw increasing attention to Helen Snow's amazing accomplishments.

Several months later, An Wei opened a message from Brigham Young University in Utah and smiled. Could he and Niu Jianhua spend a few months at the library helping to organize Helen's archives? The Bischoffs, Helen's relatives who had packed up her three hundred boxes and driven them from Connecticut to Utah, had suggested they could provide vital help in sorting the enormous quantities of papers and photos. A friend would provide them with a cozy apartment nearby, and graduate students would help with the overwhelming task.

An Wei was confident they could get away. The Americans stopped coming to Xi'an during the cold winter months, so Global Volunteers' demands were fewer and could be handled by the capable hands of the American leader and An Lin.

After a couple of weeks at Brigham Young University, An Wei stood back and looked at the array of shelves in the library filling up with Helen's valuable research. He realized they were organizing her papers in the same complex way Chinese drugstores arranged herbs and medicines.

An Wei had compiled a long list of categories to use for sorting Helen's papers: the study of Chinese women, the study of the Chinese legal system, the Gung Ho movement, letters to Chinese friends. On and on. Then after he and Niu Jianhua had labeled all the empty bookshelves, they guided the graduate students to the correct shelf categories as they sorted through every paper, letter, and memo.

Despite the heavy demand of the work, An Wei and Niu Jianhua were able to enjoy the quiet days there, cooking for themselves in a small apartment and relishing the fact that their children were now independent young adults. They even had enough free time to visit friends, including former Global Volunteers members who lived nearby and had been part of the first Xi'an team.

One amazing day, while watching the students sort through papers from Helen's well-worn cartons, An Wei noticed handwritten pages, unusual because she almost always typed everything. He walked over to get a better look and realized he was looking at *his* handwriting. He picked up a couple of pages, and then some more. He stood stock still. He was holding letters he had written to Helen years before. He pulled the remainder out of the carton, dumbstruck. It was hard to believe. She had saved them all![1]

An Lin began writing her parents to say she wanted to study English in the United States. She seemed driven by the desire, saying that although she could understand the American volunteers' specific words, she didn't always comprehend what they meant. She said she needed to know more about their cultures and their lives. An Wei disagreed and wrote back. He was sure she could best improve her English through daily interactions with the volunteers in China. But being stubborn like her father, An Lin was adamant that she needed concentrated study in the United States. She started to explore options, and she and her husband decided to postpone having a child until she could fulfill this goal.

As winter gradually gave way to spring, and with Chinese New Years celebrations approaching, An Wei and Niu Jianhua finished up their work in

Utah and headed back to Xi'an to be with family and to help An Lin make her final decision about studying English.

Spring 1999, Xi'an

The first offer to study in the United States came from Sheril Bischoff, who invited An Lin to live with her in California and study at a nearby community college. Next, Global Volunteers suggested she work at their headquarters in Minneapolis and study near there. Then her cousin, An Wenli, who lived in Michigan, urged her to apply to a language program at the state university, a plan An Lin much preferred. There she could be independent, and she thought the program would challenge her and prepare her best for further work with Global Volunteers and building bridges between Chinese and Americans.

Fall 1999, East Lansing, Michigan

Wenli was waiting for her and An Wei in the small East Lansing airport when they landed. During the brief week they spent in her apartment, An Wei was relieved to see the two cousins connect with each other.

He explored the spacious campus with them and admired the mix of old and new brick buildings sitting along the Red Cedar River, which meandered through the wooded university grounds. They toured the city and bought essentials that An Lin would need.

At registration, she nervously fiddled with a strand of hair while she awaited the dreaded interview to demonstrate her English proficiency. But she passed easily and was able to register for several classes, including US Government and American Culture. Ready for her new adventure, she and Wenli started planning a trip to New York City. An Lin hoped to finish the program in a year and rejoin her husband, and An Wei had to admit that study in the United States was probably the best decision after all.

He waved good-bye at the airport and boarded the plane for Xi'an. He would get back just in time to greet the next Global Volunteers team.

On the long flight back, he let his thoughts wander. He recalled the first time he had seen An Lin work with the US volunteers, how her smile lit up her face as she answered their endless questions.

Was it all right to drink the tap water in the hotel?
What was the proper way to greet teachers and students?
Would they have any days off?
Did the Global Volunteers office have any extra teaching materials?

An Lin in about 1998. *Source*: An Wei.

She was a natural at making them feel at home, and she thrived on using her developing English skills.

The Americans loved her. An Wei continued to suggest how she could improve, but he knew An Lin worked hard. He thought of the time when, early in the program, she overcame her fears and interpreted for the Global Volunteers leader at a ceremony. He knew that had not been easy.

Yes, he had to admit, it was good for her to learn more at an American university. Some day, he hoped, she might take over his work. He had already suggested to others that she would be able to take over his Global Volunteers responsibilities when the hundredth team arrived in Xi'an. They were already preparing to welcome the forty-fifth.

November 1999, Xi'an

An Wei picked up the ringing phone in their Xi'an home. It was an American friend in Minnesota.

"I do not have good news, An Wei."

His breath stopped. An Lin was finishing up her first semester in the United States. Was she all right? Sick? He waited for the next words.

"She had an accident, An Wei. She was driving back to school after Thanksgiving dinner and lost control of the car." There was more silence.

"She did not survive."

He forced himself to breathe.

"She didn't survive?"

"I'm so sorry. Such a wonderful person."

He heard the words but couldn't take them in.

Bright-eyed, opinionated, kind An Lin? It was impossible.

"An Wei, there are things you are going to have to do," the friend said. "You will need to come here as soon as you can."

His hands were ice cold. He put his head down. Images of An Lin flashed through his mind: her tiny hands when she was first born, her delight at reading her first characters, and her wave as they said good-bye in East Lansing just a few months earlier.

"Yes, yes. I'll make arrangements," he said. "Thank you for calling." He couldn't believe he was using that strange, unnecessary American expression.

He hung up and stared into nowhere, tears rolling down his face.

How was he going to tell Niu Jianhua? She might go mad.

He steeled himself as he walked into the apartment living room. Niu Jianhua was sitting in a chair, her white-knuckled hands clutching the arms. She had heard the conversation.

"What did you mean, 'She didn't survive?'"

"She had a car accident and didn't survive." The words stuck to his dry lips.

They stared at each other in disbelief.

As the US-bound plane took off, An Wei looked at Niu Jianhua and let his body absorb the thrust of the engines. He thought of the people he had called so far. His family and An Lin's close friends. There were many more to notify. But what would he tell Niu Jianhua's elderly parents? They would not be able to bear the news.

Xi'an, Beijing, Chicago, Michigan. A full day of travel lay ahead, with nothing to do but think. To mull over a thousand what-ifs. What if they hadn't let her go to Michigan? What if she had studied English in Riverside, California, where she first planned to go? What if she weren't as stubborn as he? Then she would have stayed overnight at their friend's house and driven back in daylight. What if he hadn't encouraged her to improve her English?

In Michigan, friends met him, Niu Jianhua, and An Lin's husband, Zhou Jing, at the East Lansing airport. Jim Swiderski, who led Global Volunteers programs in China, took him to the morgue and the police station. Images of her cold body haunted him. Her car had swerved into oncoming traffic, presumably because she had fallen asleep. He needed to take care of the matters involving the accident. He and Niu Jianhua needed to make decision after decision. In the process, they also saw how much she was loved by these kind friends. They were not the only ones who were heartbroken.

The family decided to leave her ashes in Minnesota, where she had many friends. Without children, they were sure if her remains were returned to China, she would be forgotten. In the United States, her memory could become a bridge to help unite the two countries. And so she was buried in a cemetery of expansive lawns and stately maples near the Global Volunteers office.

When the flight attendant locked the door of the plane headed back to China, An Wei felt the doors close on his life. His body ached with all-consuming grief as he looked at Niu Jianhua's pale, drawn face. How could they possibly survive?

• *13* •

Against Rural Habits

Messages poured in. An Wei had no idea how so many people knew about An Lin's death.

"Rosalynn and I were saddened to learn of your daughter's death."
—Jimmy Carter, former president.
"Tipper and I want to express our deepest sympathy to you and your family." —Al Gore, vice president.

Scores of participants from Global Volunteers wrote.

"An Lin meant so much to us."
"Her energy and smile will be with us forever."
"She helped me with all my problems, no matter how trivial."
"She has touched so many lives and helped us understand the world better."

Someone sent An Wei a book, *When Bad Things Happen to Good People*.

Then something amazing happened. Maurine Harris, who had participated in the first Global Volunteers China program, wrote with a proposal. "Another volunteer and I want to donate money to build a library in An Lin's name. How much would it take?" she asked. "We can give fifty thousand dollars."

An Wei looked at Niu Jianhua, speechless. Tears welled up in his eyes.

The women wanted to know if the library could be built in his home village of An Shang. And could they donate it through their church?

This was big money. It was illegal for him to accept a large amount from foreigners or from a church, but he and many others missed An Lin terribly. There must be a way to create a project in her name.

By evening An Wei was at his computer, thanking Maurine. It would be a memorable tribute to An Lin.

"I suggest you contact Bud Philbrook and Michele Gran, the founders of Global Volunteers. Maybe they can organize it. We have received over two hundred emails and letters from American friends. Many have asked, 'What can we do for you?'"

Global Volunteers agreed to oversee the US part of the project. They would raise funds and provide volunteer workers.

Over the months, communications flew back and forth. In lengthy phone calls with his brothers and other villagers, An Wei discussed possibilities for An Shang. They finally decided the library should be part of a new village school.

In November 2000, the Global Volunteers' country manager for China made a site visit to An Shang. She enthusiastically approved the village for the American program and suggested they name this endeavor Project Peace because 安 (An) means "peace" or "safe." Besides, the mission of Global Volunteers was "peace through service."

"What better way to remember *An* Lin and *An* Shang," she said.

An Wei and Bud Philbrook discussed how to arrange payments. Global Volunteers required that every dollar donated go directly to the project, but ensuring that happened would not be easy. "We need to stop local officials who want to *yan guo ba mao* 雁过拔毛 (to pull a feather off every goose flying by)," An Wei said. Although contrary to rural tradition, the group overseeing the project decided that the Sino-American Society would bypass local officials and transfer the Global Volunteers' funds directly to the building contractor.

The group overseeing Project Peace, which included villagers and town officials,[1] made many decisions. Some would never be honored.

They agreed the villagers would provide housing and meals for the volunteers. Moreover, the villagers would need to work alongside the volunteers, without pay. That was a new way of working.

School construction would require some farmers to trade their land, and they agreed to the group's plan to give them better fields than their current plots closer to irrigation. The town of Wujing leaders accepted responsibility to oversee the work.

Once the agreements were in place, An Wei and Niu Jianhua used their own money to have blueprints drawn up.

With the planning completed, An Wei sent a report about Project Peace to Jia Zhibang, the executive vice governor of Shaanxi Province, whom he knew from their Yan'an years. Jia approved the project with great enthusiasm.

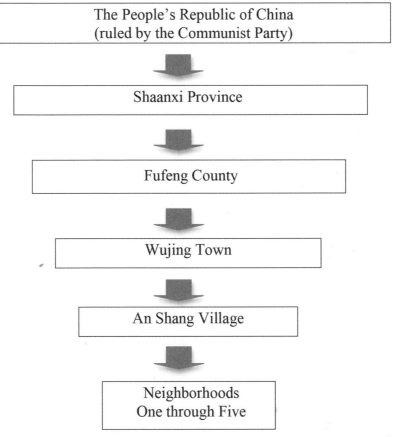

The People's Republic of China
(ruled by the Communist Party)

Shaanxi Province

Fufeng County

Wujing Town

An Shang Village

Neighborhoods
One through Five

Governing structure of An Shang village. In China, the Communist Party rules all levels of government.

April 2002, An Shang Village

An Wei headed to the site for the Project Peace groundbreaking ceremony. As he nodded hello to Brother Number Five's neighbors, he wondered what An Lin would be doing if she were alive. She would have been twenty-nine.

He inspected the final arrangements. A few villagers were putting up pastel-colored flags to catch the breezes; the speakers' platform was covered by a canvas roof in case of rain. Thank goodness the weather had held. As a white bus eased along the rutted entrance road into An Shang, An Wei could see the Global Volunteers from Xi'an peering through the windows. The village women began beating large drums and cymbals in a raucous, traditional welcome that could be heard miles away, as An Wei walked along a narrow path to greet the bus. He welcomed each American who stepped off, including his good friend, Sharon Crain, who was teaching in Xi'an for the semester.

For weeks the schoolchildren had been practicing their song-and-dance performance with pink and yellow hoops they swooshed through the air. Now they were gathered near the school grounds, decked out in their bright blue uniforms—the girls with pink pompons adorning their black hair.

Curious residents from An Shang and beyond began to gather. Soon hundreds were pouring into the main street from surrounding villages.

An Wei walked back to the speakers' platform one last time. Name cards were in place, and bottles of water sat neatly beside each one. Leaving nothing to chance, he checked the name on each card:

- Yuan Xu, a representative of the Shaanxi Province governor
- Sun Tianyi, an official at the Shaanxi Province level[2]
- Kenneth Weschsler, a visiting American who would read a message from the governor of Minnesota
- Sharon Crain

An Wei chatted briefly with the villagers who were arranging a variety of small potted trees on the stage. In the center they placed a young flowering fruit tree. An Shang might be a poor village, An Wei thought, but its people knew how to put together a grand celebration.

Soon cars with the important guests began to arrive. Before going to meet them, An Wei looked around one more time. He noticed the large pastel flags floating in the gentle breeze and took a slow, deep breath. Few people knew the significance of the date, April 10. It was An Lin's birthdate.

The speakers took their seats on the platform, and the schoolchildren burst into song, their hoops dancing over their heads. A hush came over the crowd as the representative of the provincial governor began to speak. His voice boomed over the loudspeaker, urging the villagers to make this school a model project to be proud of. He then unrolled a magnificently inscribed scroll written by Jia Zhibang, An Wei's old friend. An Wei felt his tears well up as he heard Jia's words. He had called the project "The Fusion of Love and the Crystal of Friendship." In Chinese it was a poignant description: 友谊的结晶; 爱心的融合. (*Yǒu yì de jié jing; ài xīn de róng hé.*)

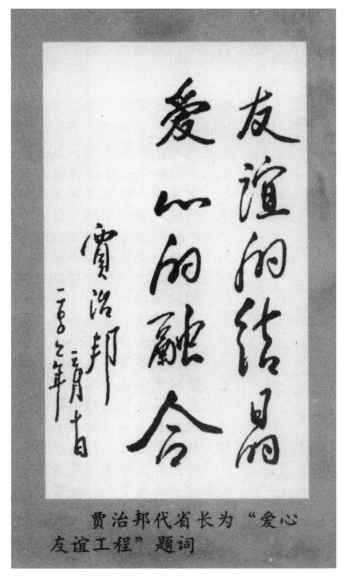

友谊的结晶

爱心的融合

贾治邦

一九九六年三月十日

贾治邦代省长为"爱心友谊工程"题词

Jia Zhibang scroll.

Sharon stepped to the podium and looked out across the crowd of villagers and the fields beyond.

"Yes, we believe in each other's dreams," she began.

She lauded An Lin and her family, the villagers and Global Volunteers, and the building of bridges between two great countries: the United States and China. Then she concluded,

Today we celebrate the dreams of all of us who are gathered here . . . who come together as family to promote this Peace Project. . . .

Shi zai ren wei. Things are done by people.

Let us all dare to believe in each other's dreams.

Days later, An Wei tried to thank the Americans who had been so kind to them after An Lin's death. He cried every time he tried to write. But after the groundbreaking, he and Niu Jianhua were finally able to finish their letter. By then hundreds of messages had poured in as well as more than $200,000. They were overwhelmed. They had read every single message with tears.

Now he wrote about An Lin's love for life and for her work. Her goal was to build bridges of understanding and friendship. In a recent dream, she had said to Niu Jianhua, "I can still help."

Brothers Number Five and Two began to paint rooms in their houses, where the volunteers would stay because they were in better shape than most village homes and had indoor toilets. Even so, An Wei knew they were hardly what Westerners were used to.

With only two weeks left before the first Global Volunteers team arrived, he hurried down the lane past a few persimmon trees to Number Two's three-story house. The ground floor was full of grain sacks and a handcart, but the upstairs had several bedrooms. The beds were made of wood slats and bricks that Westerners would never be able to sleep on comfortably. There was also a large room where the volunteers could eat, but it needed a table.

The Western-style toilet had to be reinstalled in Number Five's house. With An Wei's help, they bought mattresses and extra beds. The village purchased bedding materials, and village women sewed the quilt covers, stuffing them with leftover cotton batting from their old quilts. Showers would be a problem, though. No one in the village had a place to bathe. Water was both cold and scarce.

"Take them back," An Wei told his brothers and the village leaders who had gathered desks from the old school to create a dining room table in Number Two's house. "They are too old and wobbly."

That afternoon he took a taxi to the county seat to buy new tables.

A few days later, satisfied all the arrangements were proceeding well, he boarded a bus to Xi'an to meet the volunteers. A delegation from An Shang followed to welcome the ten Americans and tell them how much Project Peace meant to the village. It would build a bridge between China and the United States.[3]

*   *   *

The first Global Volunteers peered out the windows of the small lumbering bus. An Wei watched a village woman and her grandchild on the rutted road scurry out of the way. He could see the Americans taking in the low-slung homes made of rammed earth, the old school, and the few small shops. They'd been told to expect squat toilets and very little water, and he was sure they were apprehensive.

But they had not expected a large crowd of villagers to greet them. The drum-and-cymbal group played with abandon; several women in red jackets and black trousers carried a large bilingual sign. The English read, "May Sino-American Friendship Evergreen."

Hardly perfect, An Wei chuckled, but the sentiment was right.

Village women greeting the first Global Volunteers team in An Shang, 2002. *Source:* An Wei.

As the volunteers stepped off the bus for their several weeks' stay, the village leaders and town officials shook hands with each one. Then An Wei and the village party secretary, Feng Zhichun, a cigarette in the corner of his mouth, assigned them to the two homes. An Wei was everywhere, checking the lights, the water, and the new furniture. He was pleased at the visitors' startled response to the bright new quilts.

Feng Zhichun organized a festive gathering in the old school. After an official welcome by the village and township leaders, with An Wei translating, singing filled the room. School children sang songs, and a few villagers poured out their souls with ear-piercing strains of local opera.

The next morning, Feng Zhichun and another village leader led the eager volunteers to the new school grounds, introduced them to the construction workers, and helped them start their jobs.

The Americans carried materials and shoveled sand for the builders to lay the foundation, while An Wei took on the role of project advisor. The volunteers quickly learned their way around the village, enjoying walks along paths through the fields and chatting with children eager to learn a few English words. Once a week they returned to Xi'an for showers. By the time the team left, the school foundation was complete, the steel frame of the first floor had been started, and the Americans had made friends with several farmers. Everything had gone just as the planning committee had hoped.

May 2002

Back in the city to plan orientation programs for both Xi'an and An Shang volunteer teams, An Wei gripped the phone as he listened to his brother. A major conflict had emerged. Feng Zhichun, the village leader, refused to arrange any more welcome ceremonies for the next volunteers who would arrive in a little over a week.

"How can he do this? He agreed to be their host," An Wei said to Brother Number Five. Horrified, he took a few deep breaths to calm himself and made a snap decision.

"I'll be on the next bus to An Shang." If the village leaders would not take responsibility, he would. He would not let Feng derail this project to celebrate An Lin's life.

He knew his brothers and a few enthusiastic villagers would help. Let Feng Zhichun and his cronies drink and play mah-jongg. Political leaders were supposed to work for the good of the community, but they obviously did not think so.

In An Shang, An Wei rushed between his brothers' houses, checking to see that the quilts were clean, the toilets functioning. He inspected the tables and chairs to make sure they were strong and consulted with the cooks about meals. At night he called Ma Ke and the American Global Volunteers leader in Xi'an to confirm that an orientation had been set up for the second team. Then he double-checked with the school construction crew to make sure they had the supplies for the volunteers to work with.

As he rushed from one place to the next, An Wei was sure he knew why Party Secretary Feng Zhichun wouldn't help. The contractors had been paid their first installment, and as agreed, the money had gone directly from the Sino-American Society to the builders, bypassing village leaders. Despite all the discussions during the planning meetings and the agreements everyone had made, it was clear that Feng Zhichun had assumed the funds would pass through his sticky hands.

Feng Jiedong, a confident and congenial farmer who lived near the village entrance, offered to help with the project wherever his energy and talents were needed. Although he belonged to the same clan as Feng Zhichun, Feng Jiedong was his polar opposite. He and his wife had invited the first team members to their tidy home, provided music for parties, and taught local dances to the delighted Americans. They and the village school teachers agreed to organize the welcoming ceremony.

With his plans completed, An Wei tracked down Feng Zhichun, who often stayed close to his homestead, to invite him to attend the ceremony. Feng Zhichun agreed but made it clear he would do no more work for this project. An Wei suspected he agreed to attend only because he thought important town leaders would be there.

Once the new volunteer team was settled, An Wei wrote officials in the town of Wujing about Feng Zhichun's refusal to take any responsibility. He asked for their help, but although they had agreed to oversee Project Peace, they never responded.

October 2002, Xi'an

In his Xi'an apartment, An Wei picked up his ringing phone.

"Wei," he answered. "Hello." He closed a window by his desk to shut out noise of the trucks and buses on the street below. It was an official from the Foreign Affairs Office wanting to talk about his retirement.

An Wei smirked. It was about time they responded. He had heard nothing since 1996, when he submitted his formal application to retire and said he would wait at home for their answer. Two years ago, when he was in his late fifties, the government had said staff could retire a few years before sixty because it was trying to create jobs for younger people. Although he was eligible under this new policy, the office had never contacted him; month after month he had heard nothing.

The speaker continued. "You have been approved for retirement, and you can pick up your official document any time."

An Wei let a moment pass. They had waited until he was sixty to grant him retirement status. "I'll pick it up in a week or so," he said.

He leaned back in his chair. How long had it been? More than six years since he had applied for retirement and stopped going to the office. At least he had gotten what he was desperate for: freedom to work at home nonstop on projects he cared about.

A few weeks later, after collecting the papers, An Wei returned from the Foreign Affairs Office, made some tea, and sat down at his apartment desk to read the retirement document carefully. Anger still burned into him when he thought of all those years Zhang Kairou had kept him in an empty job, but now a smile spread slowly across his face. They had promoted him to the highest level, equal to that of a deputy director general. That meant they had awarded a salary increase and a health plan in which the government would pay 90 percent of his medical expenses.

He placed the document on a shelf with other important papers and leaned back in his desk chair, feeling satisfaction spread throughout his body.

Fall 2002, An Shang Village

The more rebar and concrete that was added to the new three-story school building, the angrier Feng Zhichun became. He almost never disagreed with anything in public, but his rage was well known enough to be a leading topic of village gossip. As village leader, he asked friends, why wasn't he allowed to touch the money for the school? Why should he support a project that bypassed traditional practices? He went to work on the families that had agreed to exchange their land.

Back in An Shang after a week in Xi'an, An Wei climbed up to the flat roof of Number Five's house where he often went to survey the village and take in the sweep of the countryside. For a long time he looked out on the main street at the new three-story school that had risen high enough to be seen. The proud structure and its promise of better education for village children would have gratified An Lin.

The next day, though, as autumn breezes rustled through the cornstalks, he heard several families complain that they had been tricked. They claimed their fields were much better than what the village had offered them in exchange. Although they had agreed to leave their old fields fallow so schoolyard construction could begin, they refused. They would not plant in their new fields. After harvesting their corn, they hitched up their oxen and donkeys, and defying the Project Peace agreement, replowed their old fields and sowed winter wheat. It meant the land could not be touched until the new crop ripened in June.

Heartbroken and angry, An Wei studied the situation. Construction would have to stop until June—maybe longer. Although Feng Zhichun had agreed to the original plan, he now insisted the land for the sports ground could not be given to Project Peace because those villagers objected.

On the way to Number Five's homestead from a meeting, An Wei ran into Feng on the dirt road near the school. He greeted the village leader, who as usual had a cigarette tucked into the corner of his mouth. He looked at An Wei and then at the school and said, "You can put the sports ground on the east side of the school, instead of the west. Just fill in the hollow there."

Feng Zhichun pointed to the area where villagers had lived in caves until recently. It was about as wide and deep as a large reservoir and much too large to fill.

If the suggestion had not been so infuriating, it would have been laughable.

The next day the school construction company packed up its equipment and left. They could do no more without the land. Project Peace was at a standstill.

April 2007, An Shang

The former village leaders hadn't been able to "pull feathers off the goose" of Project Peace. In 2007, I learned how much hatred that rebuff had produced.

"Let's go look," Niu Jianhua said to me. "We can see the caves where a lot of village families lived until the 1980s." She headed through the low grass in the clearing beside a small sawmill and stood on the edge of the large depression known as "The Hollow."

I followed, admiring the blossoms of the unfamiliar trees, when into my peripheral vision came a snarling, lunging dog.

I sprinted faster than I could imagine, flipped over a pile of concrete slabs, and landed on the other side.

I was out of his reach. His chain, free to move along a rope, had stopped him feet away.

Niu Jianhua and I looked at each other in disbelief.

For the last several days, I had been in An Shang with her and An Wei and had relished these meanderings through the countryside.

I got up, relieved I had no broken bones. I could feel an abrasion on my arm, but no blood. The layers of clothes to ward off the cold had protected me. Niu Jianhua picked leaves and sticks out of my hair as we looked around.

How were we going to get back to the road? The two narrow paths behind the mill and a house were dead ends.

The dog's neck fur was still standing high.

Niu Jianhua yelled for the owner.

Eventually a man sauntered from a nearby house, pulled the dog back a little, and stepped on the chain to hold it. Warily, we headed back toward the road, fully aware the dog was still uncomfortably close and could lunge if the man moved his foot. It turned out, the dog owner was a crony of Feng Zhichun, the former village leader. They hated An Wei for taking away their access to money and would thwart him in any way they could.

Frustrated by the actions of the five resisting families and without recourse, An Wei reported the standoff to his friend Jia Zhibang, who had become governor of Shaanxi Province. Within days, an official response raced down through the chain of command: from the provincial office to Baoji City, the Fufeng County government, and the town of Wujing. The criticism of the county and town officials was severe. How could they implement the government's policy of opening to the outside world and welcoming foreign investors if they couldn't handle a project that had been handed to them? How could they talk about improving the environment for investors, yet could not manage this *one* school?

Fearful county leaders leaned hard on the town officials to write self-criticisms and apologize for the school delay. They and Feng Zhichun also needed to promise to follow the original plan that had been agreed to by all parties.

Weeks dragged on. An Wei realized that a threat from the provincial governor might not scare Feng Zhichun, who clearly was refusing to write the required self-criticism. Farmers did not like to change their ways, and since he had managed to halt the school project so far, he probably thought he could hold out until he got some money.

Back in Xi'an, An Wei turned to pressing work for the Shaanxi Translators Association, but he worried that the school situation would never get straightened out. He knew the town officials were unhappy with the provincial reprimand. One of them had told him confidentially that Project Peace was creating big problems. The man said that if every village kept money and privileges away from the leaders, then there was no benefit in being one. Despite these sentiments, An Wei was sure the town leaders knew the provincial governor would run out of patience, that if they did not want to lose their own jobs and privileges, they would have to act.

By November, the county and town officials began repeated negotiations with An Shang village leaders. But Feng Zhichun refused to budge. In December, the town party leader Li Shuansuo asked An Wei to meet for a private talk. Curious, An Wei agreed.

"I wonder if you would take over the village leadership and become party secretary?" Li asked.

Startled, An Wei hesitated. He did not want that responsibility. He already had more than enough to do. Yet as he rode the bus back to Xi'an, he wondered how else the school would ever be finished—and An Lin's memory honored.

*   *   *

Negotiations dragged on, as did Feng Zhichun's refusals.

In January, Li Shuansuo implored An Wei to reconsider becoming An Shang's party secretary. Some people did not want to cooperate, Li said. An Wei would meet many obstacles when he tried to resume building the school. "If you have to spend a lot of time solving problems, why don't you just take the leadership position? Then you will have a say in village affairs. People will have to listen to you."

An Wei nodded thoughtfully.

"You are the right person to handle the present situation," Li Shuansuo said.

An Wei promised to think about it.

While waiting for a taxi to An Shang, he wondered how he could possibly take this on. What about his commitments to the Translators Association and to Global Volunteers? They were huge responsibilities. And how could he keep up the momentum of promoting Helen's work? Several of her books needed translating. Besides, farmers were enormously stubborn and hard to work with. He kept coming back to the same answer, though: he had no choice if the memorial to An Lin was going to be built.

Dirt tracks that thread through the An Shang neighborhoods.

An Wei rose before dawn the next day to ponder what he would need to do to get the school finished. How would Feng Zhichun try to stop him? He paced back and forth in Brother Number Five's courtyard. Then, taking a deep breath, he climbed the stairs to his room and dialed the phone. "Secretary Li, I will accept your suggestion and become the An Shang party leader."

Once back in Xi'an, he did not dare tell Niu Jianhua what he had agreed to do. They both knew that changing farmers' ideas was very nearly impossible. When villagers called looking for the party leader, Niu Jianhua said they had made a mistake. It took An Wei weeks to admit to her what he had done.

March 2003

It was March when An Wei returned to An Shang with its muddy roads and mist-laden mornings. Smoke from the dried cornstalks the farmers burned to warm their kangs hung low to the ground.

He had come to accept the party leadership, but the party officials postponed the meeting to announce the switch. Feng Zhichun had refused to leave his position, saying he was owed money. More negotiations took place; pressure on the town leaders grew.

While An Wei waited, he walked the village, visiting with friends and relatives. Rain and snow had soaked the land during the winter months, and winter wheat was beginning to turn the fields a light green.

One day he found himself standing in front of the bleak shell of the school. He noticed the curve of the overhang where the front-door entrance would be and the well-spaced openings for the windows. His eyes scanned the rest of the building and the ground around it. "I am going to get this built," he vowed. "No matter what obstacles come at me."

A few days later the town of Wujing's party leader and another official paid 50,000 yuan to Feng Zhichun, who agreed to resign.

Village rumors flew. Why would town officials pay a village leader to leave? They were his bosses and had the right to remove people who were not doing their job. Word traveled from one to another, using a familiar expression: *Chi ren zui duan.* 吃人嘴 短. (If you eat other's food, you cannot speak strongly.)

An Wei slurped the tea Brother Number Five's wife handed him and headed out the iron door in their gate. Their neighbor, who made brooms from surrounding bushes, nodded hello as he poured water-diluted pig droppings at the base of a newly planted tree. There was purpose in An Wei's stride. The day before, March 17, he had become the political leader of An Shang village.

He walked along the muddy lanes, chatted with villagers, and headed for the homes of those who had refused to give up their land. The first one was cordial but distant. When An Wei brought up the subject of the fields, the farmer did not want to listen to an explanation about the official agreement. He said he would not leave his piece of land. "It is much better than what the village is giving me."

An Wei went to the nearby homestead of a woman who was always unpleasant. She glared at him as he approached.

"Good morning," he said.

She walked to her courtyard gate and locked it from the inside. When An Wei said he would like to discuss the land with her, she turned her back and walked away, leaving him to stare at the dark blue fabric of her jacket.

He took another deep breath and gazed across the expanse of cultivated fields. A pure white goat tethered nearby nibbled peacefully at early spring grass. He walked to the next family homestead. He was not looking forward to this one. It was the home of the man the villagers called "Mouth Rot" because of all the foul things he said. A few days earlier he had stood shouting on the main road of the village, "They're using too much land for this school. They're just building a whore house."

Just as An Wei was settling into his role as party leader, orders came from the town. "Stay in your village until further notice." A deadly epidemic called severe acute respiratory syndrome, or SARS, was spreading quickly throughout China. An Wei had neighborhood leaders arrange for guards at all entrances to An Shang.

Confined to the village and with construction on the school stopped by the five hostile families, An Wei visited more farmers. Although his purpose was to find out their hopes and frustrations, he enjoyed the congenial conversations and laughter. No matter how poor they were, the villagers almost always invited him to sit in their living areas or on their warm kangs. They chatted about their children and their crops. But frustrations also emerged. They said the previous leaders had collected money from the villagers, but no one knew what had happened to it.

"It is our money, and I have a right to ask how it was used," one farmer said as An Wei drank tea from a ceramic mug the farmer's wife had handed him. Another, who talked with An Wei while fixing a hoe, looked up at him. "At the old school, they taxed us for children's chairs, but the chairs never appeared." Questions surfaced about the expensive houses of the old village party leaders. Why were they so wealthy compared with the rest of the villagers if they had no family businesses, no orchards, and no pigs? Said one man as his voice rose in anger, "Those leaders just try to squeeze the blood out of our skinny bodies, but they do nothing good for us."

An Wei didn't know how much of the farmers' accusations to believe. Where was the proof?

While he was resting in Number Five's courtyard one day, a childhood friend arrived. They sat at the worn table beside the small earth goddess shrine, soaking up the spring warmth. His friend leaned forward in his chair and asked, "An Wei, how long are you going to stay in An Shang?"

"You are the village leader, but you are from the city." If he were a local person, they knew he would be the leader for several years. Because he was from the city, they feared he might leave as soon as the school was completed.

Another friend walked through the open gate. After a hearty greeting, the second man pulled up an old wooden bench, listened to the conversation, and finally added, "People can't pour out their hearts to you. If you leave soon, they will be in trouble with the old leaders."

An Wei had to admit this might be a problem. He sensed the villagers had no hope for the future. What troubled him most, though, was that they expected him to fix their lives. If he did nothing good for them, he realized they would never trust him enough to help with the school project. At night, An Wei sat on the small bench in his second-floor room and jotted down their concerns in his tattered notebook, wondering how he could ever improve this mess.

April 2003

One day on his way back from the fields that had become a radiant green as the winter wheat kernel heads filled out, An Wei passed tall Feng Jiedong who was sweeping leaves from in front of his house. He was someone An Wei could discuss village issues with because he was more open to new ideas than most villagers.

They pulled two small benches into the afternoon sun in Feng Jiedong's courtyard. Lush vines hung from the second-floor balcony with partially grown gourds protruding from under the leaves. Feng had a couple of ideas for improving the village. The water supply was a continuous problem, and he wondered how much it would cost to dig a new well. They discussed the pros and cons, both knowing there was no money for such a project. Feng also offered the front area of his family courtyard home for future Global Volunteers team meetings and for teaching English lessons.

An Wei headed home mulling over their discussion. He decided that Feng Jiedong, with his intelligence and open, friendly presence, should help lead the village.

At the April 2003 meeting of all the village party members, Feng Jie-dong was elected a member of the three-person Party Committee[4] that over-saw village affairs, along with An Wei as the head and An Xiyuan, who was a friend of the former village leader. Short, broad-faced An Xiyuan was also chair of the Villagers Committee, which handled day-to-day responsibilities.

Traditional Village Committees

Villages throughout China had a Party Committee and a Villagers Committee.

The village Party Committee, the lowest level of the Communist Party structure, was headed by the village party secretary. An Shang's committee had an additional two members who were elected by the village party members. The committee created village policies and managed everything except day-to-day village affairs. Its responsibilities included making sure finances were carried out transparently, oversee-ing the selection of committee members and neighborhood leaders, and educating villagers about new government policies for rural areas. It supervised the Villagers Committee.

The Villagers Committee, elected by all the villagers aged eighteen and above, took care of day-to-day village affairs—for instance, control-ling chicken epidemics, assigning people to maintain the irrigation canals, and recording births and deaths in county records. It approved permits for building new homes and transferred university students' household regis-tration to their new locations.

Although committees were selected by elections, the concept of Western-style democracy with secret ballots and honest outcomes did not exist.

---

* * *

Villagers from Neighborhood Two gathered for the meeting about the prob-lem caused by the families who had reneged on trading their land so the new school could be built. Of all the village neighborhoods, this was the toughest to deal with.

An Wei eased his way into the packed ground-floor classroom of the old, whitewashed school, chatting and joking with the men and women. The room filled quickly. He hoped the gathering would start on time, for it might be a long meeting of hard negotiations.

Each family from Neighborhood Two had been required to send one representative. He was pleased to see that some young people had come and that some grandmothers had brought their grandchildren. The three Party Committee members had come too.

The husbands and wives of the five resisting families had been requested to attend, but two were missing: the woman who locked her gate when An Wei had tried to talk with her and the man the villagers called "Mouth Rot."

In an effort to resolve the sports ground issue, the five families had been offered 10 percent more than their original land if they agreed to an exchange by the end of April, which was a few days away. During repeated and hard negotiations, the three families present had accepted land near the village center. That meant the most difficult two would have to accept less desirable parcels.

Tired of sitting, villagers wandered outside to smoke and talk. Others napped. Finally, the two missing villagers arrived, well over an hour late.

The Neighborhood Two director opened the meeting and offered the two holdouts the remaining land. They were unhappy. The land, they said, was too far away. It was not by the roadside. They did not care that the parcels were larger and better irrigated than their original fields. They would not accept them. Frustrated, Feng Jiedong stood up, tall and confident.

"Individuals obey the collective," he said, his face drawn taut.

The two families resisted—getting louder with each comment. They were not going to be cheated out of their lands, they shouted. Then one looked at Feng Jiedong and said, "Don't talk big, empty words. Land beside the irrigation canal is much better for farming. Will you trade your irrigation canal land for the land we're being offered?"

Feng Jiedong looked at them steadily. "Yes, you can take my best land, and I will take what was offered you. I will obey any decision made by the village."

The crowded room erupted in applause. But Feng Jiedong's irrigation canal land was not large enough. The room hushed as one of Feng's brothers stood.

"You can have whatever piece of my land you like. I will give it to you." He sat down slowly. An Wei could feel the tension in the room.

Without missing a beat, Feng Jiedong's other brother rose. He looked at the two holdouts. "You can choose whatever piece of my land you like also." Applause erupted again.

Speechless, the two families had no choice. They stayed silent and accepted.

An Wei was stunned. Feng Jiedong's family was sacrificing its landholdings so the school could go forward. As the villagers filed out of the classroom and headed down the lanes and paths to their homes, An Wei walked to the schoolroom that housed the village loudspeaker. He pulled the microphone toward him and announced the results of the meeting. "The construction of Project Peace can resume very soon. We are all grateful to the Feng brothers for their selfless offer."

May 2003

An Wei heard the rumble of trucks and watched a construction crew climb the new building's scaffolding. What a relief. They had been blocked since October, and the cost of the project had risen with every passing month. Now that the land issue was settled, they were hard at work again. In addition, the Leading Group for Project Peace verified that the five families had accepted a generous cash payment to cover the loss of a small strip of green wheat that needed to be removed to make way for a brick wall that would surround the school property.

The earthmover driver started the engine and edged into position to clear the strip. As it neared the plants, however, members of the five families ran out yelling and stood in his path. Although they had been paid double the value of the plants, they refused to move.

An Wei called the town leaders, and soon all the town staff arrived. They filed into the upstairs meeting room of the old school along with the village Party Committee members and the neighborhood leaders to hash out the problem. They reviewed what had been agreed by everyone.

The families had been paid double the value of the green wheat that would be destroyed.

The school project was increasing in cost every month because of the penalty for breaking the original contract and because costs of materials were rising.

They discussed the options and agreed construction of the wall must continue.

The town officials decided to walk up the main street to the construction site, tell the crew to begin, and talk with any family members who were still upset. In order to prevent more arguments, they told An Wei and the other village leaders they were not allowed to go.

But as the town staff neared the site, members of the five families ran out and blocked their entrance. One man squatted in front of the earthmover, yelling, "You can't have our plants. You cannot build this wall."

Town staff dragged him into a nearby field where he lay shouting that the town cadres were beating him. The driver of the earthmover started its engine again, revving it to make sure it would run smoothly, maneuvered into place, and uprooted the green wheat.

Summer 2003

When An Wei took over village affairs, he was confronted with another complex situation. He collaborated with short, broad-faced An Xiyuan about an electricity improvement project that had been paid for by the county government. An Xiyuan was a member of the party branch, head of the Villagers Committee, and a friend of the former village leader.

The villagers needed to pay for their electric meter and the wire that ran to their homes. Two issues complicated the situation. Some farmers owed the village money, and the village owed money to some of the farmers. The Party Committee decided An Xiyuan, as head of the Villagers Committee, would collect the money for the electricity and the debts.

They estimated they would take in about 100,000 yuan, and the amount owed the villagers was about 60,000. Once the Party Committee had paid back the villagers, they would then decide how to use the remaining funds.

In June, Feng Jiedong asked An Xiyuan if he had collected the fees. "They are almost all collected," An Xiyuan reported. At a meeting a month later, An Wei asked An Xiyuan to pay 3,000 yuan to a carpenter who had done work for the village. To An Wei's shock, An Xiyuan said matter-of-factly, "There is no cash left." He said he had used the money he collected to repay the debts to the villagers.

But where were the thousands that should have been left for village projects?

In an abrupt, defensive voice, An Xiyuan added that he had used the rest—more than 46,000 yuan—to pay back "salaries" to the old village leaders, including himself. An Wei and Feng Jiedong were aghast. As far as they could guess, the old leaders had decided this was the last time money would be accessible to them, so they grabbed it.

An Xiyuan had given away all the funds they had planned to use to improve the village:

12,029.39 yuan to the former party secretary
4,380.70 yuan to the former director of the Villagers Committee
18,544.59 yuan to the village cashier
11,530.50 yuan to himself as former deputy director of the Villagers Committee

An Shang village, where a hardworking family earned a little more than 4,000 yuan a year, was left with nothing.

An Wei and Feng Jiedong went immediately to the village office behind the small shops on the main street and put a new lock on the door. In the traditional way, they then sealed it with a strip of paper pasted from the door to the doorjamb with the date and an official red stamp on it. Next they appointed an auditing committee of highly trustworthy villagers: An Dong, a former bank clerk; an older gentleman who had been the village leader many years earlier; and a villager who was a retired accountant. They carried the seven years of account books to the accountant's home, where the committee worked for hours over many weeks, finding one irregularity after another. What the farmers had complained about during An Wei's weeks of interviewing villagers turned out to be true. It was no longer a secret that the previous village leaders were corrupt, but it was even worse than the farmers thought.

Enough evidence existed to eject An Xiyuan from the Party Committee for his double-dealing. At a tense party meeting in July, he tried to defend himself, but many of the sixteen village party members spoke openly against him. He was replaced by thin, reliable An Dong, who had helped carry out the audit. The vote was fifteen against An Xiyuan and one in favor. However, he remained head of the Villagers Committee.

• *14* •

Democracy and a New School in An Shang

Summer 2003, An Shang Village

An Wei barely heard the mourning doves calling back and forth as the early dawn light outlined the trees in the neighbor's yard. He sat at his desk at Brother Number Five's. It was obvious the farmers felt hopeless about village affairs. He needed to do something. But what? And how? He looked at the tattered notebook in which he had been recording their complaints and suggestions over the past months. So much of what they said was important, and many of their ideas could be implemented with good planning. But they needed a reliable government.

An Wei heard a donkey braying in the distance. As pink streaks spread across the sky, he paced back and forth in his small room. An Shang farmers worked hard, yet they could be so difficult. They had almost no education and no understanding of how government should be run. Instead, they kept their eyes focused on their grinding mills and feeding their animals. Their opinions were ignored. Their previous leaders had run a dishonest dictatorship.

He sat down on the small wooden bench at his desk, hands on his fidgeting knees. Villagers hated corruption, yet they didn't know how to get rid of it. He had to convince them they could be masters, not just of their homes and fields, but of the village as well.

What if the farmers themselves were in charge? Could they oversee road maintenance or the irrigation system? Would they follow their own decisions? Maybe. But how could he create such a workable government?

He headed down to the courtyard, his plastic slippers slapping on the concrete steps. He nodded to his sister-in-law, who was cooking at the large wok, and poured boiled water into his tea jar. Brother Number Five pushed through the plastic strips covering the doorway to his sleeping and living space.

An Wei launched into a monologue. "Mao Zedong wrote that we have to do everything by relying on our own efforts. He also said the most important issue is to educate the farmers. These are important words." He looked at his brother and continued. "The village will never become a healthy community if it relies on just a few leaders."

An Wei unscrewed the lid of the tea jar and, teeth clenched to strain out the tea leaves, took a long drink. He walked across the loose brick courtyard and put on his outside shoes. "You villagers need to rely on yourselves."

"I'm going out to Neighborhood Three," he added as he opened the iron door of the courtyard entrance. "I haven't been there for a while, and one of the villagers has a new chicken farm."

That night An Wei switched on his florescent desk lamp and ran his hand across the top of his Lenovo ThinkPad to clean off the day's dust. Now was the time to let his mind roam, after the village had settled down. The screen cast a green glow across the room as he began to scroll through documents, looking for ideas. He sat back on the edge of the small bench, thinking more deeply about the issue of governance. An Shang villagers had to be in charge of their own decisions. That is why Helen Snow's book *China Builds for Democracy* was so powerful. The industrial-style cooperatives drew villagers together into a common project, where they collectively made major decisions. In the same way, if farmers in An Shang were going to avoid corrupt dictatorships, they all needed to participate in decision-making.

He began to hunt for something he had translated years earlier, just before President Bill Clinton visited Xi'an. The president had wanted to know about China's moves toward democracy, so the Foreign Affairs Office had asked An Wei to translate a document about village voting. What was it called? He opened Internet Explorer through his brother's phone line. Thank goodness he had an internet connection hooked up. It was slow and intermittent, but invaluable.

"Bylaws," he muttered. "It was certainly a document about bylaws." He scrolled through Chinese government sites. There it was, actually passed by the National People's Congress in 1998: "The Organic Law of the Villagers Committees of the People's Republic of China." He remembered that at the time he had translated it into English, he suspected that former president Jimmy Carter had been influential in its development. Carter had tried to help China move toward democracy after the Tiananmen Square massacre.

An Wei saved the document to his computer, took a long sip of tea, and then read it carefully. The more he read, the more he realized he had found the key to a better village: a national law that encouraged democracy in rural areas. He leaned forward, hands on his knees, and read it again to make sure he understood it.

The words could not be clearer.

Article 1 began by ensuring "self-government by the villagers in the countryside." They should oversee development of "a grassroots democracy."

An Wei walked out on the little balcony leading to the stairs. He looked out across his neighbors' rooftops and down into the darkened courtyard, exhilarated but apprehensive. This law would create radical change in the village.

He went back inside to read it again. It said the Villagers Committee could be elected by the whole village, by everyone over age eighteen. And if any committee member made mistakes, villagers could vote him out. The former leaders had probably never even bothered to read the whole law, or if they had, it was obvious they had never told the villagers about it.

He stood up again and stretched. Everything was so clear.

"Have you ever heard about a national law for the Villagers Committee?" An Wei asked the village Communist Party members gathered in one of their courtyards. They looked puzzled. He just hoped they would be as enthusiastic about it as he was. He held up the pages he had printed out.

"There *is* one, and it was adopted by the National People's Congress in 1998. It even went through a trial period before that." Voices quieted down as he began to read. By the time he got to article 2, he could feel tension rising.

"The Villagers Committee is the primary mass organization of self-government, in which the villagers manage their own affairs." It also said that they should have elections and that government supervision should be done democratically.

Party members started talking to each other. Was it really possible for the whole village to make decisions about village affairs?

An Wei skipped to article 22. The Villagers Committee should have an open administration and show its financial records. It should also "accept supervision by the villagers."

By then the party members were all talking. What did it mean, that they should have an open administration? An Shang had been ruled by a few men who made all the decisions secretly, and those men certainly weren't supervised by the villagers. If this was a national law, could they really use it in An Shang?

When they quieted, An Wei said that he could not do much by himself, but he added, "if you are interested, I can help you carry out this law."

*   *   *

A week later, after a few days at home in Xi'an, An Wei was on the bus back to An Shang with a packet of 450 copies of the law carefully tucked onto the overhead luggage rack, one copy for each family in the village.

He looked out at the bluffs rising above the Wei River, where he had learned to swim. The bus windows were open to offset the stifling summer heat. As the bus turned off the main road, he mulled over the village situation. He had to figure out an effective form of representation. Almost a third of the young men left the village for months at a time to earn money in the cities. If all decisions were made only by those remaining, it would not work. Helen Snow had introduced democratic principles in the industrial cooperatives back in the 1930s, but how could he make her ideas work now? He thought about how to create a representative government. Perhaps it could be a little like the National People's Congress. Besides, each city and province also had a representative congress. Why not a villagers congress? An Wei hummed to himself. Could a representative, elected in a neighborhood, represent several families?

The bus stopped to allow a small funeral procession to cross the road. Dressed in crumpled white jackets and wide, white headbands, several of the procession members carried a painted coffin. Others carried a many-colored floral wreath of paper to be placed near the grave. They headed down a side street that must have led to a graveyard or a farmer's field. Cremation was now the national law, but in rural areas, including An Shang, traditions were nearly impossible to shake.

The bus started up again. Many An Shang villagers were excited about a law that could give them control over village decision-making.

If he was going to work with the villagers to create a new form of government, he needed to follow the national law precisely. It said rural villages could decide their own government structure. But An Wei knew not everyone would like such a radical change. Somewhere, somehow people would object. Since Tiananmen Square, the nation's leaders had stopped talking about a democratic system, although they had not openly opposed it. Still, that packet on the luggage rack contained a powerful weapon for An Shang, one that had been approved by the National People's Congress. Nobody could say, "Oh, that law is wrong."

Nobody.

Early August 2003

"We have to see if the villagers really want to *do* something to change An Shang," An Wei said to Feng Jiedong who had dropped by Brother Number Five's.

To talk, they moved inside where brick and plaster walls gave relief from the heat.

"Many farmers are enthusiastic about the law," An Wei said. "Now we need to test them with a project."

He had been stewing about this for days. The villagers were supposed to provide volunteer labor for Project Peace. They needed to level the sports ground, which meant hauling one to two thousand cubic meters of earth a kilometer, from the fields to the new school site. Using shovels and picks, An Wei figured it would require one full week of work from more than half the village's adults. They would also need four or five of the few village tractors. It was a massive project for a small village.

Both An Wei and Feng Jiedong knew farmers did not like the idea of volunteering. Work for their families? Yes, long hours into the night. Work for others? Why?

August 17, 2003

An Wei was up before dawn, making sure everything was organized. The cool morning air ruffled his short-sleeved shirt. What if no one showed up to move the dirt? It would be a major disaster. If An Lin were here, her optimistic spirit and willingness to try new things would have helped with this radical experiment. He shut his eyes and dedicated its success to her memory.

On the little balcony outside his room, he took a sip from his tea jar and watched Brother Number Five head for the tractor shed. Well, at least one tractor would be there. At the bottom of the stairs he slipped on his shoes and walked down the dirt lane toward the village center. The corn had grown high. How different from those awful starvation years.

In the village office in the old school, Feng Jiedong and two others were already arranging the papers to keep track of those who provided tractors and volunteered. They would be recognized publicly. They also had music tapes, to be played beginning at 9:00 a.m. It was music to make you want to move.

Their careful planning with the village party members and other backbone villagers seemed to be working. If all of them plus their families came, that would set the tone for the week. They hoped that would overcome the effect of any disgruntled villagers.

Feng Jiedong pulled the microphone toward him, and his strong voice poured out from the village loudspeaker. An Wei walked out to the main street and headed toward the school construction site. A man walking by prodded his recalcitrant hog with a long stick.

Relief surged through An Wei as he heard the steady putt-putt of his brother's tractor and then the sound of more putt-putts from another neighborhood. Several party members met him at the new school grounds with spades, talking, and laughing. There were women in colorful pastel jackets and the men in tans and greys, many wearing straw hats. All wore handmade cloth shoes. An Wei could feel the enthusiasm.

Their energy seemed to grow when the music blared from the village speaker, starting with a rousing rendition of "On the Fields of Hope," which praised farmers and their fields as the hope of their country.

The group headed toward a slope on the northeast side of the village to excavate the dirt. An Wei counted twenty people, including one student who was determined to help even though he was thin and not very strong.

They had decided to announce the names of all participants each day. That might encourage others to join in. They needed scores more volunteers to finish the work in a week.

At the noon break, An Dong, the other Party Committee member, turned on the loudspeaker and read the names of the volunteers. Thirty-nine had participated.

As the early morning sun filtered through the dust of the plateau the next day, An Wei walked to the sports ground. Several piles of dirt had been carried there the day before. He picked up a handful of soil and let it run through his hands.

An Dong's strong voice carried across the rooftops, reading the names of yesterday's participants again and encouraging others to join in. Soon the low putt-putt of several tractors could be heard across the fields and down the lanes. An Wei marveled at how many farmers were headed toward the gathering point.

Come lunch break, they counted those who had signed in. Seventy.

To keep up spirits and encourage even more to help, some villagers had asked An Wei to write a daily commentary.

Tired and exhilarated, he walked back to Number Five's house and savored a bowl of soup with noodles before climbing the stairs to his room. As he heard An Dong reach the end of the list of the day's volunteers, An Wei sat down on his hard bench and began to type. "Villagers in An Shang, from young teenagers to seventy-year-olds, enthusiastically answered the call of the local Party Branch. . . ."

The excavation project gained speed. Each day An Dong read An Wei's commentaries with an enthusiasm that inspired the villagers. "The new An Shang School—the product of An Shang's volunteering work—is a treasure An Shang villagers leave to their offspring."

Music blared across village neighborhoods in the morning. The song An Wei loved the most was "A Sweet Offering of Love," sung by a popular singer. He hummed as it played.

> This is a call from the heart.
> This is an offer of love.
> This is a spring breeze for the world.
> And this is a source of human life.

Volunteer numbers grew. By the fourth day, there were 185 volunteers. An Wei could barely believe it. The careful planning by the party members and committees had worked.

Day 6: "This is the most successful mass activity ever organized in An Shang. . . . The key to this success is that the organizers have faith in the masses and rely on them."

On the seventh day, crowds of farmers worked long hours to level the heaps of earth into a packed sports ground in front of the school. They were nearly finished.

August 25, 2003, Day 8

An Wei watched An Dong help members of the village drum-and-gong group set up their red drums on black wooden frames. Farmers and their children crowded around as reporters from large provincial newspapers and the Xi'an TV station gathered in front of the rostrum. Ma Ke, An Wei's partner at the Shaanxi Translators Association in Xi'an and a former journalist, had delivered well.

An Dong cued the drum-and-gong corps, outfitted in white shirts and black pants, to begin a welcome, with their brass gongs piercing the countryside and drum rolls alerting other villages that a ceremony had begun.

Feng Jiedong stepped to the microphone. "Dear Journalists. Your arrival will become a powerful driving force for An Shang villagers to strive for a better life." An Wei listened as Feng invited them to talk with any of the farmers about their volunteering and their hopes for the future. He looked up at the school—not yet finished but well on its way. The sports ground was nearly complete.

The villagers seemed ready for more changes.

"We have to make a village plan right away," An Wei said to the village's other two Party Committee members, Feng Jiedong and An Dong, a few days later. He set his tea jar down on the small table in Number Five's courtyard. He was brimming with confidence. The villagers' pride in the volunteer effort was palpable.

"We need a five-year plan of how to change An Shang and give the villagers hope." He described the frustrations villagers shared with him during his early months as leader in the village.

Some people put garbage in the ditches, and nobody stopped them. They ran out of water all the time. Some people had four children, when they were only supposed to have one or two. Some people got approval for new housing immediately, while the leaders never responded to others' requests.

That night up in his room, An Wei opened the rumpled notebook in which he had jotted down the villagers' complaints. He hummed while he turned the dusty pages, remembering the farmers' earnest faces as they talked with him. Their problems were heartfelt, their suggestions practical, and now they were more interested in governing.

He pored over the notes. There was plenty of material for a five-year plan. His fingers touched the computer keys tentatively at first. He realized he was drawing directly from Helen's work with the industrial cooperatives. Using the farmers' suggestions, he would introduce a few new ideas. What she had called commodity circulation, for instance, could be accomplished by having a farmers' market in An Shang. If they taught villagers how to encourage their children to study at home, the multiyear plan could set a goal of fifty college graduates for the next five years.

He called a meeting of the Party Committee, and the Villagers Committee and passed out copies of his draft, "Five-Year Program for Economic and Social Development."

"This draft is a little like a sculpture," he told them. "I have given you the shape. But there is no nose; there are no eyes. You can put your own ideas on it."

An Wei then fine-tuned his proposal for electing representatives so that everyone, especially those who worked part of the year in cities, would still have a voice. When he explained that the Villagers Congress would be based on a national model, Feng Jiedong and An Dong were enthusiastic. Then, to his relief, the sixteen village party members supported the idea.

When he introduced the concept to the rest of the farmers, the great majority accepted it without hesitation. The congress would give them a voice, information, and most important, control of village decision-making. They hated the old system that left them in the dark about everything and feeling abused.

The Party Committee—Feng Jiedong, An Dong, and An Wei—hammered out crucial requirements for the village's five neighborhoods to elect their delegates for the congress. These delegates would make all the major decisions for the village. They needed to be hardworking role models willing to serve the villagers, be able to discuss official business, and be respectful of all ages. They must also be organized and should not spend long periods of time away from the village.

The Party Committee scheduled the first meeting of the Villagers Congress for the end of September, before harvest time and while a Global Volunteers team would be on hand to observe. An Wei hoped a TV crew would be there too.

Feng Jiedong and An Dong made regular announcements over the loud-speaker to keep the village updated and enthusiastic. The congress would last a day and a half, and the night before the delegates would attend a preparatory meeting.

With great care, An Wei checked the five-year plan, which if approved, would become an official village policy. He also spent hours describing to villagers how a democracy works. His Brother Number Five and inquisitive Feng Jiedong were especially attentive.

"What we are doing is just like playing chess," An Wei explained. "We will win this game, but it is not so easy."

If they got full support from *everyone* in the village, and if they got full support from the township government, they would win the game quickly. With tepid or fake support, it would take much longer; they could still win, but it would be much harder.

As the date neared, An Wei, energized by what they had accomplished, re-checked all the documents for the congress and sent them to the town governor and party leader who oversaw the village's affairs. He invited them to attend.

September 2003

The sun had set over the cornfields when the elected delegates climbed the concrete stairs to the large third-floor classroom in the old school. Their voices were serious, and the usual loud joking was absent. They were about to embark on a new government.

The sound of wooden chairs scraping against the concrete floor filled the room as the delegates took their places at the battered desks and paged through the proposal handouts. An Wei checked that the cameraman they had hired was ready and walked to the front of the room. He straightened his papers, looked at the assembled group, and opened the preparatory meeting for the delegates of the first An Shang Villagers Congress. The agenda was full, starting with the qualifications for being a neighborhood delegate.

In the midst of An Wei's explanation of their responsibilities, the town governor and party assistant leader walked in.

The governor asked An Wei to step outside.

"We advise you not to hold this meeting. It is illegal." The governor's face was drawn tight.

"Why?" An Wei asked. "It is just like the People's Congress. It is based on the national government model."

"Elections cannot be held at such a meeting. They can only be held at a villagers' mass rally that everyone attends, not just representatives."

"That's impossible," An Wei said.

He knew a villager would be cowed by these powerful men. But he was not going to give in. He continued. "Many villagers work in cities. The Villagers Congress solves this problem by having everyone select a delegate to represent every fifteen families."

"You make things too open. You are affecting the enthusiasm of leaders in other villages," the governor responded.

An Wei kept his voice steady, his fury controlled. "We are doing it our way; they can do it their way." He started to turn back to the meeting. He knew exactly what Dong Dongsheng was alluding to. If An Shang made every decision with a public vote, if they made village affairs crystal clear, and if they made the village accounting open to everyone, the leaders would have no way to grab personal benefits.

The governor seemed desperate. "On hearing what you are doing, some village leaders want to resign."

An Wei kept his tone serious and respectful. "That is not our business."

He added, "Right now we are having the preparatory meeting for the Villagers Congress. I will relay your message to the delegates." If the villagers decide not to hold the congress, then of course tomorrow's meeting will be canceled. If they insist on having it, well, there is no way to stop them. The Villagers Congress is a self-governing organization. He looked at the governor and added, "According to the national law, the town government can only advise our delegates. You cannot impose your will on them."

An Wei turned toward the classroom door. "We sent you an invitation a week ago. We welcome your presence at the opening session tomorrow."

Back in the meeting, An Wei said, "Just now two town leaders said we should not hold the Villagers Congress. What's your opinion?"

The delegates did not hesitate. They were anxious to launch the congress. They agreed to proceed.

Later, An Wei walked back to Number Five's home under the starlit sky, relieved that they had hired someone to videotape the proceedings, starting with this preparatory meeting. He was sure this first Villagers Congress was as significant to rural China as land reform had been. They were creating history.

The next day, An Wei went over his opening talk for the congress and improved a few words. He wanted to emphasize the rule of law and strengthening the economy. As he waited for it to print, he noticed some of the Global Volunteers members in the courtyard below. He had invited two to attend the congress as observers, and he spied the red observer ribbons they had already pinned on. He checked that he had everything, greeted the volunteers, filled his tea jar with hot water, and started along the dusty road to the old schoolhouse. Neighborhood representatives and committee members were already gathering and pinning on their official nametags.

The assistant party leader from the town rode his bicycle through the village gate. His pale complexion emphasized his slicked-down black hair, combed to one side. He seemed reluctant to be there. Once more An Wei invited him to attend, and offered to place him at the rostrum to say a few words as the town representative. He hesitated for a few minutes and then agreed to attend, though he would just observe, not speak.

The delegates sat down at the battered desks in the large third-floor classroom. An Wei took his place behind the red, cloth-covered tables in front. A proud banner overhead declared "The First Villagers Congress in An Shang." On his left was short, broad-faced An Xiyuan, friend of the previous leader and still head of the Villagers Committee, though he had been removed from the Party Committee. An Wei felt it was important to keep him in public view because they would eventually get around to more questions about the village's public funds that had disappeared.

An Wei opening the first formal session of the An Shang Villagers Congress, 2003. *Source*: An Wei.

An Wei, looking tense, stood to open the congress—his official name tag pinned to his short-sleeved, lavender shirt, his thinning hair neatly combed back. He checked to make sure the videographer was filming and began his speech by welcoming the participants and observers. He had worked hard to keep his speech practical, while making clear they were introducing a new government. The title, he hoped, set the tone: "Building a Civilized and Well-Off An Shang by Developing the Economy and Governing the Village by Law." When he concluded, the delegates appeared to have understood his words. They looked serious.

Next, An Xiyuan introduced the Five-Year Program on Social and Economic Development. It had already been approved by the Party Committee and the Villagers Committee, but the delegates needed to discuss it and vote for or against it at the end of the congress. Finally, An Wei introduced Jim Swiderski, the American leader of the current Global Volunteers team in the village. The cameraman swung toward Jim's friendly, round face.

"We are here as volunteer teachers, as laborers, and as friends." Jim paused for An Wei to interpret. He then gave a brief history of the American struggle to develop and maintain a democracy. An Wei knew that not everyone would understand what Jim was saying, but it was valuable to have a representative of a living democracy. Jim continued, "It was the proclamation of the people, by their elected representatives, that officially founded our government. No kings. No generals. The common people were served by people whom we chose to lead us." An Wei scanned the village delegates as he interpreted. Some of them seemed to understand. The United States had representatives too, and the common people ruled.

Jim concluded, "The Chinese struggle is and will continue to be unique to your own history and culture. . . . For the people of the timeless community of An Shang, the democratic process begins today with each of you in this room. . . . We are honored to be here to observe this important moment. Good luck to you, our friends."

After a short break and a good-natured photo session, the delegates from each neighborhood filed into a separate classroom where everyone had a chance to clarify the details of the five-year plan and state his or her opinion. They then returned to the general session where the neighborhood conveners summarized their discussions and all delegates cast their votes.

An Wei watched, his pride growing as the first villager, a woman in a dark blue dress with white polka dots, slid her ballot through the slot of the red ballot box. When the villagers had finished marking their ballots, An Wei watched thin, reliable An Dong count them. If only Helen Snow could see this, An Wei thought. She would be pleased at how he had put her ideas about democracy into practice in a poor village. But he was nervous. Even

Villager voting in the first Villagers Congress, 2003. *Source*: An Wei.

though reports from the neighborhood groups seemed positive, open elections meant the results were not predetermined. His predecessors had held fake elections, selecting the candidates behind closed doors. Today the outcome was not guaranteed.

An Dong took the microphone. The five-year plan had passed almost unanimously. An Wei breathed a deep sigh of relief.

January 2004

The annual village rally, required by the national government, turned out to be disastrous.

The morning sun crept over the roof of the old school, warming the villagers who sat on the small stools they'd brought to the school courtyard. Nearly the entire village was there. The rostrum, made of desks pushed together and topped with a red cloth, had been placed on the concrete stage partway up the school's entrance steps. Wires for the speaker system stretched across it. The three party leaders—Feng Jiedong, An Dong, and An Wei—and two members of the Villagers Committee took their seats on the platform, ready to report the state of the village. The crowd settled down.

Short, broad-faced An Xiyuan, friend of the former leader, rose and opened the rally by announcing that he was still head of the Villagers Committee, but it had taken a lot of effort to be allowed to preside over this rally. An Wei was not sure why An Xiyuan had started with such a negative tone, but he could not do anything about it now.

An Xiyuan then read the agenda. He was followed by An Wei who explained the purpose of the rally. Next, the newly elected deputy director of the Villagers Committee read the village work report. The power supply project had been finished, the new Villagers Congress had been formed, and the irrigation ditches had been upgraded by the villagers.

Then came the much awaited model villager awards. The farmers shifted in their seats, as they looked around at each other and wondered who would receive one. Being selected was a great honor. First came six farmers who earned a lot of money through hard work and could become role models for others to learn from their techniques and work habits. Each walked to the front, accepting a certificate with their callused hands. The next six awards went to daughters-in-law who, without complaint, carried out their filial responsibilities for their husbands' parents. An Wei had felt these women should be honored because so often there was friction between wives and their in-laws.

Finally, Party Committee member An Dong stood up with the audit report in his hand.

"The national law for villagers requires a financial report be made public every year. A lengthy audit of the past several years has been completed," he said.

But as he began to read the report, three men rushed toward him. They grabbed the microphone and tore away the cord. As An Dong stepped back, An Wei watched in disbelief as the men picked up the rostrum and smashed it on the concrete platform. An Xiyuan, head of the Villagers Committee, friend of the old leader and in charge of the meeting, just sat and watched. His younger brother was one of the attackers. Another was a young man called "Muddle Head" by the villagers.

Rage overcoming fear, An Wei yelled for them to stop or he would call the police station. "Smashing is illegal." He struggled for words, trying to think fast. "You will be punished for breaking the Public Security Law."

They yelled in his face and at the others.

"Why can you sit up here?"

"Who elected you?" another bellowed. "We didn't."

"We elected An Xiyuan, not you."

An Wei tried to explain that Communist Party members who lead villages are elected only by party members. But it was hopeless. The men kept yelling.

One sat down beside An Xiyuan and served him tea, shouting, "*You* are our leader," making it clear to all the farmers in attendance that An Xiyuan had helped plan the attack.

An Wei looked out at the villagers. They had sat quietly throughout the chaos and seemed stunned. As far as he knew, this kind of violence had never before happened in An Shang. But then, never before had the village government told the truth to the villagers.

He stood and addressed them, "Dark clouds cannot cover the sun. We will give out the financial report later in some other way. The meeting is adjourned." He suggested they leave without comment.

The farmers got up reluctantly, picked up their stools, and left through the schoolyard gate, leaving the thugs behind to smile at their victory.

Two weeks later An Wei had the audit report printed and gave a copy to every village household so they could learn the details of the former leaders' corruption.

Soon afterward, the Party Committee hired a law firm in Baoji City to have the village account books audited by an approved accounting firm. Their report was even more devastating than the one carried out by the village audit committee. They found that more than 95 percent of the village expenditures during the former leaders' years were illegal.

The Party Committee sent the official audit to the county office overseeing corruption reform but received no response. For the next four years, tenacious An Wei and other village leaders would call and go in person for a response, to no avail. The town officials, who appeared to have been collaborating with the former An Shang leaders, had been promoted to key county positions. They ignored the charges, An Wei assumed, out of fear they would also be implicated.

New Governing Structures of An Shang Village

The *Villagers Congress* structure was developed by An Wei, modeled on the national and provincial people's congresses. It followed the bylaws of the Villagers Committee of the People's Republic of China, adopted at the National People's Congress in 1998, and was composed of representatives from all five neighborhoods. Originally a delegate represented fifteen households; later that was changed to ten households. The congress also included members of the village Party Committee and Villagers Committee. The Villagers Congress was An Shang's legislature. All major village issues were discussed and decided by vote in the congress, and the Villagers Committee carried out the decisions made by the congress.

The *Education Committee* was developed to oversee maintenance of the new school building, support education development in the village, and oversee ongoing school projects such as completion of the teachers' living quarters. It was responsible for the awards given to students and teachers, maintaining records of who went to college, and managing the An Shang village website.

Other villages did not have a Villagers Congress or an Education Committee.

* * *

A few months before the audit report fracas, An Wei had been standing in the old schoolyard when one of the Global Volunteers walked through the gate with her laptop. A few children gathered around. She squatted down, opened it slowly, and hit a few keys, gently pushing their curious hands from the keyboard. She scrolled through photos of the school and of village children. An Wei had watched the children point and shove each other as they saw familiar faces on the screen. The more she showed, the more excited they became. An Wei was sure almost none of them had seen a computer before.

A few days later, another volunteer took her computer to a neighbor's home to show them photos of their family. The neighbor, who had a small chicken farm on the edge of the village, smiled broadly, showing two missing teeth, while his wife and daughter stroked the shiny laptop.

Later, the woman had come to An Wei. What were the Americans doing with these machines? How did the photos get into them? He explained carefully what a computer was and what you could do with one. "You can even send emails to your family when they are away."

"What do you mean, email?" she asked. He explained some more.

"You can also send photographs to people, or talk to them through the computer."

She was amazed and wanted to know how they could get a computer and learn to use one. "Could we contact our relatives in Beijing?" she asked.

"Of course," An Wei said. "Or in Shanghai. Even in other countries."

The villagers' curiosity about computers stayed with him. How could they get computer access? They would need not only a computer but also an internet connection. He had one through his brother's landline; it was slow, but he could not function without it.

He began to think about websites. Brother Number Five's son, who lived in Xi'an, worked for a computer company. Could he actually help create an An Shang website? It was a radical idea for a poor village, but it would give villagers working in faraway cities a means to stay in touch with village affairs, and a blog would give everyone a chance to comment on village events.

In early 2004, with his nephew's guidance, the Sino-American Society registered anshangvillage.com in the name of the An Shang Education Committee. For several months, An Wei assembled material for it: the school groundbreaking ceremony, the volunteer effort for leveling the sports ground, the Villagers Congress, and American volunteers working in the village. There was plenty they could show the world. An Dong wrote a history of the village, and a few Americans wrote about their experiences. An Wei and his nephew, as well as Sino-American Society members, used the site on a trial basis for several months.

April 10, 2005

An Wei watched with pride as Brother Number Five, who had been cheated of an education by the Cultural Revolution, walked to the microphone. He greeted the volunteers and visitors to the public launch of the village website.

Inscriptions from provincial leaders proclaimed the day, emphasizing that An Shang village stood out from all other Shaanxi Province villages because its farmers could now explore the whole world and be as informed as citizens in the cities.

"The word *farmer*," Brother Number Five said, "has been a synonym of poverty and backwardness. . . . Only in recent years can we fully understand that farmers can never uproot their poverty unless they are better educated and very well informed. . . . It is education, and education alone, that can change the life of our future generations."

Reporters had come to An Shang from the national Xinhua News Agency and Shaanxi TV, and by the next day *their* websites spread the news. The whole country soon knew that a tiny village in the middle of China had its own website.

September 1, 2005

An Wei was ready for the Project Peace dedication ceremony at the beautiful new school. He stood on the little balcony of his An Shang room for a few minutes picturing the village children when they had moved into the finished building in February. He had been in Xi'an then, but Brother Number Five, Feng Jiedong, and others had called him to relate every detail of the move.

"You should have seen the children's excitement when they arrived at the new school, backpacks bouncing as they walked through the gate."

"The kids wanted to break into a run, but the teachers managed to keep them in line and led each grade to its proper classroom."

The children and teachers loved the new desks, the fluorescent lights, the large windows that brightened the classrooms, the ceiling fans that stood ready to cool them in hot weather, and the awe-inspiring auditorium with enough tiers of red and blue seats to hold the whole student body.

The teachers were pleased with smooth chalkboards that weren't pitted and the promise of a teachers building, where they could live during the school week.

An Wei had been planning today's dedication for months. Bud Philbrook and his wife, founders of Global Volunteers, were to be there. Sun Tianyi would represent Shaanxi Province, and officials from the county and town had agreed to talk.

He pulled on his light blue shirt, rolled the cuffs up partway and smoothed his hair, and then picked up the dedication ceremony schedule from his printer and walked down the lane toward the main road. It was the first day of school for students all over China, and what a special one for An Shang.

Thousands of farmers from other areas crowded into the village, eager to enjoy a grand event and anxious to have a look at officials from the county and province as well as at the Americans.

Pastel flags fluttered from the school roof as An Wei made sure that the red cloth still covered the name of the new school and the schoolyard monument that had been engraved with the names of those who helped build it. He then climbed to the third floor of the new school to check the cloth covering the lovely plaque for the An Lin Memorial Library. How pleased she would have been to be represented this way.

He stood there a few moments. On many days, he was sure he would see her walk around the corner talking with a volunteer. He had to keep telling himself she was gone.

The bus arrived from Xi'an right on time. Bud Philbrook and Michele Gran from Global Volunteers, Niu Jianhua, Sun Tianyi from the provincial offices, Helen Snow's niece Sheril Bischoff, and volunteers working in Xi'an waded into a throng of welcoming villagers decked out in their good clothes. Bud, a head taller than the villagers, brimmed with quiet enthusiasm, his broad smile

Crowds gathering from many villages to watch the school dedication, 2005. *Source*: An Wei.

forming crinkles around his eyes. An Wei watched everyone inch toward the school entrance.

With the schoolchildren seated in front of the stage and reporters from national and local TV channels and newspapers in place, including some posted on the roof of the school gatehouse, the drummers gave a resounding roll heard across the countryside and the dedication ceremony began. The school gate was opened, and the many honored guests walked slowly across the schoolyard, greeting An Wei and then Number Five. Bud stepped forward and folded An Wei into a long, congratulatory hug.

Once the guests were assembled, the Chinese national anthem blared through the loudspeakers, followed by "The Star-Spangled Banner." The crowd looked up at the two flags wafting in a gentle breeze on shining stainless-steel poles—the red and yellow Chinese flag and the red, white, and blue American flag, both at the same height to honor the collaboration of people from the two nations. The flags had stood there since school construction began, but today they seemed to fly more proudly.

Sun Tianyi, representing the province, stepped to the podium. He had been at the groundbreaking ceremony three years earlier and now spoke of the

Dedication ceremony for the new An Shang school, 2005. *Source*: An Wei.

changes the An Shang villagers had made: the new school, paved roads, and new trees—and of the importance of volunteerism.

Bud Philbrook followed.

"An Lin always made us smile—in a world where smiles are too few," he began, calling up memories of her optimism.

"We will remember her every day as students who attend An Shang School gain knowledge and understanding that will offer them a new opportunity to realize the fullness of their God-given potential." He lauded the community and her parents.

He then challenged An Wei and the governors of the county and town to join in the difficult task of making the school a success. "A new school building, like a new child," he said, "can be brought into the world, but it must be nurtured and cared for if it is to realize our hopes and dreams."

· 15 ·

Pigsties, a Website, and Dedicated Desks

Over the next several years, the An Shang Villagers Congress oversaw major developments.

Everyone had worked together to turn the main dirt track into a concrete road from the village entrance, past the small shops, to the new school. Each neighborhood then paved its own roads. Within a few years, ten concrete streets replaced impassable mud paths.

There were many more changes:

- They reported village finances openly each year.
- They made decisions about village life, from fixing the drainage system to improving family planning and educational opportunities.
- They planted shade trees and flowers along some of the roads, and they attached streetlights to the electric poles.
- They standardized housing permits so that everyone received equal treatment.
- They installed a cell tower, a lattice structure of steel rising high above the village, which prompted more adults to buy cell phones since they no longer had to walk into the fields to capture a faint signal.
- They developed a village website.
- They launched an annual folk art festival to celebrate the rural area's rich traditions. A woman from nearby Baoji City turned An Shang's old school into a folk art gallery to attract tourist trade.

An Wei's enthusiasm grew as villagers talked about self-education and self-governance. He provided new ideas and resources to help bring their dreams to life. Four volunteer teams from the United States came each year to stay in villagers' homes and teach English to rural teachers and students. An

From the top: Entrance road to An Shang village before the paving project, 2005; the new concrete village entrance road, 2006; new cell tower.

From the top: Village women learning to use donated computers; a new folk art gallery that transformed the old school; Shaanxi opera, part of the folk art festival.

Wei began to notice that villagers were copying the way educated Chinese visitors talked and that they seemed to have lost their uneasiness with foreigners.

After the new school's dedication in 2005, a village Education Committee was created, headed by tall and confident Feng Jiedong. The committee oversaw upkeep of the school, hosted the volunteer teams, and planned parent education, while town and county officials were responsible for carrying out school policies and hiring teachers and principals.

Not everything went easily.

One villager, An Youren, extended his pigsty onto the grounds of the old school. Next, a few of his neighbors moved their outdoor toilets there. Regulations forbade occupying community-owned land, but they didn't care. Other villagers complained to the Villagers Congress, and the congress delegates told the families they *must* move back onto their own land.

The families resisted, especially An Youren. His given name meant "friendly" and "kindhearted," but other village farmers said he was just plain selfish.

The Villagers Congress was asked to intervene. Its delegates decided the first policy had been correct but acknowledged that the families would suffer if they had to knock down their extensions.

Why not give them a permit to occupy a little public land?

How much?

"One meter."

"No, two."

The delegates argued back and forth.

"One meter. That's all," said the first group loudly.

"Two is fairer."

They finally agreed on two meters.

An Youren wasn't satisfied. He had used more than two meters for his pigsty, so he persuaded the other families to return to the Villagers Congress and demand three.

Delegates from their neighborhood lobbied for a three-meter extension. But the delegates from other neighborhoods were adamant. The families should not be allowed to use public property, they argued. "Two meters is good enough."

By now, many congress delegates were furious.

Two meters. No, three. Two. Three is better. No, two.

Finally they arrived at another compromise: two and a half meters.

To prevent further haggling or encroachment on the old school property, the congress decided to build a wall that would run behind the old school in a straight line along the families' properties. When it reached An Youren's pigsty, though, it curved around the pen where mud-spattered pink piglets grunted and jostled with each other.

2007, An Shang

Soon another problem consumed the village.

"Shu Ji, Shu Ji," a woman called from near the front gate of Brother Number Five's courtyard. "Party Secretary, are you here?" An Wei went to the little balcony off his room and saw two village women. "I am coming."

"Our children's teacher isn't teaching them anything," the older woman said.

An Wei frowned. He had heard this from others. After several villagers had complained to him a year earlier, he went to Mr. Zhang, the town director of education responsible for assigning the village school staff, to report that An Shang had some unqualified teachers. But in September, Zhang assigned another inferior teacher to An Shang village. Now there were three.

"Our kids say their third-grade teacher talks on his phone a lot during class time," the younger woman said. On the rare occasion when homework was assigned, a student made the corrections.

"Their teacher does nothing," she complained.

An Wei was furious. After so much effort to build this beautiful school, the town—with the county's approval—was giving them incompetent teachers. One or two might be tolerated, but three out of the eight? Here were villagers, who had learned the value of education, watching helplessly as their children sat in a room without instruction.

Spring 2007

With my audio recorder and notebook safely stowed in my dark green cloth bag, I headed down the steps to the brick courtyard of Brother Number Five's house. Niu Jianhua came out of the kitchen, laughing with Number Five's wife. "Let's go," she said, sliding her arm under mine.

On the new concrete village road, we navigated around the bright red peppers spread out to dry in the sun and waved to the women shoveling sand and concrete into a mixer for a new home.

I had come to An Shang to observe classes and interview parents and teachers for a research project. Niu Jianhua stopped to chat with the attendant at the gate of the new school; then we walked across an expansive tiled yard to a small building where the Education Committee met.

Feng Jiedong, the Education Committee chairman, greeted us. "Ni hao. Ni hao." A few committee members and several parents were already seated around a table. With An Wei interpreting, they answered my numerous questions about their childhood schooling and about how they and their children were taught Chinese. As we neared the end of an hour, I asked what changes they would like to make in their children's education. The room crackled with energy.

"Computers! Our children need to know how to use them," said the mother nearest me, lines of determination creasing her face.

"We need better-educated teachers," said another.

"Our children and grandchildren need to go to college and have opportunities similar to city children," another added.

Their talk shifted into the local dialect. Their frustrations surfaced about the inequity between the privileged city children and those in poorer rural schools. An Shang teachers did not speak standard Chinese and couldn't teach it to their children. Few educated people understood the village dialect. Worse, their English teachers knew almost no English.

"All we can do is complain and make a few suggestions," one woman said. "We don't know how to change the teachers."

We had run out of time. As we cleaned up the teacups, the parents and committee members kept talking about new possibilities. I had the feeling they could have gone on for hours.

The next day, I met a few of An Shang's teachers for a group interview. We sat around a small rectangular conference table in the school meeting room. I asked them to write their names in my notebook while An Wei introduced them.

The young energetic dean, who had been at the school four years and taught Chinese to fifth graders, wrote first. I watched as he formed the characters quickly and precisely, the way well-trained urban teachers of Chinese did.

Another Mr. An was next. I recognized him from the village. After forty-two years of teaching in An Shang, he had retired but was still teaching sixth-grade Chinese. Holding the pen with his arthritic fingers, he wrote his name slowly, but firmly, with one stroke steadily following the next.

He passed the notebook and pen to Mr. Yang, who An Wei said had come to the school in September and taught fourth-grade Chinese.

While An Wei described their responsibilities, in my peripheral view I could see Mr. Yang pick up the pen awkwardly. After a long hesitation, he began his surname with one shaky stroke. Then he paused, the pen held above the paper, and moved his fingers slightly as if practicing the next stroke in his mind. I had seen beginning first graders do that. He finally made another shaky stroke with difficulty and then laboriously inscribed the rest of the characters in his name, stroke by slow stroke.

I was appalled. Even I could see that he could barely write his name.

Yet he was assigned to teach Chinese to upper-grade students.

Summer 2007

Armed with the villagers' concerns, An Wei rode his bicycle several miles to the town office of Zhang Changsheng, the director of education who assigned An Shang teachers.

"Good day, Director Zhang," An Wei said. He wanted to be as diplomatic as possible and not offend the officials, but he needed to make clear that the villagers were unhappy about the teachers assigned to An Shang. He reported the parents' complaints and asked the director to please remove at least one of the poor teachers. The new An Shang school had many foreign visitors, he said, and it was a loss of face for the town and county to have so many unfit teachers in one place. Mr. Zhang seemed to be listening.

"Just assign average teachers to the school," An Wei said. "But not so many who are good for nothing." The director said he would work on it.

As the new school year approached, the village sent a report to the An Shang school principal listing some of the problems—among them, that students were directed to teach classes while their teachers went for a nap and that some punished the children physically. Villagers hoped the report would reinforce what An Wei had told Director Zhang.

On September 1, the official day for school to start, the villagers watched expectantly as the teachers arrived. To their dismay, not only were the same three bad teachers there, but also an additional one had been assigned who was well known throughout the area for being incompetent.

Now half the school's eight teachers were useless.

Fury drove An Wei as he paced in his brother's courtyard after he learned about the newest teacher. He was village leader, but he had little power over the school. The town government, with county approval, assigned staff to village schools and oversaw school quality. He decided, however, that being village leader gave him the right to inspect the school.

He climbed the stairs to the upper-grade classes. As he stepped onto the outdoor corridor on the third floor of the new school, he stopped for a moment to let the cool autumn breeze refresh him. He imagined An Lin commenting about the beautiful building. But she would also have been determined to improve the poor teaching.

He looked out at the thriving trees and bushes the volunteers and villagers had planted on the school grounds. Then he turned and walked slowly, looking into each classroom through large glass windows. The first teacher was instructing fifth graders who were eagerly raising their hands to respond to his questions.

At the next classroom, the teacher was squatting in the hallway talking on his cell phone. He seemed unconcerned that An Wei was there, although inside his room the students were laughing and joking, and two were throwing wads of paper back and forth.

An Wei was shocked. The town officials were making it impossible for these poor village children to change their lives.

He tried to push the hurt away as he walked down the concrete steps to the second floor. There he found two teachers helping students read pages in their textbooks. Yet in another room, the teacher was yelling at the children who sat hunched over, looking at the floor.

The first-grade class had no teacher at all.

For the next two weeks, An Wei returned every afternoon he could. The energetic dean and three others were always teaching. But several were not. And the first-grade teacher was never there.

One day he opened the classroom door.

"Is this your class time?" he asked the first graders.

"Yes," they yelled.

"Well, where is your teacher?"

"In his room in the back building."

On a final inspection tour several days later, An Wei stepped into the first-grade room to look around. Still no teacher. He spotted a smashed electrical socket, its wires hanging out while children played and fought next to it.

He hunted down the principal who was, as usual, polishing his motorcycle, to report what he had found. "You have to fix the electrical problem, and until you do, the room should be locked. The class can meet in the auditorium."

The principal was furious. "You do not appoint us and cannot supervise us."

On his walk back to Number Five's, stepping over cornstalks drying on the road, An Wei reassured himself that, as village leader, he should intervene as much as possible because parents had complained to him about the poor teaching. According to the Chinese education act, every Chinese citizen should care about children's education and about their safety.

He called a Party Committee meeting, and they dug up the Chinese education laws on student safety on his computer. That afternoon, over the village loudspeaker, committee members described the unsafe first-grade room and asked the farmers to study the law that stated children were not allowed to be in unsafe environments.

The principal must have reported An Wei's complaint to the town, because the director of education and the governor, who oversaw staffing in the area schools, soon asked to meet with the Party Committee members. The An Shang school principal, saying his blood pressure was too high, chose not to attend.

Villagers poured out their anger about the unsafe classroom and about the increasing number of irresponsible teachers. One teacher had not written a single Chinese character on the board the whole year, they complained. Their school was being ruined. Director Zhang Changsheng told them that all the teachers in the Wujing area were about the same.

An Wei could not believe the gall of this man. Trying to control his fury, he made a recommendation. "Since the An Shang villagers are so distressed by these teachers, but you believe they are *good* teachers, I suggest you exchange all the teachers in An Shang with all the teachers at the school in the next village, An Xia. That way we will take all of their teachers, and they will take all of ours."

Zhang Changsheng was silent.

An Wei watched him as a slight redness spread across Zhang's face, hinting at his anger. An Wei was confident he had trapped him and that his silence confirmed his suspicion that the bad teachers had bribed him to transfer them to An Shang because the new school's facilities were the best. If Zhang removed them from An Shang, those teachers would expose him.

An Shang's leaders were relentless. They insisted that the county officials who supervised the town staff, including Zhang, meet with them.

The next evening two county junior officials from the Bureau of Education arrived in An Shang. Long into the night, An Wei and the other leaders described their observations and complaints in detail. The school was now so bad that some parents had sent their children to live with relatives in Baoji City so they could get a decent education. The officials seemed sympathetic and said their director was out of town but that they would report to him as soon as possible.

Optimistic, An Wei and the other villagers waited. But after several months, when the county officials had not responded, all the village committees and the Villagers Congress collaborated on a report documenting the problems. They named several teachers and their misconduct, including sexual harassment of the school girls and failure to teach classes. They asked for help to resolve the issues. An Wei hand-delivered the report to the county and town officials and met with the leaders of the education department, repeating his concerns and requesting a solution.

The village then posted the report on its website.

Soon afterward, two county officials drove to the school and strode across the yard. For over three hours, they talked with the principal and teachers.

A few days later, the An Shang principal announced that according to the county's thorough inspection, "Everything is okay. The teaching plan is good, everything is good. You have no problems to worry about."

The villagers felt desperate, as nearly another school year had passed. It was obvious the Fufeng County officials were working in league with the town to cover up their corruption. They were stealing the children's education.

But what was the solution? The village committees discussed the situation from every angle they could think of. They were certainly not going to visit those officials again. They were through begging. They needed a plan before the town made final teacher assignments at the end of August.

At a meeting, the Villagers Congress passed a resolution saying their children's future should not be destroyed by bad people. They decided that if, before the end of August, the town said they were replacing the principal and at least three bad teachers, they would do nothing. If the town did not make these changes, however, the village would lock the teachers and principal out of the school, and on September 1 the children would stay home.

To do this they needed the principal's key. They sent two Education Committee members to talk with him. They explained that, because there were many valuable items in the school, it must be guarded throughout the summer break. They suggested two solutions: the teachers could take turns being on duty during the summer, or the villagers would take full responsibility for the school.

The principal gave them his key.

On August 31, a few teachers arrived to move into their rooms, found the gate locked, and left.

On September 1, the first day of school, the teachers returned to find no children and the gate still locked.

Feng Jiedong and other villagers waited and watched.

The next day the good teachers returned, along with the town governor, four new teachers, a new principal, and Mr. Zhang, the director of education.

In Xi'an, An Wei's phone rang. It was the town governor.

"Mr. An, the school gate is locked. What's the problem?"

An Wei smiled.

"Your request has been filled," the governor said. "The teachers and principal have been transferred."

An Wei called Feng.

With the key in his hand Feng Jiedong, chair of the Education Committee, walked up the street from his home. He nodded to Director Zhang and the governor, put the key in the lock, and swung the metal gate open.

Zhang exploded, hurling curses at Feng Jiedong.

Feng yelled back.

Zhang Changsheng lunged at Feng. The town governor grabbed him with both hands and pulled him back.

The new principal was in his thirties, enthusiastic, strict, and fair. Within a few months, An Wei noticed a change in the school atmosphere. The teachers, old and new, began taking online government courses to upgrade their skills. They corrected the students' homework. Staff and students cleaned up the sports ground, which had been allowed to turn to weeds, and students soon began playing basketball. In the mornings in the schoolyard, children sat in circles on their small stools reviewing their lessons before classes began. The older students practiced speeches and won competitions at the town and county level. The Education Committee reinstituted prizes for high-achieving students and for excellent teaching. A foreign researcher observing classes met with the teachers. Scheduled to last an hour, the meeting extended well into dinnertime because the staff wanted to discuss ideas for improving their teaching.

Fall 2008

But the education controversy continued to cause tumult in the town and county.

In an attempt to undercut the villagers, the former An Shang principal and Zhang Changsheng, the town director of education, lied to the Shaanxi Province TV crew assigned to investigate the story of the locked gate. They told the TV crew that the villagers had broken the hearts of the four teachers, and that's why they no longer wanted to teach in An Shang.[1]

Furious, a village commentator took to their community website. Writing anonymously—a common practice in China—he said Director Zhang knew exactly why the incompetent teachers were removed from An Shang. He wrote that town and county corruption had led to the locked gate.

More villagers aimed anonymous attacks at Zhang and pointed fingers at county administrators for collaborating with him. They also posted a detailed explanation of why the school gate was locked. That infuriated Zhang and the other officials.

An Wei knew that the leaders wanted to destroy the village website, but they couldn't because it was registered with the government. Instead they tried to destroy the village Education Committee, which oversaw the site. They claimed the committee was illegal and accused its members of siphoning money from Global Volunteers.

Village commentaries continued to attack the town and county leaders, who then pushed back harder against the Education Committee. Then one day, an article appeared in the Xi'an evening paper heralding the accomplishments of the An Shang Education Committee.[2] It praised the committee for connecting parents to their children's schooling and making helpful suggestions to the village elementary school.

The story spread from one news source to another, leaving the angry officials no choice but to stop their attacks.

The village website continued to harass them about corruption. To a Westerner, the commentaries were often oblique, full of innuendoes and loaded questions that don't easily translate across cultures. One commentary raised questions about a former town governor, identified as "D," though everyone knew who it was. He had been promoted to a powerful party position in the county and was being honored for excellent work in building a clean government, although he had been part of corrupt maneuverings when he worked in the town. Other commentators chimed in. Although the village website usually garnered thirty or so visitors, one day they numbered more than three thousand.

Despite the villagers' successes, trouble lay ahead. The new school was being threatened by social forces that were sweeping across China.

From the start, the new An Shang school was a symbol of hope for the village children. Their parents and grandparents were proud of the hard work and love they had poured into it.

- They had built the school grounds with dirt from their fields.
- The students had performed amazing songs and dances for the groundbreaking ceremony, and they were bursting with pride when they finally moved into their new classrooms.
- American Global Volunteers teams had spent thousands of hours helping to build the school, carrying materials, digging ditches, smoothing plaster, planting trees, and creating goodwill in the village.
- One of many battles over the school's location ended when Feng Jiedong and his brothers traded their good farmland to make construction possible.
- The village had won the locked-gate confrontation.
- The good teachers and principal were providing a quality education that was changing the children's lives.

An Wei's life had changed too. Since he agreed to become the An Shang village party secretary, he had devoted every ounce of energy to building bridges between the US volunteers and the Chinese farmers, and to improving the farmers' lives. He had done it not solely for the village and the future of China but also to honor the short life and dreams of his beloved daughter, An Lin.

But the school's population was shrinking. In fact, the rural school population across China was dwindling as increasing numbers of migrant workers from the countryside took their children with them to urban worksites. Even with its improved educational offerings, the new An Shang school was down to thirteen students in a class. Some rooms were empty.

The villagers began to consider how to use the extra space in their magnificent new building. An English language school in the county seat had asked An Wei about renting classrooms; farmers from other villages were showing interest in having their children attend the school. Could the village accept them and charge them a fee? The school could house a cultural center for the county, following the central government's initiative to create enjoyable, healthy places for farmers to relax. An Wei worked on several viable ideas.

Then came the directive from the provincial government. The town of Wujing must close all but one of the sixteen village schools it oversaw. The national government had been consolidating rural schools for several years, and now it was speeding up closures.

An Wei investigated other communities and found that several were keeping younger children near home in village schools and sending the older students to central boarding schools. He accelerated his efforts to keep An Shang's modern school open with its auditorium that seated 150 people.

He thought of the teachers' comments, that they loved seeing youngsters learn the new skills of asking questions in class and working in pairs or groups. One teacher enthused about how many students had become active learners, unlike earlier days when they just memorized everything. Another had explained with a smile, "I observe my pupils and learn their shining points so I can build their self-confidence."

There must be a way to use the new school and preserve some of this good teaching.

Some officials looked at the An Shang school as a possible site for the area school because it already had the necessary land and they would not need to build many more classrooms. But the committee that oversaw the town's decisions said no. An Shang was not centrally located and was too far from many villages. The committee decided to close all sixteen existing schools in June 2010, including the new An Shang school, and build a new one in the town of Wujing.

The villagers were heartbroken. The improved instruction by the current teachers had already shown results. They were proud of their school now.

"We've seen big changes in the last couple of years," one parent said.

"My son has greater interest in studying now," another added, smiling.

Parents from other villages said An Shang had good teachers and hard-working students.

"The kids no longer just sit and listen," a farmer observed.

In the past, students were afraid to speak. Now they spoke up in class, raised questions, and gave presentations.

"At other schools, they don't give speeches," said one mother. "But here the teacher helped my daughter improve and polish a speech, and she gained a lot of self-confidence."

Fall 2009

It was at this point that An Wei's protégé Feng Jiedong began to go his own way.

An Wei was reelected party secretary of the village. Two terms were normal, but a new county official had insisted that he serve a third term until Feng could be trained to be the leader. Since An Wei needed to return to work in Xi'an full time, the party members chose Feng for vice secretary, with responsibility for managing all the day-to-day work. He would consult regularly with An Wei.

Back in Xi'an, An Wei settled into his projects while spending hours on the phone mentoring Feng Jiedong about how to carry on the reforms he had helped An Wei achieve. Though time consuming, it seemed a good arrangement to An Wei.

As Feng was confronted by one issue after another, he and An Wei hashed them out together. Should they lease the abandoned reservoir site to farmers for fields? If so, how? What should they do about the cell phone towers? How should they handle the dwindling number of representatives for the Villagers Congress? Their discussions seemed endless to An Wei, but he felt that Feng Jiedong was learning a lot and doing a good job.

They had plenty of amicable disagreements, especially recurring ones about democracy versus the old ways.

"The villagers know nothing about democracy," Feng said. He complained that when he gave them a chance to speak up, they didn't know what to say. "The old way was easier," he often said.

An Wei argued back. Democracy was more time consuming, but when a decision was finally made, the majority of villagers would follow it because they all had a say in creating it.

As the first year slid into the next, they continued to hammer out solutions to village issues, from regulating chicken farms to paving more neighborhood roads, but Feng Jiedong found the democratic process increasingly cumbersome. He thought it simpler to tell people what to do.

He also worried that he would antagonize those men who oversaw An Shang village. One day he said, "If we offend town and county officials by following your ways of managing affairs, the village will be in a very difficult position in the future."

An Wei made angry notes on a well-used pad while he listened. Feng just wanted to please those officials. After a pause, An Wei said, "We *never* offended those people. They offended us with their corrupt practices."

But Feng Jiedong was headed in another direction.

April 2011, Xi'an

An Wei sat in my somewhat-worn hotel room on the outskirts of Xi'an. Exasperation animated him as he talked, lines creasing his forehead and his leg jittering impatiently. He told me about the unsettling things Feng Jiedong was doing in the village and how Brother Number Five was trying to protect the An Shang school as best he could. It was still open because the replacement school being built in the town of Wujing was well behind schedule.

An Wei during a 2011 interview.

Through the window behind An Wei, I watched as paddleboats meandered across a small lake. Blooming cherry trees, interspersed with weeping willows, made up for the view of dilapidated carnival rides beyond them. His wife, Niu Jianhua, was recovering from back surgery, and it was best that I stay in the hotel rather than at their home.

Leaning back and nearly shutting his eyes, An Wei reflected on the past. He had given years to the village. With the help of Feng and other villagers, he had laid the foundation for democracy and honest government, but to keep that going was a full-time job. The reforms went against tradition. His term as leader would soon be up. The village needed to be led by someone who lived there, and that would be Feng Jiedong. An Wei was not optimistic.

He paused, took a long drink of tea, and edged forward in his chair to sit straighter; pointing into the air with his left hand, an expression of enthusiasm began to soften his face. He seemed infused with new energy.

I had begun to realize that when things were not going well, An Wei's attention turned to the future and other goals he hoped to accomplish. He often focused on what should be done to improve life for new generations. If one effort was stymied—his job, his translations, or the school—he would barrel toward what was possible and expand other projects he had already started.

At first his words seemed studied. "I have to find talented young people who want to do research on the Snows and continue my work." He had begun that process, but it was already taking considerable time and would take even longer to mentor them and help them find the needed resources. He had also promised Helen Snow that he would retranslate her book Inside Red China *because the original translation omitted sections. It was a promise he had mentioned to me more than once, and he seemed haunted that he had not yet fulfilled it.*

Suddenly he chuckled and sucked in more tea. Inching closer to the edge of the upholstered chair, he began to enumerate more plans.

"I need to write a pile of books—starting with a picture book in memory of An Lin." The next one would be about his years introducing new ideas in An Shang. "I want to write about this experience because I want to tell the future generation what kind of society, what kind of psychology, and what kind of culture they will confront in today's China as it opens more and more to the outside world. They need to see what kind of resistance will confront them, starting with corrupt local officials."

He leaned forward and spoke with greater intensity. He jabbed one hand into the air and then the other. For over an hour, he laid out his plans for the next decade, all aimed at connecting China to the rest of the world.

Finally he let his shoulders relax and leaned back. In a quieter voice, he added that he wanted to spend time with his wife and their granddaughter. He had been busy all his life and did good things for many people, but he felt he had neglected his family. He wanted to do more that was meaningful for them.

Summer 2011

Feng Jiedong was drifting ever further from the democratic government he had helped An Wei so carefully construct. Feng began to hold meetings with only a small group of villagers—a few party members and a few delegates he knew would agree with him. And they were expected to agree. No discussion, no objections.

Next, he discontinued the Villagers Congress and then the neighborhood committee meetings.

Soon afterward, An Wei learned about a disreputable practice Feng Jiedong had begun.

The government provided yearly benefits for farmers who lived below the poverty level. But before each family could receive its government stipend, Feng required them to work in his own fields for a full day during the busiest summer and autumn harvest seasons.

When he heard about Feng's requirement, An Wei called him to object. Gripping his phone tightly, An Wei said, "That's unfair. Those families should spend their time bringing in their own crops."

Feng protested. He wasn't taking their money like the last leaders. He was just getting his due for being village leader.

An Wei, his body stiffened in anger, his shoulders tight, responded. "Forced labor is a bribe. The practice is disgusting."

Once more, the farmers had to put up with the old practices. They knew it was wrong, but they kept silent.

Feng Jiedong took even greater advantage. He sold many of the computers that had been donated to the village by the Americans and were used to familiarize villagers with the internet. Worse, he began to cut down and sell timber from the trees planted at the school by the Global Volunteers and rural English teachers as a gift to the village.

When An Wei visited An Shang and talked with farmers that he knew well, they laughed at Feng Jiedong. He was the kind of person, they said, who wants to be an emperor. He was becoming a dictator. An Wei asked why they didn't speak up, but he already knew.

Sucking tea through his teeth, one told him, "We have lived in the village for hundreds of years, from generation to generation."

His cousin added, "We don't want to offend anybody."

One farmer said as he sat down on his kang, "If I offend my neighbor, he will be angry with me for many years. Then if I need his help in the future, he won't come to my aid."

An Wei nodded and sighed internally at each comment. Their words repeated centuries of practices. He thought of a particular young woman who had become a leader in the Villagers Congress. He wondered what she thought. And what about the dedicated Education Committee members who had worked so hard to make the school the best possible? He knew they did not like what was happening.

It's so hard to change farmers' ways, he thought. So hard. They would just stay silent and let the new idea go.

And he had to let it go too.

In March 2012, An Wei's term ended as party secretary of An Shang village. Feng Jiedong was officially elected to replace him.

An Wei never heard from him again, although he would sometimes hear about what Feng was doing.

The new An Shang school ultimately improved village life, even though its existence had been challenged by graft, corruption, and entrenched practices.

The few extra years that it remained open, the teachers and principal kept up their efforts to provide their students with a good, modern education. The last year before it would close in June 2012, fifteen village students were accepted into college, the largest number ever. Some were going to nationally recognized universities such as Beijing University of Science and Technology and the Beijing Military Academy. And the village Education Committee was pleased to tell the teachers that they could take home the computers they had been using, the ones that had not been sold by Feng Jiedong. "They belong to the school, but you can use them forever."

Spring 2012

Even though the An Shang school was soon closing, political corruption in the town had one last insult to heap on the village.

By closing all sixteen schools in the area and building a new one, the town and county officials had managed to get a large project that gave them funds from the town, county, province, *and* national governments. When the school construction money arrived, these officials all plucked some of it for themselves. Now they had no money for desks and chairs.

With the new school about to open and local officials finally able to hire a principal, they made him call An Shang's new party leader, Feng Jiedong. They wanted the village to give them its new school desks and chairs—for free. Feng, who wanted to please the town and county administrators, asked Brother Number Five, who was in charge of the An Shang school property, to arrange the transfer.

Unlike the other schools that still used old, heavy wooden double desks, An Shang students worked at individual tan-and-grey metal desks with matching chairs. Adjustable to a student's height, the desks even had hooks on the side to hang jump ropes and pencil boxes. Each desk and chair set had been sponsored by an American in honor of a beloved person. An Wei's good friend, Sharon Crain, for instance, had donated one in honor of her mother.

Brother Number Five did not need to think long about his response to Feng Jiedong and the principal. "The school in Wujing cannot have our desks and chairs," he said. Everything in the new An Shang school was donated to the village by American friends. "If they are to be used in other schools, you must seek permission from the many American donors spread across the United States."

He added that the desks and chairs were given for the An Shang villagers' use. They were not for the town school that had already received government funds to purchase their own. "Once the An Shang school closes this June, the desks and chairs will stay in the village."

· *16* ·

Let's Teach Them Together

September 2017, Cedar City, Utah

My encounter with An Wei at a conference in Utah showed once again that he just won't quit.

Squeezing into an empty place at a table in the rustic lodge high in the mountains for a dinner opening the conference, I scanned the dining room for An Wei. He was nowhere to be seen. I noticed Sharon Crain and others, but no An Wei. Then as I stood to let someone pass, I realized he was the elderly looking gentleman in a heavy jacket at a table against the wall.

His complexion was gray. He sat still and spoke only occasionally to the person next to him while coughing persistently. In all the years I had known him, An Wei was always in the middle of things, talking energetically, introducing people to each other, and taking charge. Four months earlier in Xi'an, he was his usual energetic self. Certainly he had had health concerns for a long time. Heart issues that had plagued him finally required a pacemaker. His lung problems had diminished since he and Niu Jianhua had moved from the center of polluted Xi'an. But these seemed not to slow him down.

Now, however, he definitely looked sick.

Once dinner was over, Sharon and I headed for the parking lot. We were concerned, given that the mountain restaurant was at 7,500 feet, an altitude not recommended for heart patients. After considerable dithering, An Wei's hosts found a driver to take him to his hotel room in Cedar City, but even that was at 6,000 feet.

"I'll be all right," An Wei said, stopping to gulp a little air.

"My medicine is . . ." He stopped again for a breath.

"It's in my hotel room." Again he paused.

"I'll be all right . . . once I take it."

In characteristic style, he had been making the most of his trip. The day before, a several-hours drive north at Brigham Young University, he had negotiated an agreement for the translation of descriptions Helen Snow had written on thousands of photos in their archives. He had agreed to help find translators, and Brigham Young agreed to digitize the photos with bilingual descriptions and then make them available free to the public.

When An Wei and the driver pulled out of the lodge parking lot, Sharon and I both breathed a sigh of relief. He was scheduled to give a major speech the next day, and he would be the center of attention throughout the conference hosted by Southern Utah University. He had orchestrated the event and was eager to talk with all of Helen's relatives, as well as the many donors who supported studies of Helen Snow. We hoped he would be better after a good night's sleep.

But later, when Sharon and I entered a hall on the Southern Utah campus in Cedar City for a late evening program, there sat An Wei in the front row, stubborn to the core. He had taken his medicine and had someone accompany him to the campus.

At breakfast early the next morning, though dogged by a persistent cough, An Wei talked ardently about passing his work about the Snows on to younger scholars who might be motivated—just as Helen had inspired him—to build a bridge to future generations. His enthusiasm mounting, he said that the papers, translations, books, and copies of audio recordings and videos had all been transferred from the Edgar and Helen Snow Studies Center at the Translators Association to the School of Foreign Languages at Xi'an's Northwest University. Some of their staff members were already translating Helen's materials.

Peeling a hardboiled egg, he smiled, obviously pleased. I knew that the transfer of the materials had taken a load off him. He'd worked long and hard to find young people who were interested in Helen's work and willing to carry on her legacy. Much to his delight, the dean of the School of Foreign Languages was a huge supporter of the project.

By afternoon, with the help of a jitney transporting him from one conference location to the next, An Wei made it through his speech without much coughing and mingled with the guests.

The next day as I prepared to leave, I talked with him briefly. He looked sick but was planning to visit an elementary school in Cedar City and then fly to Minnesota to visit An Lin's grave before returning to Xi'an.

Back home in Los Angeles, I waited a tactful period of time before writing him, and then only sent him a simple question because I didn't want to tax him. An Wei almost always answered within twenty-four hours, but this time a week passed, and then another. I was relieved when an email finally arrived: "In this information age, 'no news is probably bad news,'" he wrote. "Having returned home I was immediately hospitalized for two weeks. Now I am at home, having a rest cure."

October 2017, Xi'an

An Wei did not remain at home long.

Defying doctors' orders, he headed for Shaanxi Normal University in Xi'an. Sharon Crain, who had taught there periodically for more than three decades, was hosting a twentieth-anniversary celebration of its English Club. She had helped students found the club, and almost all of its former student presidents had traveled long distances for the event.

Back in 1997, clubs had not really been allowed, and the students struggled to create a space where they could practice English. For years, An Wei had served as a key advisor for the club, given speeches to them in English, and emphasized how important it was for them to learn anything they could from people in English-speaking countries. He taught them about Helen Snow's ideas for China, how she initiated industrial cooperatives that helped people work together in war-torn China and heralded the importance of individuals' contributions to society. He shared with them his experiences of creating exchanges with Americans. To the students, he seemed to hold deep, steady beliefs despite the country's political tensions pulling first in one direction and then another. Many of them wanted to be just like An Wei.

Now, twenty years later, the club needed his support even more as new assertions from China's powerful president, Xi Jinping, poured forth:

Don't follow Western ideas.
Don't use Western books in schools.
Turn to Chinese thought and traditions.

Dictums were issued. Human rights lawyers were jailed and independent think tanks shut down. As Mao Zedong had done decades earlier, Xi Jinping had his new ideology written into the Chinese constitution. He declared that China had developed an economy without Western values and pressed Communist Party members to "solidify economic and political influence" throughout the world.[1] At the October 2017 National Congress of the Communist Party, held just days before Sharon's anniversary celebration, the president laid the groundwork to have himself appointed ruler of China for life—with no term limits.

Groups such as the English Club were anathema to Chinese thought as promoted by Xi Jinping.

A nationalistic surge had begun to permeate the country. The new president of Shaanxi Normal University ruled that students should not participate in clubs but instead focus entirely on classroom studies. Even so, the anniversary celebration proceeded, albeit with caution.

Many Communist Party officials would be attending the event. Although the English Club had always held its programs in both English and Chinese, the department overseeing it decided this time everything should be in Chinese.

An Wei arrived at the university with a different perspective.

On October 28, An Wei, Niu Jianhua, and their nine-year-old granddaughter arrived at Shaanxi Normal University. He looked in better health than he had in Utah, but he still appeared frail. A big smile lit up his face when he saw Sharon. As they walked to Sharon's room, An Wei shuffled noticeably.

Left to right: An Wei, Niu Jianhua, Sharon Crain, and Bill Crain (Sharon's husband), at Shaanxi Normal University, Xi'an, October 2017. *Source:* An Wei.

He had come out of deep loyalty to Sharon and their shared love for Helen and for the English Club. To him, the club's goals were critical—to emphasize the importance of learning English and building strong friendships between the Chinese and American people. While Xi Jinping was pushing to have all of China speak in one voice and follow his increasingly autocratic pronouncements, An Wei was promoting the belief that *individuals* such as Helen Snow made the difference.

An Wei walked slowly to the podium, looked directly at Sharon, and said he was going to speak in English because that is how he had always spoken with her for more than thirty years. No one stopped him.

He talked of the importance of the club and its being "an incubator of bridge builders and a cradle for folk ambassadors." For decades he had urged people to get acquainted with other cultures. He had encouraged college students from the city to spend time in An Shang village learning about farmers' lives and urged farmers to become acquainted with the American volunteers. The students in the club were potential bridge builders, he said, not just between China and the United States as Helen Snow had been but also to future generations in both countries.

During the celebration, the enthusiastic former English Club presidents initiated the Dream Maker Foundation, donating their own funds to help new students follow their dreams. In honor of An Wei's continuing support, they asked him to be one of the primary judges in the foundation's first event, a translation contest.

It was one more demonstration of how respected An Wei was. Earlier, at the Utah conference, Minna Gao, a self-assured young Chinese professor from Xi'an's Northwest University, had spoken of An Wei's influence on her. When she was a young teenager in a rural middle school near Xi'an, Americans from a Global Volunteers team that An Wei had hosted introduced conversational English classes to her school. Those lessons with native English speakers dramatically changed her life. Moreover, she was from a poor village where no one had attended college, and every time An Wei visited her school, he encouraged her to strive for excellence.

"Without his generosity and vision," she said, "I would never have become the first in my village to go to college." That was the first step in her journey to become a professor at a prestigious university.

No one had ever had so much faith in her, not even herself, she told the conference participants.

Early November, 2017

A week after the English Club celebration, An Wei stepped from Minna Gao's SUV, again defying doctors' orders to rest. This time the event was a symposium at Northwest University on the outskirts of Xi'an to celebrate the anniversary of Helen Snow's 110th birthday and the eightieth year of her 1937 visit to Yan'an where she interviewed fledgling Communist Party leaders such as Mao Zedong and Zhou Enlai.

An Wei spoke to the gathering briefly, but poignantly, as he donated to the university's growing Snow Studies Center the original photograph, often used by the media, of him with Helen Snow at her house in Connecticut.

At the end of the day, symposium guests gathered in front of the almost-completed building that would house the School of Foreign Languages as well as the new Snow Center.

An Wei, Sharon, and a few dignitaries were handed ceremonial shovels to help plant a tree in honor of Chinese and American friendship. For An Wei, who had been showing fatigue, it was more than a symbolic planting of a tree. He pushed the shovel deep into the earth, turning the soil onto the sapling's roots. For him it was also an important farmer's job.

An Wei and Sharon then unveiled an enormous stone monument, taller than they were, that had been designed by the Snow Center staff. Positioned proudly in front of the building, the monument had a message carved on one side in Chinese, the other in English:

> The seeds of a tree are planted by one generation
> The shade is enjoyed by the next.
> This tree was planted in honor of Helen Foster Snow and An Wei
> and others who also devote their lives to nurturing Chinese-American
> Friendship and Understanding for the benefit of future generations.

Sharon Crain, An Wei, and School of Foreign Languages staff unveiling the ceremonial stone monument at Xi'an's Northwest University, November 2017. *Source*: An Wei.

July 2018

Several months later, increasing regulations and political pressures in China hounded the English Club and the Dream Maker Foundation. In late July, Sharon sent An Wei an email, suggesting that in the fall they could team-teach, giving a series of lectures at both Shaanxi Normal University and Xi'an's Northwest University. Together, she wrote, they could help the students cope.

Within hours, An Wei's response landed on her computer screen. "I completely share your proposal. Let's teach them together."

Who would have thought that the little boy with almost no chance to leave the poverty of a peasant village in the middle of China could accomplish all this? He had picked up the books his brother threw down and dusted them off with eagerness to find out what was in them—to explore whatever they might offer.

At the dawn of modern China, that impoverished young boy of eight years old longed to explore the unknown world beyond the village paths. Becoming literate drew him into new worlds. Stubborn persistence pulled him through upheavals and obstacles: his grandfather's refusal to pay his tuition, starvation during high school, and all the turmoil he dealt with throughout his life.

As so many millions of Chinese have done, An Wei worked hard like his parents. Because he came from a rural family, though, perseverance was even more crucial for survival. He worked twice as hard as most students, committed not only to succeed but also to be the best, to be a leader. Throughout his life, he constantly observed everything around him and asked why.

Driven by curiosity and a desire to give a talented and forgotten woman her due, he immersed himself in reviving Helen Snow's work and cementing her legacy as one of the first Westerners to document the very birth of modern China. In the process he drank deeply from her wisdom and took on her cause to promote the far-reaching importance of Chinese-American relations, mutual understanding, and cooperation.

He was determined to see as far into the future as possible and to figure out what would happen if he tested new ideas. He created new ways of doing things in his village, from developing a technique for grinding flour as a boy to establishing a groundbreaking local democratic congress that functioned for more than five years. When confronted with unexpected changes and obstacles, he doubled down on work, learned new skills, and used every task he was given to make connections between people and help foreign visitors understand China better.

That has been his life's mission, and he has never given up.

Notes

Chapter 1: Beginnings

1. Rammed-earth walls were made of loess packed into a frame by hand and then painted with lime to help keep them from disintegrating in the rains.

2. Jack Chen, *New Earth* (Carbondale: Southern Illinois University Press, 1972; Peking: New World Press, 1957); Robert L. Worden, Andrea Matles Savada, and Ronald E. Dolan, eds., *China: A Country Study* (Washington, DC: Federal Research Division, Library of Congress, 1987), http://www.country-data.com/cgi-bin/query/r-2564.html.

3. Patricia Buckley Ebrey, *Cambridge Illustrated History: China*, 2nd ed. (Cambridge: Cambridge University Press, 2010), 308–9.

Chapter 2: A System Unraveling

1. Jonathan D. Spence, *The Search for Modern China* (New York: Norton, 1990), 579–81.

2. Ralph A. Thaxton Jr., *Catastrophe and Contention in Rural China: Mao's Great Leap Forward, Famine and the Origins of Righteous Resistance in Da Fo Village* (Cambridge: Cambridge University Press, 2008), 106–16.

3. Martin C. Yang, *A Chinese Village: Taitou, Shantung Province* (New York: Columbia University Press, 1945), 253, 255; Isabel Crook and David Crook, *Ten Mile Inn: Mass Movement in a Chinese Village* (New York: Pantheon Books, 1979), 157, 162, 186; Oliver J. Todd, "Taming 'Flood Dragons' along China's Hwang Ho," *National Geographic* 81, no. 2 (February 1942): 209, 222–23; Walter C. Lowdermilk, "China Fights Erosion with U.S. Aid," *National Geographic* 87, no. 6 (June 1945): 661, xxiii, xxiv; Adam Warwick, "Farmers since the Days of Noah: China's Remarkable System of Agriculture Has Kept Alive the Densest Population in the World," *National Geographic* 51, no. 4 (April 1927): 473–82, 493–98.

4. Martin Bernal, "Mao and Writers," *ChinaFile, New York Review of Books*, NRYB China Archive, October 23, 1969, https://www.chinafile.com/library/nyrb -china-archive/mao-and-writers.

5. Jasper Becker, *Hungry Ghosts: Mao's Secret Famine* (New York: Henry Holt, 1998), 100–111.

6. State Statistical Bureau, ed., *China Statistical Yearbook, 1984* (Beijing: China Statistical Publishing House, 1984).

7. Spence, *Search for Modern China*, 583.

Chapter 3: Moving On

1. 西安外国语学院, *Xi'an Wai Guo Yu Xue Yuan*. It later became the Xi'an International Studies University.

2. Debate continues as to whether his diary was authentic or fabricated by a Communist Party official.

Chapter 4: Into the Maelstrom

1. Gu Hua, *A Small Town Called Hibiscus*, trans. Gladys Yang (Amsterdam: Fredonia Books, 2003), 137.

2. Ebrey, *Cambridge Illustrated History*, 314; Han Suyin, *Eldest Son: Zhou Enlai and the Making of Modern China, 1989–1976* (New York: Konansha International, 1994), 319–21.

3. Feng Jicai, *Ten Years of Madness: Oral Histories of China's Cultural Revolution* (San Francisco: China Books and Periodicals, 1996), 105.

4. Estimates vary widely of how many "Red Guards" traveled to Beijing, from one to eleven million. Regardless of the actual number, photographs show them packed into the vast ceremonial area of Beijing.

5. Mao Tsetung, "'Talk at a Meeting with Chinese Students and Trainees in Moscow,' November 17, 1957," in *Quotations from Chairman Mao Tsetung* (Beijing: Foreign Languages Press, 1972), 288.

6. Feng, *Ten Years of Madness*, 21.

7. Chen XiaoBo, ed., *Xiao Zhuang's Photography: The Irrational Times* (Beijing: 798 Photo Gallery, 2004).

8. Yongyi Song, "Chronology of Mass Killings during the Chinese Cultural Revolution (1966–1976)," *Online Encyclopedia of Mass Violence*, August 25, 2011, https:// www.sciencespo.fr/mass-violence-war-massacre-resistance/en/document/chronol ogy-mass-killings-during-chinese-cultural-revolution-1966-1976, ISSN 1961-9898.

9. "Beating in Beijing Described by Gray," *New York Times*, October 14, 1969.

10. A cadre was a government worker trained to be active in China's revolutionary movement.

11. Named for a major directive issued by Mao Zedong on May 7, 1966, at the beginning of the Cultural Revolution.

Chapter 5: Clinging to Shattered Dreams

1. Alexander Casella, "The Nanniwan May 7th Cadre School," *China Quarterly* 53 (March 1973): 153–57.

Chapter 6: Unshackled

1. The resources for this period are legion. Three that are quite accessible for the general reader are Dean King, *Unbound: A True Story of War, Love, and Survival* (New York: Little, Brown, 2011); Anthony Lawrence, *China: The Long March* (Hong Kong: Intercontinental Publishing, 1986); and Harrison Salisbury, *The Long March: The Untold Story* (New York: McGraw-Hill, 1987).

A couple of other readable sources that provide in-depth assessment of the complex events surrounding the Long March and the Yan'an years are Richard Bernstein, *China 1945* (New York: Vintage Books, 2015); and Rana Mitter, *Forgotten Ally: China's World War II, 1937–1945* (New York: Mariner Books/Houghton Mifflin Harcourt, 2013). I have also drawn from Audrey Topping, "Return to Changing China," *National Geographic* 140, no. 6 (December 1971), 801–33, and from a comprehensive review of Bernstein's book and that period by Jeffrey Wasserstrom, "The Generalissimo and the Chairman," *Wall Street Journal*, January 2, 2015, http://www.wsj.com.

2. An Wei and Helen Snow, *Ageless Friends: Helen Snow and An-Wei Letters*, English ed. (Xi'an, China: Shaanxi Tourism Press, 2007). [《忘年之交——海伦与安危两地书》，英文版，作者：海伦·斯诺 安危， 陕西旅游出版社2007年9月西安出版。]

3. A review of their two books, *Red Star Over China* and *Inside Red China*, in "Reports from China," *Saturday Review*, February 25, 1939, 10, said that besides being vivid personal narratives, "the two volumes constitute an invaluable source book of historical materials on the Chinese communist movement."

4. Chen, *Xiao Zhuang's Photography*.

5. Edgar Snow, "A Conversation with Mao Tse-Tung," *Life* 70, no. 16 (April 30, 1971), 46–47.

6. John Saar, "A Whole Country Being Worked Very Hard," *Life* 70, no. 16 (April 30, 1971): 33.

7. Saar, "Whole Country," 33.

8. Known to Americans first as Formosa and then as Taiwan.

9. Erik Bao, "'Ping-Pong Diplomacy': The Historic Opening of Sino-American Relations during the Nixon Administration," 2011, http://www.ohiohistory.org/File Library/Education/National History Day in Ohio/Nationals/Projects/2011/Bao.pdf; James Lilley and Jeffrey Lilley, *China Hands: Nine Decades of Adventure, Espionage, and Diplomacy in Asia* (New York: Public Affairs, 2004), 164–65.

10. "The Mao Years," part 2, in *China: A Century in Revolution* (Ambrica Productions and WGBH Educational Foundation, 1997), DVD.

11. *Yenan* is the earlier, Wade-Giles spelling of *Yan'an*. In 1979, *pinyin* replaced the Wade-Giles system.

12. Audrey Topping, *Dawn Wakes in the East* (New York: Harper & Row, 1973), 146.

Chapter 7: Building a Future

1. Worden, Savada, and Dolan, *China: A Country Study*.
2. Jonathan Kaiman, "Witness to Mao's Revolution," *Los Angeles Times*, April 16, 2016.
3. Gao Wenqian, *Zhou Enlai: The Last Perfect Revolutionary* (New York: Public-Affairs, 2007); Han, *Eldest Son*; Frederick C. Teiwes and Warren Sun, "The First Tiananmen Incident Revisited: Elite Politics and Crisis Management at the End of the Maoist Era," *Pacific Affairs* 77, no. 2 (2004): 211–35, https://www.jstor.org/stable/40022499.
4. Similar to the Great Rectification Movement of the 1930s–1940s, "Make It Clear" or "Say Clearly" [Shuo Qing Chu 说清楚] lasted for months or for a couple of years in large organizations.
5. Helen Foster Snow, *My China Years: A Memoir by Helen Foster Snow* (Beijing: Foreign Languages Press, 2004).
6. An and Snow, *Ageless Friends*, 12.
7. This letter has been lost. The rest of those written between Helen Snow and An Wei, plus relevant documents, have been published in *Ageless Friends: Helen Snow and An-Wei Letters*.
8. Roald Dahl, *Charlie and the Chocolate Factory* (New York: Puffin Books, 1964), 6.

Chapter 8: American Connections

1. Tim Considine, interview with author, March 2, 2016.
2. Ann Crittenden, "Helen Foster Snow and China: A Renewed Relationship," *New York Times*, February 6, 1979.
3. An and Snow, *Ageless Friends*, 11.

Chapter 9: Setting the Record Straight

1. David Barboza, "Huang Hua, 97, a Diplomat Who Served China, Dies," *New York Times*, November 24, 2010, http://www.nytimes.com.
2. An and Snow, *Ageless Friends*, 237.
3. A number of sources are available on the Chinese cooperative movement, such as Kelly Ann Long, *Helen Foster Snow: An American Woman in Revolutionary China* (Boulder: University Press of Colorado, 2006); Snow, *My China Years*; Robert Ware, "Gung Ho and Cooperatives in China," *Grassroots Economic Organizing (GEO) Newsletter* 2, no. 7 (2011), https://geo.coop/node/603.
4. Sheril Foster Bischoff, comp., *Bridging: The Life of Helen Foster Snow*, trans. An Wei and Mary Niu (Beijing: China Center for Edgar Snow Studies, Peking University, Beijing Publishing Group, 2015), 312. [《架桥——海伦·斯诺画传》，中英双语版，谢莉尔·福斯特·毕绍福主编，安危牛曼丽翻译，北京出版集团北京出版社2015年7月北京出版。]
5. The next several pages include quotes from the letters in An and Snow, *Ageless Friends*, 41–44, 248–62.

6. Helen wrote to An Wei on November 12, 1985, and then not again until March 1986. An Wei continued to write her, however, and they talked by phone about various issues.

7. Long, *Helen Foster Snow*, 162.

8. Edgar Snow, ed., *Living China* (New York: John Day Company, 1936).

9. An Wei, "The Beginning of Indusco: The Hitherto Untold Story of Helen Snow in the Chinese Industrial Cooperative Movement, February 26, 1987," in An and Snow, *Ageless Friends*, 369–80.

Chapter 10: Gathering Storm Clouds

1. Some of the nationally known writers and poets who attended the forum were Tan Tao, Bian Zhi-lin, Xu Nai-xiang, Zhang Da-ming, Chen Shu-yu, Zhang Xiao-ding, and Chen Zao. An Wei knew two personally: Xiao Qian, a well-known writer, journalist, and translator who was a friend of the Snows, and Zhang Xiao-ding, who was editor of the People's Literature Press.

2. The following letter excerpts are from An and Snow, *Ageless Friends*, 70–91.

3. Thomas Moore, "Old Friends Return to China" (Iowa Public Television, 1989), accessed May 28, 2016, http://v.youku.com/v_show/id_XMTU4NzYyNDUwOA==.html?from=s1.8%E2%80%931-1.2.

4. Hundreds of sources address this period. A few in English that are easily accessible are as follows: James Miles, *The Legacy of Tiananmen: China in Disarray* (Ann Arbor: University of Michigan Press, 1997); Dingxin Zhao, *The Power of Tiananmen: State-Society Relations and the 1989 Beijing Student Movement* (Chicago: University of Chicago Press, 2001); Spence, *Search for Modern China*, 712–47; Antony Thomas, "The Tank Man," *Frontline* (WGBH Educational Foundation, 2006), DVD; Nicholas D. Kristof, "Units Said to Clash: Troops in Capital Seem to Assume Positions against an Attack," *New York Times*, June 6, 1989; *China: A Century of Revolution*, part 3 (Ambrica Productions and WGBH Educational Foundation, 1997), DVD.

5. *Peking* is the old, Wades-Giles way of romanizing Chinese names. The Chinese government began moving to *pinyin* romanization in 1979.

6. An and Snow, *Ageless Friends*, 297.

Chapter 11: Working in Limbo

1. An and Snow, *Ageless Friends*, 352–53.

2. Niu Jianhua, conversation with author, Xi'an, China, May 2016.

3. An and Snow, *Ageless Friends*, 354.

4. Bischoff, *Bridging*, 255; Sharon Crain, correspondence with author, May–June 2017.

5. Helen Foster Snow, "Eternal," in *A Great Woman: Helen Foster Snow in China*, comp. An Wei, Chinese ed. (Xi'an, China: Shaanxi Tourism Press, October 1997), 40. [《伟大的女性》——纪念海伦·福斯特·斯诺，中文版，安危主编，陕西旅游出版社1997年10月西安出版。]

Chapter 12: Stately Maples

1. These two sets of letters were published in a Chinese and then an English edition of *Ageless Friends*. The Chinese edition, translated by Ma Ke, was published in 2003; the English edition was published in 2007. The letters from both An Wei and Helen Snow were all written in English.

Chapter 13: Against Rural Habits

1. The Leading Group for Project Peace consisted of the two village leaders plus three other villagers including An Wei's Brother Number Five, two leaders from the town of Wujing who oversaw the governing of An Shang village, and the Sino-American Society represented by its president, An Wei, and his colleague, Ma Ke.

2. Sun Tianyi was at this time the vice chairman of the provincial Chinese People's Political Consultative Conference.

3. Chloe Ryan Winston, "Helped Build a School in China," *International Travel News*, accessed October 31, 2016, https://www.intltravelnews.com/2004/01/helped-build-a-school-in-china.

4. I have shortened this for readability. The Chinese term is 党支部委员会 (*Dǎng zhī bù wěi yuán huì*), which translates as "Party Branch Committee." The Chinese for "Village Party Branch Committee" is 村党支部委员会 (*Cūn dǎng zhī bù wěi yuán huì*).

Chapter 15: Pigsties, a Website, and Dedicated Desks

1. "Stories behind the Locked School Door," *Today News Program*, Shaanxi Television Station, September 19, 2008. ["学校大门被锁的背后," 今日点击栏目, 陕西电视台, 9/19/2008.] Referenced in *My Life* (blog), http://blog.sina.com.cn/s/blog_5c4ba8210100aj7h.html.

2. "To Support Elementary Education: An Shang Village of Fufeng County Establishes First 'Village Education Committee,'" *HSW News*, October 18, 2008. [为支持小学的基础教育，扶风县安上村成立了国内首个"村教委"], http://news.hsw.cn/system/2008/10/18/006344670.shtml.

Chapter 16: Let's Teach Them Together

1. Xi Jinping, "Secure a Decisive Victory in Building a Moderately Prosperous Society in All Respects and Strive for the Great Success of Socialism with Chinese Characteristics for a New Era," Report at the 19th National Congress of the Communist Party of China, October 18, 2017, http://www.xinhuanet.com/english/download/Xi_Jinping's_report_at_19th_CPC_National_Congress.pdf.

Bibliography

An Wei. "The Beginning of Indusco: The Hitherto Untold Story of Helen Snow in the Chinese Industrial Cooperative Movement, February 26, 1987." In An and Snow, *Ageless Friends*, 369–80.

An Wei, and Helen Snow. *Ageless Friends: Helen Snow and An-Wei Letters.* English ed. Xi'an, China: Shaanxi Tourism Press, 2007. [《忘年之交——海伦与安危两地书》，英文版，作者：海伦•斯诺 安危，陕西旅游出版社2007年9月西安出版。]

Bao, Erik. "'Ping-Pong Diplomacy': The Historic Opening of Sino-American Relations during the Nixon Administration." 2011. http://www.ohiohistory.org/File Library/Education/National History Day in Ohio/Nationals/Projects/2011/Bao. pdf.

Barboza, David. "Huang Hua, 97, a Diplomat Who Served China, Dies." *New York Times*, November 24, 2010. http://www.nytimes.com.

Becker, Jasper. *Hungry Ghosts: Mao's Secret Famine.* New York: Henry Holt, 1998.

Bernal, Martin. "Mao and Writers." *ChinaFile, New York Review of Books*, NRYB China Archive, October 23, 1969. https://www.chinafile.com/library/nyrb-china -archive/mao-and-writers.

Bernstein, Richard. *China 1945.* New York: Vintage Books, 2015.

Bischoff, Sheril Foster, comp. *Bridging: The Life of Helen Foster Snow.* Translated by An Wei and Mary Niu. Beijing: China Center for Edgar Snow Studies, Peking University, Beijing Publishing Group, 2015. [《架桥——海伦·斯诺画传》，中英双语版，谢莉尔·福斯特·毕绍福主编，安危牛曼丽翻译，北京出版集团北京出版社2015年7月北京出版。]

Casella, Alexander. "The Nanniwan May 7th Cadre School." *China Quarterly* 53 (March 1973): 153–57.

Chen, Jack. *New Earth.* Carbondale: Southern Illinois University Press, 1972. First published, Peking: New World Press, 1957.

Chen XiaoBo, ed. *Xiao Zhuang's Photography: The Irrational Times.* Beijing: 798 Photo Gallery, 2004.

China: A Century of Revolution. Parts 2 and 3. Ambrica Productions and WGBH Educational Foundation, 1997. DVD.

Crittenden, Ann. "Helen Foster Snow and China: A Renewed Relationship." *New York Times*, February 6, 1979.

Crook, Isabel, and David Crook. *Ten Mile Inn: Mass Movement in a Chinese Village.* New York: Pantheon Books, 1979.

Dahl, Roald. *Charlie and the Chocolate Factory.* New York: Puffin Books, 1964.

Ebrey, Patricia Buckley. *Cambridge Illustrated History: China.* 2nd ed. Cambridge: Cambridge University Press, 2010.

Feng Jicai. *Ten Years of Madness: Oral Histories of China's Cultural Revolution.* San Francisco: China Books and Periodicals, 1996.

Gao Wenqian. *Zhou Enlai: The Last Perfect Revolutionary.* New York: PublicAffairs, 2007.

Gu Hua. *A Small Town Called Hibiscus.* Translated by Gladys Yang. Amsterdam: Fredonia Books, 2003.

Han Suyin. *Eldest Son: Zhou Enlai and the Making of Modern China, 1989–1976.* New York: Konansha International, 1994.

HSW News. "To Support Elementary Education: An Shang Village of Fufeng County Establishes First 'Village Education Committee.'" October 18, 2008. [为支持小学的基础教育，扶风县安上村成立了国内首个"村教委。"] http://news.hsw.cn/system/2008/10/18/006344670.shtml.

Kaiman, Jonathan. "Witness to Mao's Revolution." *Los Angeles Times*, April 16, 2016.

King, Dean. *Unbound: A True Story of War, Love, and Survival.* New York: Little, Brown, 2011.

Kristof, Nicholas D. "Units Said to Clash: Troops in Capital Seem to Assume Positions against an Attack." *New York Times*, June 6, 1989.

Lawrence, Anthony. *China: The Long March.* Hong Kong: Intercontinental Publishing, 1986.

Lilley, James, and Jeffrey Lilley. *China Hands: Nine Decades of Adventure, Espionage, and Diplomacy in Asia.* New York: PublicAffairs, 2004.

Long, Kelly Ann. *Helen Foster Snow: An American Woman in Revolutionary China.* Boulder: University Press of Colorado, 2006.

Lowdermilk, Walter C. "China Fights Erosion with U.S. Aid." *National Geographic* 87, no. 6 (June 1945): 642–64, ix–xxiv.

Mao Tsetung. "'Talk at a Meeting with Chinese Students and Trainees in Moscow,' November 17, 1957." In *Quotations from Chairman Mao Tsetung.* Beijing: Foreign Languages Press, 1972.

"The Mao Years." Part 2. In *China: A Century in Revolution.* Ambrica Productions and WGBH Educational Foundation, 1997. DVD.

Miles, James. *The Legacy of Tiananmen: China in Disarray.* Ann Arbor: University of Michigan Press, 1997.

Mitter, Rana. *Forgotten Ally: China's World War II, 1937–1945.* New York: Mariner Books/Houghton Mifflin Harcourt, 2013.

Moore, Thomas. "Old Friends Return to China." Iowa Public Television, 1989. Accessed May 28, 2016. http://v.youku.com/v_show/id_XMTU4NzYyNDUw OA==.html?from=s1.8%E2%80%931-1.2.

New York Times. "Beating in Beijing Described by Gray." October 14, 1969.

"Reports from China." *Saturday Review*, February 25, 1939, 10. Review of *Red Star Over China* by Edgar Snow and *Inside Red China* by Helen Foster Snow.

Saar, John. "A Whole Country Being Worked Very Hard." *Life* 70, no. 16 (April 30, 1971): 33.

Salisbury, Harrison. *The Long March: The Untold Story.* New York: McGraw-Hill, 1987.

Snow, Edgar. "A Conversation with Mao Tse-Tung." *Life* 70, no. 16 (April 30, 1971): 46–47.

———, ed. *Living China.* New York: John Day Company, 1936.

Snow, Helen Foster. "Eternal." In *A Great Woman: Helen Foster Snow in China.* Compiled by An Wei. Chinese ed. Xi'an, China: Shaanxi Tourism Press, October 1997. [《伟大的女性》——纪念海伦·福斯特·斯诺，中文版，安危主编，陕西旅游出版社1997年10月西安出版。]

———. *My China Years: A Memoir by Helen Foster Snow.* Beijing: Foreign Languages Press, 2004.

Song, Yongyi. "Chronology of Mass Killings during the Chinese Cultural Revolution (1966–1976)." *Online Encyclopedia of Mass Violence*, August 25, 2011. https://www .sciencespo.fr/mass-violence-war-massacre-resistance/en/document/chronology -mass-killings-during-chinese-cultural-revolution-1966-1976. ISSN 1961-9898.

Spence, Jonathan D. *The Search for Modern China.* New York: Norton, 1990.

State Statistical Bureau, ed. *China Statistical Yearbook, 1984.* Beijing: China Statistical Publishing House, 1984.

Teiwes, Frederick C., and Warren Sun. "The First Tiananmen Incident Revisited: Elite Politics and Crisis Management at the End of the Maoist Era." *Pacific Affairs* 77, no. 2 (2004): 211–35. https://www.jstor.org/stable/40022499.

Thaxton, Ralph A., Jr. *Catastrophe and Contention in Rural China: Mao's Great Leap Forward, Famine and the Origins of Righteous Resistance in Da Fo Village.* Cambridge: Cambridge University Press, 2008.

Thomas, Antony. "The Tank Man." *Frontline.* WGBH Educational Foundation, 2006. DVD.

Today News Program. "Stories behind the Locked School Door." Shaanxi Television Station, September 19, 2008. ["学校大门被锁的背后," 今日点击栏目, 陕西电视台, 9/19/2008.] Referenced in *My Life* (blog), http://blog.sina.com.cn/s/ blog_5c4ba8210100aj7h.html.

Todd, Oliver J. "Taming 'Flood Dragons' along China's Hwang Ho." *National Geographic* 81, no. 2 (February 1942): 205–34.

Topping, Audrey. *Dawn Wakes in the East.* New York: Harper & Row, 1973.

———. "Return to Changing China." *National Geographic* 140, no. 6 (December 1971): 801–33.

Ware, Robert. "Gung Ho and Cooperatives in China." *Grassroots Economic Organizing (GEO) Newsletter* 2, no. 7 (2011). https://geo.coop/node/603.

Warwick, Adam. "Farmers since the Days of Noah: China's Remarkable System of Agriculture Has Kept Alive the Densest Population in the World." *National Geographic* 51, no. 4 (April 1927): 468–500.

Wasserstrom, Jeffrey. "The Generalissimo and the Chairman." *Wall Street Journal*, January 2, 2015. https://www.wsj.com/articles/book-review-china-1945-by-richard-bernstein-1420237669.

Winston, Chloe Ryan. "Helped Build a School in China." *International Travel News*. Accessed October 31, 2016. https://www.intltravelnews.com/2004/01/helped-build-a-school-in-china.

Worden, Robert L., Andrea Matles Savada, and Ronald E. Dolan, eds. *China: A Country Study*. Washington, DC: Federal Research Division, Library of Congress, 1987. http://www.country-data.com/cgi-bin/query/r-2564.html.

Xi Jinping. "Secure a Decisive Victory in Building a Moderately Prosperous Society in All Respects and Strive for the Great Success of Socialism with Chinese Characteristics for a New Era." Report at the 19th National Congress of the Communist Party of China, October 18, 2017. http://www.xinhuanet.com/english/download/Xi_Jinping's_report_at_19th_CPC_National_Congress.pdf.

Yang, Martin C. *A Chinese Village: Taitou, Shantung Province*. New York: Columbia University Press, 1945.

Zhao, Dingxin. *The Power of Tiananmen: State-Society Relations and the 1989 Beijing Student Movement*. Chicago: University of Chicago Press, 2001.

Index

About the Author

Nancy Pine holds a PhD in education focused on young children's learning in the United States and China, has done cross-cultural research in China and the United States for more than twenty years, and has published more than thirty education and research articles, many related to China or cross-cultural learning. She has given talks and workshops throughout the United States and internationally and has spent extended periods in rural China, including five lengthy visits to An Wei's village to teach teachers from neighboring communities and consult in the local school. She has been appointed an honorary member of the village and has interviewed An Wei over a period of ten years, traveling to many of the important locations of his life including the reeducation camp, Nanniwan. She has worked on historical projects in the Chinese archives of the Claremont Graduate University and on ancient literacy practices in China.

Her book *Educating Young Giants: What Kids Learn (and Don't Learn) in China and America* (2012), described by reviewers as "brilliant" and "loaded with vivid descriptions," was nominated for an Outstanding Book Award of the American Association of Educational Research and recommended by *Choice*, the American Library Association publication. Based on *Educating Young Giants*, a traveling exhibition, *Two Roads, One Journey: Education in China and the United States*, has been mounted by the Museum of Teaching and Learning.

Pine has taught in public elementary and high schools for fourteen years; directed the Elementary Education Program and the Bridging Cultures Program at Mount Saint Mary's University, Los Angeles; and has won numerous awards, including a City of Los Angeles award for her cross-cultural efforts.